Of Missing Persons: A Warning to Those Left Behind to be Faithful to Jesus Christ, Even Unto Death

By Timothy & Sabrina Medsker

1

Of Missing Persons: A Warning to Those Left Behind to be Faithful to Jesus Christ, Even Unto Death

Cover Photo: Timothy, Sabrina & Joshua Medsker, 2011, Our Home, Petoskey, Michigan

All Scripture taken from the VW Edition (www.a-voice.org), with permission.

www.ofmissingpersons.com

Final Edition

Cover Photos: (1) ABC Good Morning America screen shot of our family.* (2) A photo taken during an execution of a search warrant at our home in Michigan. (3) A portion of an email received by a friend during an investigation into our whereabouts.

*Copyright Disclaimer under section 107 of the Copyright Act 1976, allowance is made for "fair use" for purposes such as criticism, comment, news reporting, teaching, scholarship, education and research.

ISBN 978-0-9906958-5-1

Of Missing Persons: A Warning to Those Left Behind to be Faithful to Jesus Christ, Even Unto Death

Contents

Introduction

In 2016 it seemed good to me to once again release this book in what will be the final edition. I had embarked on a mission in 2015 to once again go through the entire FOIA process which took nearly a year and a half. As of this writing in late 2016, the process is still ongoing with U.S. Senator Steve Daines and U.S. Representative Ryan Zinke's, both of Montana, working with us to try and get the Department of Justice (DOJ) to comply with my FOIA request. In this entire process we had uncovered a few bits and pieces of information that required some additions to the former edition of the book. During the course of time I pondered and thought about how crazy this whole world has become, the threat of World War 3 looming, a house of cards economical conditions worldwide and the immorality of mankind that is getting worse and worse.

I considered these things and thought of how it appears that the Rapture is imminent. I wondered who it is that would try to give a final warning to anyone who might listen and it seemed good for me to do so and not only that, but to provide a truly Christian warning to those who are actually Left Behind. Realizing that most everything out there that calls itself Christian is often times far off the mark of being a biblical viewpoint in regards to the events of the Rapture, those Left Behind and the "time of Jacob's trouble" (Jer. 30:7), most commonly known as the Great Tribulation or Tribulation.

After much thought on our situation and the events that led to it, we realized that there were two sides to our story. On one hand we had certainly aroused the interest of state and federal law enforcement, having had evidence of problems years prior to our flight, on the other hand we are both convinced that without the holy and righteous chastising of Almighty God, our family would not have been singled out by the federal government. God's chastening in regards to our unholy behavior as Believers was not only deserved, but merciful. Considering what the world will go through in the Great Tribulation, our flight is but a mere drop in the bucket of God's upcoming judgment. I realized that God's judgment against mankind is not only just, but deserving. Yet in all of this I also know that God's mercy will extend to all who are able and willing to listen to Him. There is yet hope.

While it is understood that many will not believe the things in this book, there are those who will. In the near future I expect that more and more people will believe what is detailed out in our story, until finally most will believe it. By then society will be in the final days, most will understand that God is real and what a lot of people secretly feared would eventually happen, catastrophe, disaster, judgment, economic collapse, wars, earthquakes, martial law, concentration camps, etc., will be into full play. Let it be known at that time, God may still help, but even if not, without accepting Jesus Christ as your Savior, all will be lost. Our story is such a story that shows how a family, who were truly deserving of God's judgment, could trust and hope in God Almighty's mercy during trying times.

We would like to dedicate this book to those who helped us along the way. To my best friend Brandon: without your assistance the situation would have been disastrous quickly. Your sacrifice in helping us, almost losing your job and ending up deeply engrained with problems thereafter is remarkable. Inevitably having to also move thousands of miles away from your home and family with a new wife is a deep price to pay.

Also to that special family member Kathy. Your assistance and getting involved with a major situation of which you didn't even comprehend will always be appreciated more than words can convey. The fact that you still have problems associated with having helped us, provides the testimony of the sacrifices that you made for us.

This book is also dedicated to our family who became worried sick and did not know what became of us. For them it was a tragedy in the making. We would like to thank you for your support afterwards and also your assistance in trying to get answers and information about our ongoing situation. Without your believing, understanding and helping us through this situation, it would have simply made it much worse for us. We understand that all you can often do is throw your hands in the air and say that you don't know what can be done about it. Likewise, our feelings are often the same.

We also dedicate this book to attorney Peter O'Rourke. Your kindness in helping us, who were strangers to you at the time, in being able to make a brief safe return to our home in Petoskey, Michigan and safely out of the hands of the people who sought us, will never be forgotten. The fact that you did not ask that we pay you any fees, except your actual expenses, (if even that) is beyond belief. Your assistance and counsel afterwards showed even more kindness. A true professional you are, you will always be remembered.

Finally we dedicate this book to the Most High God who keeps those who are His safe, despite the odds against them. Let it be known that without God this story would never have been written. In fact the headlines on the news about us would have been entirely different. The Most High does save and He does offer Salvation through His Son, Jesus Christ. It is our belief that the Lord wants this story to be known to the world.

Tim & Sabrina Medsker

"O Jehovah my God, many are the wonderful works which You have done, and Your thoughts which are toward us; they cannot be recounted to You if I were to declare and speak of them, for they are more than can be numbered." Psalms 40:5

The Time Will Come

"For the time will come when they will not endure sound doctrine, but according to their own lusts, desiring to hear pleasant things, they will heap up for themselves teachers; and they will turn their ears away from the truth, and be turned aside to myths." 2nd Timothy 4:3-4

The apostasy of the Church did not happen overnight, nor was it done in the dark. There has always been false religions throughout the world, just as there are today. The original Church did not have a institutional name attached to it, but was simply defined as a body of Believers, disciples of Jesus Christ.

"Now you are the body of Christ, and members individually." 1st Corinthians 12:27

People simply do not want the truth and the world makes it just too easy to go along with the lie. Constantly our education system teaches children humanistic values, evolution theories and sways around from allowing discussion regarding on whether or not there is a God. They go so far that they actually teach children about other religions found throughout the world, including their holy days, practices and suggesting that the children should find one, if any, that fits their desire.

Growing up I went to a lackluster churches that did not have a zeal for following God's truths, for loving Christ and living a life that was fully obedient to Him. There were compromises on every level in the church. The music was not honoring to God, the activities for the youth group were more geared to entertainment than learning about God and the majority of the congregation, not all, were there out of social obligation and personal gain. This, however, was what the people wanted.

The people did not want to hear the truth, they did not want to hear sermons that were truly given to the pastor from the Holy Spirit, ones that convicted their hearts. They heard want they wanted to hear. In today's society the remaining strongholds of Churches that still hold true to God's Word are shattering one by one and joining the apostate ranks. This reminds me of Jesus's words:

"Nevertheless, when the Son of Man comes, will He find faith on the earth?" Luke 18:8b

There are many false religions out there that lead many people astray and ultimately, if they do not realize it, repent and believe into Jesus Christ, to Hell. The Roman Catholic Church, Hindus and Muslims alone, all false religions, claim to have over 4.4 billion followers. Right there is way over half the world's population following a false religion, to say nothing of spiritualism, Jehovah Witnesses, Mormons, Seventh Day Adventists and many others. This is only more complicated when the institutional Christian organizations are considered.

There are many different venues of Christianity, which one is correct? There are Apostolic, Assembly of God, Baptist (American, GARBC, General Conference,

Independent, Non-Affiliated, Southern), Bible, Christian, Disciples of Christ, Christian & Missionary Alliance, Christian Science, Church of Christ, Church of God (including Cleveland-Tennessee), Community, Episcopal, Evangelical, Evangelical-Free, Foursquare Gospel, Independent, Lutheran (ELCA, LCA, Missouri Synod), Mennonite, Methodist-United, Nazarene, Non-Denominational, Pentecostal, Pentecostal United, Presbyterian (Presbyterian in America, PCA, USA), Reformed, Religious Science, Salvation Army, Unitarian, Unitarian Universalist, United Pentecostal -- just to name a few. So if someone really says that they want to learn about God, they want to follow God, they want to associate with a group of Believers, becoming a Believer into Jesus Christ, where or how does one decide which Church to attend?

All things must be weighed against the Holy Scriptures *(Acts 17:11)*. While most mainstream denominations can quickly be erased off of the list of acceptable, even the more conservative biblical churches are a church by church basis. If the church does not have believers in it or a truly godly pastor, then of what use is it to attend?

"And I heard another voice from Heaven saying, Come out of her, my people, so that you not share in her sins, and so that you not receive of her plagues." Revelation 18:4

As we get closer and closer to *"the time of Jacob's trouble" (Jer. 30:7)*, more commonly known as the Tribulation or Great Tribulation, things are simply going to get worse and worse. The Holy Scriptures states the following:

"But evil men and pretenders will grow worse and worse, leading astray and being led astray." 2nd Timothy 3:13

"And as it was in the days of Noah, so it will be also in the days of the Son of Man: They ate, they drank, they married wives, they were given in marriage, until the day that Noah entered into the ark, and the flood came and destroyed them all. Likewise as it was also in the days of Lot: They ate, they drank, they bought, they sold, they planted, they built; but on the day that Lot went out of Sodom it rained fire and brimstone from heaven and destroyed them all. Even in the same way will it be in the day when the Son of Man is revealed. In that day, he who will be on the housetop, and his goods are in the house, let him not come down to take them away. And likewise the one who is in the field, let him not return back. Remember Lot's wife. Whoever seeks to save his life will lose it, and whoever loses his life will preserve it. I tell you, in that night there will be two in one bed: the one will be taken and the other will be left. Two will be grinding together: the one will be taken and the other left. Two will be in the field: the one will be taken and the other left. And they answered and said to Him, Where, Lord? And He said to them, Wherever the body is, there the eagles will be gathered together." Luke 17:26-37

If you are reading this and the world has already entered the Great Tribulation, then you need to understand something very clearly. At the very moment that the Rapture happened, there were no more true Christians left in the world, the Lord Jesus took them to be with Him. So while multitudes will be Saved throughout this time, understand that you no longer have to guess or wonder which church might speak the truth, all of the godly pastors and Believers are gone, there are NONE to chose from. If you believe into Christ during this time period and find other Believers, you may very well find it useful to do what the original disciples did after Jesus rose from the dead and went to sit at the Father's right hand, churches that are in Christian's homes *(Acts 2:46; 20:20)*.

"After these things I looked, and behold, a great multitude which no one was able to number, of all nations, tribes, peoples, and tongues, standing before the throne and before the Lamb, clothed with white robes, with palm branches in their hands, and crying out with a loud voice, saying, Salvation belongs to our God who sits on the throne, and to the Lamb!" Revelation 7:9-10

So what about the Rapture? As this is written in 2016, nearly 2017, more and more churches and those who call themselves Christians are getting away from what is referred to as the pre-tribulation Rapture. They are either for mid-tribulation or a post-tribulation Rapture theory, the post theory being by far the most popular, of course there are other theories out there. What the Holy Scriptures clearly teaches is that the Rapture (the term coined for our Lord Jesus appearing to gather us to Himself) happens -before- the Tribulation. Below is a list of verses that teach this truth and though there are naysayers that have arguments against such truth, understand that those who are reading this book or the articles found online after the Rapture will understand clearly whether what God's Word teaches or man's theories is true. I am absolutely certain that God's truth will prevail, though I only have sorrow that so many people will have been led astray by such a deception.

"Then we who are alive and remain shall be caught up together at the same time with them in the clouds to meet the Lord in the air. And thus we shall always be with the Lord." 1st Thessalonians 4:17

"looking for the blessed hope and glorious appearing of our great God and Savior Jesus Christ"... Titus 2:13

"Hereafter, there is laid up for me the crown of righteousness, which the Lord, the righteous Judge, will give to me on that Day, and not to me only but also to all the ones loving His appearing." 2nd Timothy 4:8

"Behold, I tell you a mystery: We shall not all sleep, but we shall all be changed; in a moment, in the twinkling of an eye, at the last trumpet. For the trumpet will sound, and the dead will be raised incorruptible, and we shall be changed." 1st Corinthians 15:51-52

"For God did not appoint us to wrath, but to obtain salvation through our Lord Jesus Christ, who died for us, that whether we watch or sleep, we should live together with Him." 1st Thessalonians 5:9-10

"Because you have kept the Word of My perseverance, I also will keep you from the hour of trial which shall come upon the whole world, to test those who dwell on the earth." Revelation 3:10

"And if I go and prepare a place for you, I will come again and receive you to Myself; that where I am, there you may be also." John 14:3

Will the deception end there? I strongly suspect no. I've heard numerous things that those evil powers that control this world will purport against those who have been Left Behind. The deception will be great and they will likely try to undermine the Event, by telling even more lies, perhaps lies that many would like to believe, so that they might deceive themselves that they have not been Left Behind. Yet I would ponder that as time goes on, those who are still alive would understand that indeed the Rapture had taken place as other events unfold that are known among some of the general public in certain forms to take place. Don't believe the media and officials if they tell you that aliens have invaded or abducted many people, research Project Blue Beam to see just how great the deception could be, including the use of holographic images by those in power to deceive even further the majority of mankind that will have been Left Behind. Let me end with a VERY strong warning to those who are reading this prior to the Rapture having taken place.

If you know the full true Gospel, fully understanding and believing, yet you refuse to repent and believe into Jesus Christ, do not think that you will suddenly be able to quickly come to the Lord during this time. The Holy Scriptures says otherwise:

"The coming of the lawless one is according to the working of Satan, with all power, signs, and lying wonders, and with all unrighteous deception among those who are perishing, because they did not receive the love of the truth, that they might be saved. And for this reason God will send them strong delusion, that they should believe the lie, that they all may be judged who did not believe the truth but had pleasure in unrighteousness." 2 Thessalonians 2:9-12

"Do not be led astray, God is not mocked; for whatever a man sows, that he will also reap." Galatians 6:7

For those of you with this mindset, I can only say the following:

"For He says: In an acceptable time I have heard you, and in a day of salvation I have helped you. Behold, now is the accepted time; behold, now is the day of salvation." 2nd Corinthians 6:2

Amen!

Nowhere to Hide!

"And the kings of the earth, the great men, the rich men, the commanders, the mighty men, every slave and every free man, hid themselves in the caves and in the rocks of the mountains, and said to the mountains and rocks, Fall on us and hide us from the face of Him who sits on the throne and from the wrath of the Lamb! For the great day of His wrath has come, and who is able to stand?" Revelation 6:15-17

"Then they will begin to say to the mountains, Fall on us! and to the hills, Cover us!" Luke 23:30

"And they shall go into the caves of the rocks, and into the holes of the earth, for the terror of Jehovah, and from the glory of His majesty; when He rises up to make the earth tremble. In that day a man shall throw his idols of silver and gold, which they made each man to bow down to, to the moles and to the bats; to go into the crevices of the rocks, and into the clefts of the cliffs, from the terror of Jehovah, and from the glory of His majesty; when He rises up to make the earth tremble." Isaiah 2:19-21

A book could be written on the ways that governments and private corporations data mine every single individual in existence. The mass surveillance (both public and private), the loss of privacy and how to actually work around that system would make for some interesting reading material. The only problem is that such a book or series of articles would need to be updated quite frequently, with the eventual end update simply being: nowhere to hide.

Technology increases exponentially year after year and with this the ability for a private corporation or the government to collect information, surveil or spy on its citizens, including dissidents. Take Edward Snowden and the amount of documents that are still being released that show the inner working of the National Security Agency (NSA) and surveillance programs against not only foreign governments, but citizens of the United States. A few examples should suffice regarding the seriousness of just how out of control and against the Fourth Amendment the spying has gotten in this country.

The NSA has what is called Tailored Access Operations (TAO). The full scope of what the TAO does is not known, but what is known is that they are responsible for intercepting certain electronics and replacing it with bugged electronics to spy on individuals who are of interest to the NSA. A prime example would be if a watchlisted individual purchased a laptop computer through a major company online. That individuals name is going to be run through the NSA, with a secret partnership, and if flagged, when the laptop is shipped, it will be intercepted. At interception a computer component or two will be replaced with spy equipment that looks identical to the original parts. The package will then continue on its way to the receiver, the assumption that the end user is none the wiser, with the NSA now able to data mine valuable information, even eavesdropping in the dissidents home or office. Another example is vehicle travel.

In 2012 the United States government started publicly testing license plate reading cameras connected to federal databases in both Washington state and Michigan. Secretly beforehand the Drug Enforcement Agency (DEA) had been doing the same thing, the scale of both operations were somewhat limited in scope. Fast forward to nearly 2017 and much of the country is a grid connected to cameras that can be accessed by federal agencies.

In many places the license plates of vehicles are captured to show when and where a vehicle was spotted. To further complicate things, now Bluetooth is being used to also track vehicles in major cities across the United States. Face recognition cameras are being used to go along with license plate readers and identify not only the driver, but the passenger of the vehicle by matching them to digital driver's license photos. As a final example there are surveillance blimps floating above most major cities watching all of their inhabitants 24/7. Don't believe it is that bad, do your own research!

This is primarily written for those who will have been Left Behind, the *"time of Jacob's trouble" (Jer. 30:7)*, more commonly known as the Tribulation or Great Tribulation will have begun. To a certain extent it appears that governments around the world want people to know that they have these capabilities, at least partially.

As of this writing the movie Snowden is showing in movie theaters. Talking about President Obama and the police surveillance state, director Oliver Stone stated, *"the most massive global security surveillance state that's ever been seen, way beyond East Germany's Stasi, way beyond that."* The Holy Scriptures tells us the following:

"And he causes all, both small and great, rich and poor, free and slave, to receive a mark on their right hand or on their foreheads, so that no one may buy or sell except one who has the mark or the name of the beast, or the number of his name." Revelation 13:16-17

Would not such a system require surveillance to control all the financial transactions of the world? For those who are Left Behind, things are going to be tough, get worse and there is only one solution, believing into Jesus Christ as your Lord and Savior. For a time you might be able to hide, for a time you may have sufficient supplies, food and other necessities. Yet without Jesus, you have nothing.

So what happens if you find yourself Left Behind and in the midst of the Great Tribulation? This is serious stuff. Understand that you CAN NOT take the mark of the beast or do homage to the beast or his image and receive Salvation through Jesus Christ. If you take the mark, whatever it may be (you will know when it is time to know), or worship (do homage) to the beast or his image, you have made your choice, you are eternally doomed and will be judged by God accordingly. There will be those who resist taking the mark or doing homage to the beast or his image, but will still not receive Salvation by believing into Jesus Christ.

"And a third angel followed them, saying with a loud voice, If anyone does homage to the beast and his image, and receives his mark on his forehead or on his hand, he himself

shall also drink of the wine of the wrath of God, which is poured out full strength into the cup of His anger. He shall be tormented with fire and brimstone before the holy angels and before the Lamb. And the smoke of their torment ascends forever and ever; and they have no rest day or night, who do homage to the beast and his image, and whoever receives the mark of his name. Here is the perseverance of the saints; here are those who keep the commandments of God and the faith of Jesus. And I heard a voice from Heaven saying to me, Write: Blessed are the dead who die in the Lord from now on. Yes, says the Spirit, that they may rest from their labors, and their works follow with them." Revelation 14:9-13

For them in the end they still lose. Even if they are able to evade detection, have years of food, supplies and weapons holed away in some hidden remote spot and are able to effectively fight off any enemies that might detect and try to stop them, without accepting Salvation, they are lost and will ultimately end up in Hell, just as those who take the mark and worship the beast. While it can not possibly be known what the best form of advice for those who do believe the Gospel, in terms of conduct in a totalitarian society, understand you will most definitely lose your life for Jesus Christ, you will be a martyr.

"And when He opened the fifth seal, I saw under the altar the souls of those who had been slain because of the Word of God and because of the testimony which they held. And they cried with a loud voice, saying, How long, O Lord, holy and true, until You judge and avenge our blood on those who dwell on the earth? And a white robe was given to each one of them; and it was said to them that they should rest a little while longer, until both the number of their fellow servants and their brethren, who were about to be killed as they were, was filled up." Revelation 6:9-11

"And it was granted to him to make war with the saints and to overcome them. And authority was given him over every tribe, tongue, and nation." Revelation 13:7

The question that can not be answered beforehand, is simply how long do you have until things get that bad? Just because you are in the Great Tribulation doesn't necessary mean that it starts off with harsh conditions and continues all of the way through the seven year period. In fact, the guess would be that the first half of the Tribulation might not be so bad at all, there could be no mark of the beast for awhile, things could be relatively calm, after all a peace treaty would just have been signed. The Antichrist would have been unveiled and many would probably now have a firm name on who he is, without all of this guessing that has been going on amongst so-called Christians for years. As time goes on the Antichrist will be known, but he might not be so obvious to most at first. The best advice that could be given from a Believer now to one who becomes a Believer in that time period is simple: trust in God, learn about God, follow Christ...even unto death.

"And he shall confirm a covenant with many for one week. And in the middle of the week he shall cause the sacrifice and the grain offering to cease. And on a corner will be abominations that cause horror, even until the end. And that which was decreed shall be poured out on the desolate." Daniel 9:27

If you have or can find a King James bible, a New King James bible, even a New International Version bible, guard it, hide it, keep it safe. They will come for the bibles, likely they will be outlawed. Don't just keep the bible, read it, spend time in it, allow God to prepare your heart for what you will be going through. Prepare to give your life for Jesus Christ and tell others about Salvation, as the Lord leads.

"Behold, the days are coming, declares the Lord Jehovah, that I will send a famine into the land, not a famine for bread, nor a thirst for water, but rather a famine for hearing the Words of Jehovah. And they shall wander from sea to sea, and from the north even to the east; they shall roam to and fro to seek the Word of Jehovah, and they shall not find it." Amos 8:11-12

"Who shall separate us from the love of Christ? Shall affliction, or distress, or persecution, or famine, or nakedness, or peril, or sword? As it is written: For Your sake we are killed all day long; we are accounted as sheep for the slaughter. Yet in all these things we more than conquer through Him who loves us. For I am persuaded that neither death nor life, nor angels nor rulers nor powers, nor things present nor things to come, nor height nor depth, nor any other created thing, shall be able to separate us from the love of God in Christ Jesus our Lord." Romans 8:35-39

The world you live in is very dangerous and will become more and more dangerous. You will have to decide whether the Lord is leading your heart to openly proclaim your faith at the current or to meet in secret with others in order to try to evade the Antichrist surveillance state.

"But whoever denies Me before men, I will also deny him before My Father in Heaven." Matthew 10:33

Eventually it will simply become impossible to evade detection and whether out of economic necessity, snitches, police state surveillance or other means, you will stand before man and most likely be beheaded. The Lord will give you strength and the words to speak during that time. You made the correct choice, you chose to serve the Lord.

"And I saw thrones, and they sat on them, and judgment was committed to them; and I saw the souls of those who had been beheaded for their witness to Jesus and for the Word of God, who had not done homage to the beast or his image, and had not received his mark on their foreheads or on their hands. And they lived and reigned with Christ for a thousand years." Revelation 20:4

"Fear not, for I am with you; be not dismayed, for I am your God." Isaiah 41:10a

"Jehovah is on my side; I will not fear. What can man do to me?" Psalms 118:6

"He who finds his life will lose it, and he who loses his life on account of Me will find it." Matthew 10:39

"For we walk by faith, not by sight. We are confident, yes, preferring rather to be absent from the body and to be at home with the Lord." 2nd Corinthians 5:7-8

"Do not fear any of those things which you are about to suffer."..."Be faithful unto death, and I will give you the crown of life." Revelation 2:10

"For this God is our God forever and ever; He will be our guide even unto death." Psalms 48:14

Amen!

Left Behind

"Jehovah said unto my Lord, Sit at My right hand, until I place Your enemies as Your footstool. Jehovah shall send the staff of Your strength out of Zion. Rule in the midst of Your enemies. Your people shall be volunteers in the day of Your power; in the splendor of holiness, from the womb of the dawn, You have the dew of Your youth. Jehovah has sworn and will not regret it: You are a priest forever according to the order of Melchizedek. The Lord at Your right hand shall shatter kings in the day of His wrath. He shall judge among the nations, He shall fill them with dead bodies; He shall greatly shatter the heads over the earth. He shall drink of the brook by the wayside; therefore He shall lift up the head." Psalms 110

Over the years I have seen many different takes on what happens when the Rapture occurs and during the *"time of Jacob's trouble" (Jer. 30:7)*, better known as the Great Tribulation or Tribulation. There has been many fanciful charts made up lining all of the catastrophes and judgments from God throughout a seven year period. Numerous books have been written on the subject, even movies made depicting crisis after crisis after Christians have been Raptured. Yet with the vast majority of these books, movies, studies and articles, while interesting, I have a large problem with.

"Remember this, and be a man; refresh the memory of your heart, you who rebel. Remember the former things from a long time ago; for I am the Mighty God, and there is no other; I am God, and no one else is like Me, declaring the end from the beginning, and from antiquity things which are not yet done, saying, My counsel shall stand, and I will do all My pleasure; calling a bird of prey from the east, the man who executes my counsel from a distant land. Indeed, I have spoken it; I will also bring it to pass. I have formed it; I will also do it. Listen to me, you stubborn-hearted, who are far from righteousness; I bring near My righteousness. It shall not be far off, and My salvation shall not delay. And I will place salvation in Zion, My glory for Israel." Isaiah 46:8-13

"But you, O Daniel, shut up the words and seal the book, to the time of the end. Many shall run to and fro, and knowledge shall be increased." Daniel 12:4

"For we walk by faith, not by sight." 2nd Corinthians 5:7

Some are clearly wrong in terms of accurate biblical prophecy, others make the assumption of devastation right from the beginning, including an immediate mark of the beast system that is up and operating. Others separate judgments where they are lumped together and most assume to simply have it all charted out. The Holy Scriptures declares what will take place throughout Revelation and numerous other books of the Bible, but for man to declare he can make known exactly how these things are going to play out is wrong.

The take on this book or article is to provide a warning to those who have been Left Behind. A terrible thing has happened to the world, God has removed the restraining of the Holy Spirit, ALL true Christians at the moment the Rapture occurred ARE GONE, at that time there is only darkness on the earth. How many people who are suddenly so startled at what has occurred can barely contain the shaking of their hands and the knocking of their knees! This is the mindset that a person should have who has been Left Behind!

So exactly what is going to take place and when? While I certainly have many speculations on what might be technology that would allow for the mark of the beast to prevent man from buying and selling without it, how could I declare what it will be? I don't know, preciously the same when it comes to exactly how God's judgment against mankind plays out and the timeframes for those ordeals. What I do know is that most people will die throughout the Great Tribulation.

I have seen an article about numbers computed by a friend who showed that it appears 90% of all humanity will die during the *"time of Jacob's trouble" (Jer. 30:7)* or 70th Week *(Dan. 9:26-27)*, better known as the Great Tribulation, with Israel this will be lower at 2/3 of all Jewish people, with 1/3 remaining at the time of Christ's Second Coming.

"And it shall come to pass in all the land, says Jehovah, that two parts in it shall be cut off and perish, but the third shall be left in it. And I will bring the third part through the fire, and I will refine them as silver is refined. And I will try them as gold is tried. They shall call on My name, and I will answer them. I will say, It is My people, and they shall say, Jehovah is my God." Zechariah 13:8-9

"I will purge out the rebels from among you, and those who transgress against Me. I will bring them out of the land where they dwell, but they shall not enter into the land of Israel. And you will know that I am Jehovah." Ezekiel 20:38

So if you are looking for a roadmap of events during the Great Tribulation, it would make no difference if someone could preciously declare exactly what/when/how/where the judgments would take place. You need to be focusing on the 'why' and understand that God's hand of mercy STILL extends to you, if you are willing to hear and obey, even unto death. Even with such a roadmap, there is a 90% chance that you would not make it to the end, even then what are your odds of making it to the end without accepting the mark of the beast? For those who accept the mark of the beast or worship the beast or his image are UNABLE to accept Salvation and be Saved, therefore they will ultimately be cast into the Lake of Fire. I would dare say that your chance of making it to the end, unscathed, is near zero, if not just numerically impossible. So verses from the Holy Scriptures about what will occur are as follows:

"And unless those days were shortened, no flesh would be kept safe alive; but for the elect's sake those days will be shortened. Then if anyone says to you, Look, here is the Christ; or, There; do not believe it. For false christs and false prophets will arise and show great signs and wonders to lead astray, if possible, even the elect. Behold, I have told you beforehand." Matthew 24:22-25

"And I heard the angel of the waters saying: You are righteous, O Lord, the One who is and who was and who is to be, because You have judged these things, for they have shed the blood of saints and prophets, and You have given them blood to drink, for they are deserving. And I heard another out of the altar saying, Even so, Lord God Almighty, true and righteous are Your judgments." Revelation 16:5-7

"Terror and the pit and the snare are upon you, O inhabitant of the earth. And it shall be that he who flees from the sound of terror shall fall into the pit. And he who comes up out of the midst of the pit shall be caught in the snare. For the windows from on high are opened, and the foundations of the earth quake. The earth has been badly broken! The earth is split open and cracked through! The earth has shaken greatly and is tottering! Like a drunkard the earth is staggering back and forth! And it sways to and fro like a hut! Its transgressions have been heavy upon it; and it shall fall and not rise again." Isaiah 24:17-20

"And I saw another angel flying in the midst of heaven, having the eternal gospel to preach to those who dwell on the earth; to every nation, tribe, tongue, and people; saying with a loud voice, Fear God and give glory to Him, for the hour of His judgment has come; also, do homage to Him who made the heavens and the earth, the sea and springs of water. And another angel followed, saying, Babylon is fallen, is fallen, that great city, because she has made all nations drink of the wine of the wrath of her sexual perversion. And a third angel followed them, saying with a loud voice, If anyone does homage to the beast and his image, and receives his mark on his forehead or on his hand, he himself shall also drink of the wine of the wrath of God, which is poured out full strength into the cup of His anger. He shall be tormented with fire and brimstone before the holy angels and before the Lamb. And the smoke of their torment ascends forever and ever; and they have no rest day or night, who do homage to the beast and his image, and whoever receives the mark of his name. Here is the perseverance of the saints; here are those who keep the commandments of God and the faith of Jesus. And I heard a voice from Heaven saying to me, Write: Blessed are the dead who die in the Lord from now on. Yes, says the Spirit, that they may rest from their labors, and their works follow with them." Revelation 14:6-13

"And I saw the dead, small and great, standing before God. And books were opened. And another book was opened, which is the Book of Life. And the dead were judged according to their works, out of the things which were written in the books. And the sea gave up the dead who were in it, and Death and Hades delivered up the dead who were in them. And they were judged, each one, according to their works. And Death and Hades were cast into the Lake of Fire. This is the second death. And anyone not found written in the Book of Life was cast into the Lake of Fire." Revelation 20:12-15

If you are reading this and you have been Left Behind, you must quickly understand that if you are seeking answers, you must turn to your Creator and His Son, Jesus Christ. You must repent and believe into Jesus Christ, accepting God's free gift of Salvation, understanding that you will lay down your life for the Lord Jesus Christ, but in doing so you will save your life.

"For whoever desires to save his life will lose it, but whoever loses his life on account of Me will save it." Luke 9:24

"He who finds his life will lose it, and he who loses his life on account of Me will find it." Matthew 10:39

This is a VERY serious matter, one of utmost importance. There is no more serious matter than the eternal destination of each soul and every man, every woman, every child of understanding age, must equally consider the importance and understand that they are lost, destined to and deserving of Hell and without Christ, who died on the Cross for your sins, Salvation is impossible. There is no other way to Heaven than through Jesus Christ our Lord and Savior. If you are reading this and already in the midst of the Great Tribulation than understand at the moment the Rapture happened there were no more Christians left on the earth, despite the fact there are numerous people left who call themselves Christians, but those who truly knew Jesus Christ are gone.

Do not seek after the knowledge of those who were Left Behind, they didn't get it right the first time, seek rather after the Most High and He will be found.

"Enter by the narrow gate; for wide is the gate and broad is the way that leads to destruction, and there are many entering in through it. Because narrow is the gate and distressing is the way which leads unto life, and there are few who find it. Beware of false prophets, who come to you in sheep's clothing, but inwardly they are ravenous wolves. You will know them from their fruits. Do men gather grapes from thornbushes or figs from thistles? Even so, every good tree produces excellent fruit, but a corrupt tree produces evil fruit. A good tree is not able to produce evil fruit, nor is a corrupt tree able to produce excellent fruit. Every tree that does not produce excellent fruit is cut down and thrown into the fire. Therefore from their fruits you will know them. Not everyone who says to Me, Lord, Lord, will enter the kingdom of Heaven, but he who does the will of My Father in Heaven. Many will say to Me in that day, Lord, Lord, have we not prophesied in Your name, cast out demons in Your name, and done many works of power in Your name? And then I will declare to them, I never knew you; depart from Me, you who work out lawlessness!" Matthew 7:13-23

"Seek Jehovah while He may be found; call upon Him while He is near. Let the wicked forsake his way, and the unrighteous man his thoughts; and let him return to Jehovah, and He will have mercy on him; and to our God, for He will abundantly pardon." Isaiah 55:6-7

Time is running out, do not delay!

"And I saw another angel flying in the midst of heaven, having the eternal gospel to preach to those who dwell on the earth; to every nation, tribe, tongue, and people; saying with a loud voice, Fear God and give glory to Him, for the hour of His judgment has

come; also, do homage to Him who made the heavens and the earth, the sea and springs of water." Revelation 14:7

Amen!

Waking Up

"For in much wisdom is much grief; and he who increases knowledge increases sorrow." Ecclesiastes 1:18

I was married to Sabrina at the age of 19 in 1997, our son Joshua was born to us in 2011. For most of our lives Sabrina and I did not pay much attention to politics or the news. As we got older we began to look at local news, but unless it was a major ordeal we often ignored it.

After the events of 9/11, we became convinced that the event was an evil scheme purported by certain tyrannical people in our own government. Who they were, we didn't know, we didn't have names, but we knew that the official story was a lie. Many hours of research went into making such conclusion, as we reviewed excellent work by numerous independent movie makers and writers. I had always been an avid reader and recalled reading a quote years prior from Henry Ford about the banking system that raised an eyebrow or two, but I was never a conspiracy theorist. In fact I had always thought those people had a couple of nuts and bolts loose.

Growing up in Michigan, Henry Ford had always been a man whom I studied when I was a student in grade school. Some of the Ford's lived in Harbor Springs, close to where I grew up. So when I read his quote, *"it is well enough that people of the nation do not understand our banking and monetary system, for if they did, I believe there would be a revolution before tomorrow morning,"* naturally I wondered what it meant. I had mentioned this quote to a few people and no one seemed to know the meaning of it. I had searched on the computer and read a bit about banking, but still didn't understand the meaning of the quote.

One day, while thinking of this quote again, I finally found an author who wrote about the banking subject, Eustace Mullins. I quickly ordered a used copy of his book, *The Secrets of the Federal Reserve*. Finally after having read the book, I understood that the banking system was indeed flawed. There was too much power pushed into the hands of a few people that allowed them to have too much control over the affairs, of not only the United States, but the world. Money talks, the whole world knows that, and our system in the United States is flawed. For the next several months I would order and read books, trying to begin to understand the society that we lived in, this was in the spring of 2006.

Some would say that a distrust in the government is nonsense, others would say that it is natural, we are of the later group. The government should not be trusted. As both of us began to learn how the congressional system worked and what our elected officials were doing, we began to see that there is indeed a conspiracy against the American people. Our government doesn't like people looking into what they are really up to. They try to create a left-right paradigm show that goes on election after election. We are expected to simply go on with life, ignore the facts, watch the show and be distracted by every trinket or new app that is available, too busy to realize that our world is starting to fade.

There are always extremes to those who know such things. There are those who are preparing for war against the government. There are those who think that the world is going to end abruptly, as in 2012, or that the poles are going to shift and the world will be turned back into the stone age. Another group of people think that a nuclear war will be unleashed and yet others see an attack against those Americans who are patriotic and stand by their rights, exercising free speech to try and get things to be run on a more constitutional level. If we were to be categorized, as we now know somewhere we are, we would fall into the later group. We did not want our rights to continue to be eroded, yet we did not advocate, promote or speak of violence.

Not only did we not want our rights to continue to be eroded, but we also wanted things like NAFTA and other original trade agreements, to stop taking away our good American jobs. We knew how hard it is to make it financially in this world without a good college degree and we always struggled to figure out how to beat the system, to earn money independently. We didn't want our food irradiated, sprayed with tons of poison toxins and all of these dangerous chemicals added to it, many of these poisons having been banned in European foods. For each of these topics we bought well known and good reviewed books. Suddenly the mainstream news stations didn't seem so appealing anymore, so we turned to what is called alternative media. We wanted the truth or closer to the truth, not a bunch of lies that was bordering on what could be called propaganda.

Is it wrong to want a redress? Is it wrong to think that the government might have some conspiracy against those Americans who could still think for themselves? As I often relayed to people about what would become our bit of political activity, the following analogy: if we were to stand on the side of the highway with signs that said aliens run the Whitehouse, people would just think we are crazy, no one would do anything. So how is it that if we want to hand out some DVD's that show the official story of 9/11 is a lie, whether or not people agree with us, that we are now considered terrorists?

Once we began to look underneath the rocks, as to what the government, corporations, food companies, banking or anybody else was doing and seeing that things were not as they were perceived, we began to question everything. Suddenly Sabrina's makeup was in the trash, replaced with much more natural products from another company, that was also much more expensive. My deodorant stick really did have a lot of aluminum, as I had read. I was worried that all of that aluminum could cause Alzheimer's in my old age. A simple ten dollar salt crystal worked well enough as a natural deodorant replacement and lasted nearly a year, saving us money. Changes were happening.

We sold our microwave, had thrown out our non-stick cookware, we began to eat some organic food and tried to get some fresh produce from Bill's Farm Market in Petoskey during the summer months. We purchased canning goods and tons of canning jars, anticipating that we would eventually have a small garden or buy some fresh local products and can them for the winter months. Our desire to get involved in politics seemed to be a necessity and our duty as American citizens to get involved. No longer should we be partly responsible for our eroding society, by doing such things as voting for whichever name that we recognized the most, as we had done when we were 18. And yes, for those Americans who do not realize this happens, a lot of misguided and uneducated young people, who are convinced that they should vote, will vote for whichever name they recognize the most.

There were changes made in our life that we deemed necessary. While it was much easier said than done, both of us eventually quit drinking pop. When we saw a study in the news about how nearly half of corn syrup contained mercury, we knew we just had to stop. Whether an organic apple is really better that a non-organic apple or an apple from a local orchard is best, that is up to the reader to decide, we don't know. What we knew, was the choices we were making with the products that we used and consumed did have consequences to our health. Ignoring political events and the news did effect our businesses, with laws being passed that could either help or hurt our monthly revenue. Being a Christian wasn't what most churches claimed it was, there is simplicity in Christ, but the standards set out by God in the Holy Scriptures were much different that what was preached from most pulpits.

Armed with having now read tens of thousands of pages of news, hundreds of books, listening to those involved patriots explain how things work, we were resolute to truly be pleasing to God, as well as being patriots in America. There would be labels for us, we were dangerous, right-wing terrorists, according to some talking heads. At the time we didn't even own a gun, both of us had only shot one a few times. We had fishing poles and pocket knives.

This is not written to convince the reader that we know exactly what is right or wrong in terms of politics or that those who read this should immediately investigate such things as 9/11, rather that you think for yourself. We are not trying to convince the world that they should think as we think or do as we do. Rather there is a conclusion to the matter.

Hours and hours, days and days, years and years, can be spent studying anything. At the end of our lives we will each stand before the Most High God. At that point all of mankind will give an account, the Book of Life will be opened and whoever's name is not written in that Book will be cast into the Lake of Fire. Time would be much better spent seeking God, finding Jesus Christ and learning as much as possible about Him; to be in complete subjection to Him. These other things are simply vanity.

"Let us hear the conclusion of the whole matter: Fear God, and keep His commandments; for this is for every man. For God will bring every work into judgment, including every secret thing, whether good or evil." Ecclesiastes 12:13-14

From the realization that not everything was as it appeared regarding most churches, to 9/11 being a wake up call towards harsh tyrannical revelations and finally researching miniature topics, years went into reading books, making changes and trying to grasp how the world really worked. Finally having opinions of our own rather than repeating like a parrot what was said on mainstream news stations, we decided to become a little bit political active. We decided to become, in the eyes of the government, domestic terrorists.

Political Dissidents

What is a political dissident? Would it be correct to say that a rough definition would be an individual or a group of people who are in disagreement with policies of the government? If so, there are many political dissidents, in fact each one of our elected officials could be considered a political dissident because they are there to speak out against this or that and make changes regarding laws and policies. What a political dissident is not, is a terrorist. While it would be true that a terrorist, by nature, is a political dissident, they are not interchangeable both ways.

By time someone researches deep enough into what is going on in our country, they will sooner or later realize that these terrorist watchlists they read about in articles or hear about on a Youtube clip, are for them. Who else is it? This is not to suggest that the United States government doesn't have the responsibility to keep people secure, but shouldn't these things be in line with the Constitution. While we are not suggesting that the Constitution be opened and changed, more bad would come than good, it is within the rights of the States to amend the Constitution. The debate has raged on for years about whether or not these new police state powers, like the Patriot Act, are infringing on civil rights.

Edward Snowden released tons of documents that are still coming to light. The debate here is not whether he is guilty of some crime, irregardless of what is thought, his documentation definitely shows crime, crimes that the United States government is committing against its own citizens. What has been done about that yet? The Freedom Act? What a joke! Where is the line drawn with civil liberties verses securing our country against terrorism, both domestic and international?

By 2007 our businesses were doing well. Our pooper-scooper service, The Weekly Scoop, was in its peak with 46 regular customers and a bunch of seasonal, one time or spring clean up customers. Aardvark Janitorial, our commercial custodial service had boomed. In 2006 we began to work for Boyne USA cleaning one of their golf clubhouses in Harbor Springs. This was a seasonal account, but ran seven days a week during the golf season, almost six months of the year! We also picked up a computer software office and were cleaning for the Beaver Island Boat Company, a ferry boat that provides service between Charlevoix and Beaver Island, Michigan. Sabrina kept her job at the local hospital as a housekeeper because our money was decent during half of the year, the other half of the year was more difficult. If we were to lose any work one of us would have to get a job anyway. Things were going in the direction that we had hoped for in our lives, just a bit more slowly than we anticipated.

Bible studies were held at least once per week at our house. By now we would all meet for hours each time. The first portion would be dinner, which was often pizza and then we would have a bible study that would last up to 2 hours, going over various topics, complete with homework that most of us found time the week prior to complete. Afterwards we would play basketball, laser tag or even go bowling as a weekly routine. We would normally meet up around 8pm at night and sometimes hang out until 1am or

2am in the morning, before bidding each other farewell. Our lives were going well, but we noted there seemed to be political trouble brewing, things were drifting away from freedom to slavery, we decided to do our duty as American citizens and not just sit on the sidelines.

Our political activism started with handing out a few DVD's about 9/11. Some of our friends also did the same. There seemed to still be a chance back then that enough people would find out about what really happened on 9/11 and the government would be forced to open a new investigation, an independent investigation. Looking through online forums and news articles, there seemed to be a consensus among those who felt the same about 9/11 also thought that Ron Paul was the man for the job as President. We eventually became Ron Paul supporters.

A local website, with a nice community forum, called Northern Michigan Update started up. I quickly signed up to the forum and began to post articles and links to movies, mostly about 9/11 and also about the banking industry. Many other local issues were discussed, some of which was political. It would be through this website that I would make a couple of friends and eventually help Kyle, the website owner, by becoming an administrator at the website, helping to run it and keep the forum clean.

The website had a decent amount of viewers, but not a horrible amount of people posting in the forums. Some people posted a lot, others not so much. A lot of the members would eventually meet those who they talked to within the forums on the outside. In my case, I would eventually become friends with one of those posters on the forum, a man named Ken. He and I would on occasion meet up to talk about politics and a large company that was trying to push their way into Pellston, Michigan, just north of Petoskey, where we lived. We also discussed our views of where we thought this country was heading. As we would sit at a buffet in the south end of Petoskey, filling up on endless plates of food, we realized that despite our age difference, as he was much older, we had a lot in common. The website became a casual pastime and I would spend about an hour on it per day. One day the Petoskey News-Review, the local newspaper, had an article about this large company that was looking to setup its headquarters in Pellston, potentially bringing up to 500 new jobs to the area.

My first thought as a businessman was what did they do and what would their need be for a janitorial contract. We kept a close eye on new developments, realizing that even if we didn't get the cleaning contract, someone else would and this would mean they might give up other accounts. So the opportunity to advertise when big changes were coming in town was at those precise moments. This particular company, which we will call Company X, had gotten my suspicion right away.

Disclaimer: We do not have any proof that Company X, Person X or Person Y did anything wrong against us. They just had the connections where the ability might have been there to do so, if they desired.

One of the conspiracy theories or a conspiracy fact that is out there is that there are concentration camps in America that are built or being built for the eventual roundup of political dissidents. As we began to look into these things, my wife and I, plus a few friends tried to find the ones that supposedly weren't that far away from our house in Michigan. There was a seemingly very outdated map online that was tossed from website to website showing locations of where these camps supposedly were. To this day we have only seen proof of a few smaller holding facilities, like Pier 57 in New York City. It is not to say it is beyond the realm of possibility, as it would be imagined that any such facilities would be tucked away on government military bases and property. We searched out these supposed ones that were near us and did not see anything of concrete evidence worth noting, but there is also another intriguing portion to the story.

The Federal Emergency Management Agency (FEMA), the Department of Homeland Security (DHS) and other federal governmental agencies put out bids to private contractors to have emergency tent cities that could be erected within a matter of days. I've personally viewed some of the plans and requirements for such things and seen that, in theory, using a public-private partnership, camps could literally be erected nationwide in a matter of days. There are also companies that produce mobile prison cells made out of reinforced cement. These mobile prison cells can be stacked one upon another. Small towns all across America have received surveillance vehicles, tanks, SWAT vehicles, machine guns, sophisticated surveillance equipment, military type uniforms, drones, endless amounts of federal grants, a lot of it from the DHS. What are they preparing for or rather what is the federal government preparing them for? On top of that, many police and fire stations have been hardened against a potential domestic attack. They have bullet proof windows, concrete barriers and other preventive measures put into place, in case of total civil unrest. It doesn't end there.

One thing there is very strong evidence for is a prison grid being built all around us. Talk to a few handful of Canadians and see what there response is to the United States building up and securing the northern border. They see it as overkill, some see it as a way to keep Americans locked in, others think the US is paranoid. The Customs and Border Protection (CBP) as well as the Immigration and Customs Enforcement (ICE) have been busy building new terminals at most border crossings, complete with interrogation rooms, machine guns and holding cells. There are hidden medal detectors in our national forests, as well as along the border with Canada that can detect someone crossing into the United States. People seriously under estimate the drone capability, long range sensitive camera equipment and the fact that there is nearly an acre wide opening cut right near the northern border, running nearly the entirety of the wooden portions of Canada's shared border with the United States, to aid in all of this surveillance. If you ever thought of running to Canada if things ever got rough, you got a big surprise awaiting you, we've just scratched the surface. As if that wasn't bad enough, it gets worse.

For years we have known that the government is tracking locations via cell phones. We've known that conversations can be listened to in real time. There is substantial evidence that all calls are even recorded and the amount of evidence that calls are screened for certain key words is overwhelming. The Central Intelligence Agency (CIA) or the Federal Bureau of Investigation (FBI) do not need to sneak into your house and place a bug, you purchased one yourself and pay the monthly payments for them! Of course, you don't have anything to hide, or do you? We didn't. Computers have never been very secure, but it is very easy for the government to request all of your online usage, the keys you type, the websites you view, using different programs that are in place with the proper warrants or oversight required by these federal agencies. For these federal agencies it is often as easy as rubber stamping the request, the paper work is often minimal. Remember that ongoing debate between civil liberties and security?

Each printer places yellow dots hidden on your paper as a document comes out. These can be used by the federal government to track who actually printed something. People used to be impressed with the way the Soviet Union had a copy of how a typewriter would type, essentially a fingerprint of the typewriter. As all typewriters had to be registered in the Soviet Union, it would only be a matter of time before the political dissident, who dared to speak out against the government, was dragged off to a gulag, likely to die. This is world history, these types of things happen over and over again.

Cars now have satellite and Bluetooth technology that can tell a governmental agency exactly where the car is currently located or where it had been. There is even features that could allow eavesdropping in the car, unbeknownst to the passengers. On the side of the roads in America there is a sophisticated Intelligent Transportation System (ITS) that has been being built up for years now. These cameras scan the license plate of cars and upload it to databases. In fact a national database run by the Federal Bureau of Investigation (FBI) has more and more States being connected to it. Recently it was disclosed that the Drug Enforcement Agency (DEA) has been tracking vehicles via license plate reading cameras for years! Want to know where someone is at or has been, even if they don't have satellite system built into their vehicle? Run their plate number through the National Crime Information Center (NCIC). In 2016 it was made known to me that the technology has even advanced further, where now there are not only cameras that read your license plates, but at the same time there are cameras taking digital photographs to match who is the driver and front passenger in the vehicle.

Further, much computer software comes with built-in back doors. If you have the software registered in your name it can reveal a lot about your computer and internet usage that could be passed off to any requesting governmental agency. Spend a lot of times on social networks? So do police agencies throughout the United States, the FBI, DHS, DEA and a host of other federal and state agencies. Don't assume because your information on social networks is marked private that you are untouchable, you're not.

Tracking is also completely possible through the use of RFID chips, Wifi or Bluetooth technology; the identity of customers can be known the second they walk into a retail store. Customer movements, what they look at and what they purchase can all be recorded to their permanent record stored in private company databases. Right now there are large retailers who use face recognition cameras, having done so for years, to record every single purchase that a customer makes into their database that can be accessed by federal agencies through the proper channels and legal requests. Ever use a credit or debit card at one of these retail stores? If that is the case, cash will no longer work for anonymous purchases, your face is the only further identification they need to know your identity, forever. Ever carry your smart phone into the same store, same thing.

Credit card companies and banks keep tabs on all of your usage, they have to, but that information also gets stored in databases. When a gun is purchased through a regular dealer that information also must be databased by federal law. Any gun registration required by local or State municipalities can also be requested from federal agencies. Online purchase all have information that can be requested by a federal agency. Each year there and tens of thousands of National Security Letters (NSL) sent out, many of them by the FBI. Google themselves received nearly 15,000 requests for users information in the first half of 2012 alone. There were over 1.1 million requests in 2012 for information regarding wireless phone users usage by law enforcement agencies.

The FBI also began to place Global Positioning System (GPS) tracking devices on cars of suspected criminals and terrorists, many without any warrants. Though the Supreme Court has forbidden this practice, without an official warrant, other methods are being put into place, where the need for such devices may be unnecessary to the FBI or DHS in the near future. Drones have been used by both the FBI and DHS in watching and tracking individuals throughout the United States. Exact numbers and targets are still forthcoming from these federal agencies. The point is, much of what you do is being tracked and traced, databased and scanned for whatever flags the government determines makes you suspicious or worth watching. Whether or not you don't mind or think that you have nothing to hide, it is an infringement against your 4th Amendment rights, which have not yet been revoked.

The infamous Patriot Act allows the government to do a 'sneak and peek'. This is where a federal agency, like the FBI, comes into your house when you are gone, looks around to see if there are things in your home that match the profile they are making against you and leave, without you ever knowing about the search and with no warrant. Through this same Patriot Act, the government can also request a library hand over all of the names of the books you have been reading. The John Werner Defense Authorization Act allows the government to declare you a non citizen. This is particularly of concern because if you are stripped of your citizenship you can lose all of your rights, the right to an attorney or even a right to a trial by your peers. It could be a military tribunal trial for you or anyone else that the government believes is a threat to national security and labels a domestic terrorist. Look at what happened in Guantánamo Bay! Have you ever heard about the CIA floating prison ships or the torture prisons operated by the CIA in Europe? Americans are far too ignorant about the events that take place right around all of us. They are right in front of our eyes, the documents that provide evidence of these abuses can be pulled up online, often right from their respective federal agencies websites. Federal legislation can also be read online and then their is Obamacare. With that legislation all of your medical records now can become viewed by the federal government. In fact the government has you sign HIPPA that has you agree that they can use your medical usage to track you down. Get sick and go to a clinic or hospital, if your wanted badly enough, they will know where you are at in real time. What if the government had a personal vendetta against you? Are you really going to go through with that surgery? Are you sure it will work out?

Truly the rabbit hole is endless. A book could be written on just the types of surveillance activities that the government does against its own citizens. The technology would blow the mind of many Americans who would not even realize it is possible to do this type of tracking and surveillance of individuals. If you want an example simply search online Stringray and FBI or tracking users online with battery usage. Each year the police state prison grid quietly grows stronger in the United States, with only a few people speaking out against it. Probably, with the release of the Snowden documents, an encyclopedia set would have to be written to cover all of the technology used by federal agencies to track and database people. In order for readers to understand our story some of this must be conveyed. One thing that must be understood, as it is key to these agencies discovering us, are the fusion centers.

Each state of the union has one primary fusion center. Every major city also has their own fusion center. Recently small fusion centers have been showing up across the country, in small towns, throughout the United States. These fusion centers normally operate a bit differently, under emergency management programs, through state and federal grants. The small fusion centers that are in place don't have the access to federal databases that the larger ones do in the major cities and the state run centers. A fusion center is simply a collaboration between state and federal law enforcement and intelligence collecting agencies.

At these fusion centers, information is disseminated, databases are accessed by the federal law enforcement agencies and departments, such as CBP, ICE, DEA, FBI, US Marshal Service, the National Guard, the state police and all other law enforcement agencies in their respective city or state, collect and share information. While they can be great tools to help solve crimes, prevent further crimes and otherwise keep the public safe, they can also be tools used to watch and harass American citizens whom the government has declared dissidents, usually by calling them domestic terrorists. The information pours into these fusion centers, but it doesn't always pour out.

All of these fusion centers are kept under hush-hush circumstances. Each state has, by legislation, set their own rules regarding the balance of civil liberties verses national or state security interests. In some states a fusion center could be much less likely to be used as a political tool of the FBI or another federal agency against a dissident. In another state the fusion center could give these same federal agencies free reign. A fusion center will assist local law enforcement agencies or sheriff departments. These local law enforcement agencies don't have access to much of the information kept in federal databases, accessible at the state run fusion centers.

Fusion centers are connected to databases that are only accessible by certain federal agencies, state police and certain major cities where a regional fusion center is located. When a state trooper pulls you over, they may have certain other information regarding you than if your local city police department had pulled you over. All of this information from these fusion centers is confidential and not shared with the public openly. Getting partial access, while technically possible, to your information in your fusion center file is highly unlikely. Each state is different, depending on the legislation that created the state run fusion center, but a request for information to the fusion center about yourself would likely prove impossible to get, especially if your name is on a federal watchlist that labels you as a suspected terrorist. These state fusion centers contain special databases that are accessible by only the state police, made available from the federal government.

One such federal agency is called the Terrorist Screening Agency (TSC). When a suspected terrorist or domestic terrorist is pulled over by a state trooper and the driver's information is run through the trooper's onboard law enforcement information system, a special notice may appear on the computer screen inside their police cruiser. The trooper is not allowed to tell the person that they may be suspected of terrorism, but will have three choices, as determined by TSC, that will be mandated on their onboard computer screen.

The first choice the officer could receive, after running the pulled over driver's information who turns out to be flagged as a suspect on the federal watchlist, is to contact TSC after the encounter is over with the individual and answer any questions posed by a TSC agent regarding their suspect. The second is for the officer to call the TSC during their encounter with the suspect. When the call is made to the Terrorist Screening Center, TSC can ask the officer to detain the person, but more likely, will have the officer ask a simple question or two, to the unsuspecting driver and relay those answers back to the TSC, after the encounter is over. The third and final option, as these are the only three that have been made public through Freedom of Information Act (FOIA) requests, is to arrest the suspect on the spot. Here is where it gets tricky.

Most Americans are going to assume that their name is not on some sort of terrorist database and most Americans would be completely correct. However, what if you are an avid gun enthusiast who purchased a couple of extra AR-15s before the prices shot up in 2012? Or what if you got sick and tired of having to find ammo and just bought a thousand rounds off an internet retailer? What if you decided you wanted to buy ten pressure cookers to give out as graduation gifts? Don't realize that people are now getting raided for buying pressure cookers? Think again, they are. The possibilities are endless. Whether or not you made an innocent purchase, whether you wanted to stock up or store food or whether you decided that ammo would be the new currency in twenty years, these decisions and thoughts don't make you a terrorist. With these innocent decisions made, your name could possibly get added to a federal database or the watchlist. There are now over a million names on the terrorist watchlist, the far vast majority of these being United States citizens, the minor part being foreigners who move to America on a visa, temporary or otherwise.

This terrorist watchlist, as many people call the database, is operated by the FBI. With over a million people on that watchlist, if we were to exclude children under the age of 16, that would mean that up and down your street, someone is on the watchlist. What for? You tell me! Did you ever visit a website that talked badly about the government or conspiracies? Did you buy too many cans of food at once? Have you posted anti-government comments on your social websites? What books have you read? What movies or music do you keep in the cloud online? What digital files have you downloaded? Who are your friends?

Each one of these claims can be researched on the internet, but perhaps you better read the remainder of our story before you get busy doing so. This is the same sort of police state tactics that the Stasi did. This is the same sort of things that Mao tried to do. This is what the KGB did. This is what the United States government is doing. While masses of people are not missing or being killed in suspicious accidents, there are some stories here and there, like our story, where the government is using these lists to find and do various things to people. Whether false imprisonment, missing persons or accidents, some of these stories have a smell of tyranny. Never forget that drones have now been used to kill American citizens. This is a fact, not a theory.

So if you are reading this and find yourself having missed the Rapture, Left Behind and in the midst of the *"time of Jacob's trouble" (Jer. 30:7)*, better known as the Great Tribulation or Tribulation, than realize that these lists will go far above and beyond what is publicly known about them at the time of this writing, not only in the United States, but worldwide.

During the Great Tribulation you will be sought after, tracked down and killed for such things as owning a Bible, reading the Holy Scriptures, believing into Jesus Christ as your Lord and Savior or even trying to gather information about Jesus. Remember that at some point during the Tribulation no man can buy or sell without the mark of the beast *(Rev. 13:17)*. Be VERY aware of the reality of the police state you now live in and take precautions, knowing what you face.

Armed with this new information, we will now continue our story or rather document what the government apparently thought that our crimes were.

Standing Up

Company X had become troublesome to us. Here was a company that we thought could actually be part of this plan to build private interment camps in the United States. Their national response center was to include 2,000 parking spots, large on-site facilities, a water tower, all hidden behind Pellston Regional Airport in Emmet County, Michigan.

Pellston, a small village, just a few miles north of Petoskey, was home to the local regional airport. Bart Stupak, the former U.S. Representative from Michigan, had managed to secure grants for Pellston Regional Airport. The airport became nicely remodeled with many well carved, wood-working features, local animals on display from taxidermy services, modern looking carpet, a new restaurant and a large airport parking lot. The airport property was on hundreds of acres, but behind the airport were some two tracks on property that was owned by the state of Michigan. For those who live in places like Chicago, two tracks are dirt roads that usually have a grass track down the middle of the otherwise dirt road. Off these two track roads behind the airport, you could find a beautiful deciduous forest, where we had once searched for morel mushrooms, black and red raspberries and even took a peek or two at the beautiful Maple River that runs along the property. In this very spot a small ghost town once stood, having been long forgotten about. We knew our local area, we knew our local history and this was a very rural area of Emmet County. This is where Company X wanted to put their first national response center.

A discussion about Company X on a local forum website, Northern Michigan Update, became very popular. There was a group of people who believed that Company X was after all of the rich water resources, natural pure aquifers, that could be found around Pellston. Others on the forum simply believed there was more to the story than the locals were being told. We were skeptical of Company X because the construction plans didn't make sense to us in comparison to the services that they would offer. Company X was advertising to provide an exclusive service, primarily to upper class individuals and families in the United States.

The service they provided would be the following: a customer of Company X would pay them a one-time fee of $50,000, then a yearly maintenance fee of $15,000. Depending on exactly what service the customer signed up for, their new client would be handed a satellite phone. This satellite phone came with a promise, that if there was ever an emergency situation, Company X would rescue them wherever they were, in an area like Chicago for example, getting them or their family out of the emergency situation. If that client had a second home or another place they had prearranged, like northern Michigan, Company X would provide the necessary transportation to those locations. Company X would also provide them with food, water, medical supplies and other necessities. Essentially Company X was providing an insurance policy against the unknowns to the wealthy. As potential devastating scenarios were suddenly making there way on the news around the same time, a potential client could purchase this service, providing them assurance of having a back-up plan, if the need ever arose. Should chaos happen, whether due to a major terrorist attack, widespread civil unrest or a collapsed economy, Company X would be there to rescue them.

We knew that Company X would also be applying for federal grants from such agencies as the Department of Homeland Security (DHS). We questioned whether or not there was a different motive that Bart Stupak had when he secured the federal grant for the Pellston Regional Airport expansion and remodeling project. Was Stupak making the airport desirable to Company X? The airport expansion had been seen by many locals as overkill, in comparison to the relatively little major airline traffic the airport received. Pellston, we were being told, was one of three choices, in terms of towns around the country, that were in the process of being selected by Company X. The local elected county officials were scrambling to provide local policies that would make Company X favor and select Pellston for their national response center. This would bring a huge economic boost to the area, where the economy was already waning. A non-disclosure agreement was signed by Jim Tamilyn, the then Emmet county commissioner and Company X. The initial negotiations between the county and Company X would be largely secret, as well as many details about the agreements being formed with the county. There was a clause that would cause legal repercussions, should any county worker breach that secrecy. Even the state of Michigan would become involved, with the then Governor Granholm cheerleading the way.

Downstate Michigan, particularly the Detroit area, was running into deeper troubles keeping jobs from leaving the state. The Michigan Legislature was in the process of trying to entice businesses into coming into the metro areas of Michigan. The Michigan Legislature would get involved in trying to make sure that Pellston was selected by Company X, instead of the two potential alternative choices declared by the company, that were each in separate states; the other choices we were told were Saint Clair County, Illinois and Racine County, Wisconsin. In record time, the Michigan Legislature pushed through an amendment on PA 198 that included adding a "strategic response center" that allowed tax abatements for companies that created jobs and fell under the investment criteria of PA 198. The DNR had also, in record time, lifted the reverter clause on the land behind the Pellston airport, to also entice Company X to select Pellston. It appeared everyone was on board.

All of the chambers of commerce in the local area, the Northern Lakes Economic Alliance, Cheboygan County and the local college, NCMC, were all in favor of trying to secure Pellston as the national response center for Company X. Frequently on the front cover of the local newspaper, news stories printed by the Petoskey News-Review were pushing all of the great things that would happen in our area, with these new jobs that would be created by Company X. With many locals convinced of the 500 plus, $22 an hour jobs that could soon be available in the area, they also wanted Company X to select Pellston, hoping to apply for these new careers themselves. Person X, the Chief Executive Officer of the company, told of his ties to the military, he spoke of himself having been a former army intelligence officer.

Person X had an impressive resume, he touted about having started one of the first private para-military forces in the country, Triple Canopy. Triple Canopy would send their private mercenaries into Iraq, to help with Operation Iraqi Freedom. Person X's relationship with Triple Canopy faded and he eventually resigned from the company, for reasons that are unknown. Person Y was the vice president of Company X, who at one time was a Brigadier General for the United States Marines. I managed to find a picture of Person Y online standing with, at the time, President George W. Bush. (To the best of my knowledge, Person Y still serves his country.) These weren't just any ordinary men running Company X, they were well known, well respected and very well connected.

Not in my backyard! These were our thoughts. We demanded answers to questions that arose about Company X before they secured their national response center in Pellston. Sabrina and I knew to change things on a federal level is nearly impossible, but when the battle was to be fought locally, there was a chance. As patriotic Americans we had to step up to bat, no one else was.

Everything I could dig up about Company X seemed suspicious to us. The company would hire a private mercenary force to get the rich out of an emergency situation quickly. Company X even promised that with the $50,000 initial fee and the $15,000 annual fee, they would use their intelligence center from the national response center, that would be built in Pellston, to get the wealthy and the corporate heads out of places like Chicago, placing those clients and their families out of danger. This seemed to be a big gamble for a relatively new company. How could they support 500 full time jobs that paid $22 an hour and a national response center, full of potential air traffic from their planned usage of military transport jets? How many people would have to pay the fees in order to make this economically feasible? We thought this could possibly be a front used for some sort of ill schemed plan by the federal government.

With private mercenary forces being sent into Iraq to do the dirty work, would the federal government possibly use private contractors in the United States to help control the population, should it fall into mass disorder due to a major terrorist attack or another large event? After all, the federal government could then point the finger at private companies should abuses of the general public come out in the news afterwards. We did know that FEMA and DHS were in the process of advertising for temporary shelter, camp-like facilities, to be provided by private contractors in the event of a national emergency.

Money was arguably a problem for Company X. Richard Rainwater, who according to Forbes is one of the richest persons in the United States, was the main financier behind the company. In fact, it was Rainwater's investment company that had control over the Bush family investments. Rainwater's management of investment income had helped to make the Bush family wealthy. Rainwater was the top contributor to the Bush election campaign. As long as Person X could keep Rainwater pouring in unknown amounts of money, could there have been any short term financial problems for this new company? Company X was also planning on using funding from federal and state grants. The national response center would cost an estimated $10.2 million dollars worth of infrastructure to be built. Newspaper accounts varied with either 600, 640 or 700 acres on land behind the Pellston regional airport to be used for the national response center. Something seemed off.

The discussions on the Northern Michigan Update forum kept rolling along. I had started the discussion on the forum about Company X and it was already the most popular topic on the board. Someone had to stop them, they needed to answer questions. How could this be done? We had thought about going to the county meeting to try to get some answers, but our work schedule was always in the way. We worked evenings into the late night, nearly every day, cleaning commercial buildings. Finally one of the other members of Northern Michigan Update, Ken, whom I had befriended, gave me a phone call one day.

"Look," he said, *"I want you to meet with a group of people. You know more about"* Company X *" than anyone else. I think that you are right about it, but I can't do anything about it."* Ken knew the county commissioner Jim personally, they were extended family. Ken had been trying to get to the bottom of what was really going on with Company X. He had voiced his opinion to Jim several times about why he thought that Jim shouldn't allow Company X to build a national response center in Pellston. One day while Ken and I were talking, he told me of his latest discussion with Jim. Jim had told him, *"look Ken do you want to be able to go to Oleson's and buy groceries or not."* According to this conversation relayed to me by Ken, Company X would provide some armed paramilitary guards to ensure that those with money could continue to buy their groceries. This conversation pushed me over the edge. I agreed, even though I absolutely hated speech class in high school and hated speaking in front of groups of people, to meet with them. The meeting was setup in the Noggin room bar and restaurant at the Perry hotel in downtown Petoskey.

Arriving to the meeting, very nervous, but prepared, I walked into the Noggin Room with my paperwork in hand. A round of introductions at the table were made and I felt out of place amongst these people, as my wife sat next to me. At the table were a group of people with mixed professions; doctors, university professors, a journalist, even a member of the Michigan militia was present. This group of a dozen or so people had common ground, they were largely from the Northern Michigan People for Peace group. The man who was leading the meeting that had been setup to discuss Company X, at behest of Ken, told me that since I knew the most of anyone at the table about the topic I should speak first. I thanked them, as Sabrina and I had to get off to work soon after the meeting, our summer work was in full peak at the moment.

I started off giving all of the facts that I knew about Company X, passing along all of the articles and information I had about them. I told them of Person X's ties with Triple Canopy and explained the reasons I was suspicious about this project. During the final part of my speech I mentioned some executive orders Bush had signed and the Patriot Act, Defense Authorization Act, the current state of political affairs and simply stated point blank that I thought this was being built to possibly setup a national wide internment camp system, all while wearing my 9/11 truth hoodie. Thinking that the group would probably laugh me out of the room, I instead was surprised to see that they took my speech very seriously. We exchanged email addresses with some at the table and headed off to complete our janitorial tasks. They stayed continuing to talk about whether or not Company X was something they wanted to get politically involved against.

The next day I would hear from Ken that this group of people would take a stand against Company X. They formed a group specifically to stand against Company X called No Need for Company X. With their local connections, a voice of dissent finally hit the newspapers. The public would learn that not everyone was happy with Company X. People wanted some answers to many questions that were arising about this new national response center. The response from Company X came quick, Person X agreed to have a town hall type meeting at the Pellston high school auditorium. Person X publicly blamed internet forums for causing all of this trouble and spreading lies and rumors about Company X. He would get rid of these rumors by having this meeting to clear things up, to answer questions. We arrived at the auditorium for the meeting, armed with about fifty 9/11 truth DVD's to hand out afterwards. Taking a seat in the back of the high school auditorium, we prepared to video tape the meeting.

The meeting began with the announcement that Person X had not been able to make it to the now packed out meeting in the auditorium. Person Y, the vice president of Company X took his place, promising to explain what their company did. We were told by Person Y that he wouldn't end the meeting until all the questions were addressed. During this speech we would find out that Company X was much more troubling than we had ever thought. Company X had much bigger plans, the national response center in Pellston was just the beginning.

At the meeting Person Y discussed how this national response center was the first phase of Company X's plans. Company X planned on opening two more national response centers, Pellston would be the first. They would also have storages and regional response centers near many major cities in the United States. They were thinking big and would be working to get grants from the federal government to fund much of this. The meeting would last just over an hour. Person Y would only answer a few questions and despite his earlier promise to answer all questions, left the stage to boos from the public, refusing to do so. Now we thought there was evidence to back up our suspicions about them. These new revelations from the town hall meeting ensured us that we would continue to demand answers from Company X.

I continued to post on the Northern Michigan Update forum against Company X, but late one night as I was standing up on the top of the hill outside of our apartment, looking to the street down below, I noted an unmarked undercover car just sitting there. Having lived in the area most of my life and having grown up mostly in Petoskey, I, like many others, knew each and every single patrol car that the city of Petoskey police department owned. Sabrina and I had always been night owls, working at night, driving around at night, walking around at night, for years. This undercover car was not the city of Petoskey's, this car was a different law enforcement agency. This undercover car was sitting at the bottom of the hill, where the property line from our converted house apartment met our neighbors. At the time I still had some friends over. We were in the middle of playing Super Mario Kart on the Nintendo Game Cube, having finished with our bible study. What was this person sitting in the undercover car doing?

Making sure the driver in the car saw me, I looked right at him while standing at the top of the hill. With my eyes fixated on the undercover car, I watched as the headlights suddenly turned on. I walked along the edge of the hill that followed the street, keeping my eyes fixated on the car, as they slowly drove off into the night. Returning to play some more Super Mario Kart, I briefly mentioned to my friends what I had just seen.

The next day I spoke to one of my friends, Joe, who seemed to know just about everything that happened in regards to law enforcement activity in the area. He told me that my description of the undercover car sounded like the FBI car that worked the Petoskey area. Petoskey didn't have an FBI office, but they had one full time employee devoted to the area who would come from their office in Traverse City. Our problems had begun.

Sabrina and I talked about this and we could only figure that it was due to our political activity regarding Company X, nothing else made sense to us. This happened within days of the public town hall meeting that was held at the Pellston high school auditorium. Fear came over us and I did something that I would later regret.

I sent an email to Person X, the president of Company X, telling him that I would back off and no longer cause trouble for him. The email was never replied to. On the forum I no longer talked about Company X, I had quit all public political activity against Company X, but only for a bit of time.

I was still receiving emails about the activities of the group, No Need for Company X, about their political activities against Company X. The group was moving along in fighting the company from building a national response center in Pellston. Myself, now a silent participator, hadn't actually been in communication with these people, I was just keeping up on the news I read from the emails I received. My new silence about Company X was about to change.

Suddenly the front of the Petoskey News-Review declared that Company X had chose Pellston. The deal was set, everything was good to go. Now that it appeared to be set in stone, a lease having been signed by Company X for the use of the property, the building of the national response center would soon begin. It was now late into 2007.

The fear that came after I had caught the undercover agent at the bottom of my hill instantly disappeared. I could be silent no more, not in my backyard! I decided to email the group and ask them about whether or not Company X was really trying to get into these other cities. I had never once seen a news article from other prospective cities while I searched for information online about Company X. I told the group that I didn't think it was true, I thought Person X was lying about it. I began to post once again on Northern Michigan Update, this time I wouldn't back down, I wouldn't budge a bit.

A bombshell hit an online alternative news website, the Michigan Messenger, from one of the members of No Need for Company X. This very popular website had tons of news from all political points of views. Person X had no record of ever having been in the military. There was no evidence found to validate Person X's claim whatsoever. Person X was lying about being a former intelligence officer, at least where public records were shown, apparently he had been using this storyline for business startups for years. Person X was a creative man, he had over 400 patents to his name. With these new revelations, Person X responded back harshly. The local newspaper printed that he was thinking of filing a lawsuit against those who were starting all of these lies and rumors about him. There he mentioned forums as being responsible for starting many of these rumors. No lawsuit ever came, in fact Company X was about ready to become extremely compromised.

Someone from the group against Company X did check into whether or not these other towns were even in the running for a national response center, competing as Person X had claimed, to secure Company X's promise of jobs. Not one person in these other areas, from airport officials, county workers, local economic teams, NO ONE, had ever heard of Company X, Person X or Person Y. Now the news hit once again on the Michigan Messenger. The whole story about Company X was full of lies. How embarrassing to the Michigan Legislature, Governor Granholm, local county officials and everyone else involved in trying to secure Pellston for the national response center! There was no competition against other states for the national response center and not one person ever checked up on Person X's supposed military background. Michigan legislature had been duped or they were part of a collusion of a bigger conspiracy behind the scenes.

In fact, a few local Emmet county elected officials, including the commissioner, had been flown out on behalf of Company X, wined and dined, at meetings in Washington, DC. In Washington, DC, these local officials were told of the importance of Company X and how it was necessary for them to allow Company X to build a national response center in Pellston. The full details of their conversations were never made public, but the meeting was mentioned in an article in the Petoskey News-Review. There had always been a cloud of suspicion about Company X, this simply added to it. A freedom of information act (FOIA) request was filed by an individual in the No Need for Company X group to get some paperwork regarding the 99 year lease that the company would have on the hundreds of acres. That FOIA request was cited with an exemption, denied. The cloud of secrecy about Company X and Emmet county agreements would remain.

Company X was now beginning to get bad publicity from news articles written about them, even in the Petoskey News-Review, which had been there most outspoken media proponent. The public had awoken to what seemed to be a scheme against our beautiful area, being purported by Company X. Now there were enough people demanding answers, despite the fact that a lease had already been signed for the property behind the

Pellston regional airport. For nearly a year and a half Company X would try to get things to calm down and proceed on as planned. Even on their company website they apologized to prospective customers and blamed people on forums for having started rumors and lies against them. Finally in 2009, the company would disappear from attempting to make an appearance anywhere in the United States, they were finished. After the first bombshells hit in the newspapers around the state, Person Y quietly resigned from Company X. Apparently he was smart enough to realize that Company X would only be going downhill from the new revelations of lies released in the news and didn't want to have his good name associated with this upcoming failure.

We really believe that had a stand not been taken by us, starting with the questions and concerns being relayed through the forum, to a final meeting with this group of well educated people, Company X would have been successful, starting with their national response center in Pellston. As with any type of proposed change in a given city or neighborhood, there are always people for and against it. In a state like Michigan, each piece of legislation had its supporters and those who were against it. Some people would win with a piece of legislation, some would lose. The voting process of passing legislation always showed how things run in a democratic society, not forgetting that we truly live in a republic. Nonetheless, without my portion, my voice, though I did not do it alone, Person X would have won his bid to have a national response center in Pellston. Whatever Company X would have turned out to be, if they hadn't been stopped, is unknown.

The whole thing showed us that this is exactly why Americans should do their patriotic duty. Sometimes we are called to do something for this country. Sometimes that something might be taking a stand against a piece of legislation or in this case a company who was in bed with the government.

In January 2008, as the campaigning for the primary elections was beginning, we started to hand out some flyers about Ron Paul once in awhile, while also walking around downtown Petoskey in the evenings. We spoke to other business owners that we personally knew, telling them that we felt Ron Paul would be good for our businesses also. Like many Americans, we knew that there needed to be change in this country. Ron Paul to us seemed to be the only candidate worth putting into the Oval Office. The others just appeared to have the same smoke and mirror show that has been going on for so long in this country. In the meantime I would meet another very avid Ron Paul supporter, a man named Bill.

Bill was handing out some political material at the local college in Petoskey, NCMC, but was kicked off the property by the college. Being a public community college he got involved with the Rutherford Institute who pointed him in a direction to a local constitutional attorney. This attorney wrote to the college and they eventually apologized, once again allowing Bill on the property. When Sabrina and I read about this in the Petoskey News-Review newspaper, we thought it would be good to give Bill a call and tell him of our support.

I called Bill and spoke to him, we would eventually meet up and he would hand us numerous signs and information to hand out for the Ron Paul presidential bid. We agreed to help, along with our friend Brandon. Not that long after I received a call from Bill wanting to know if our business, Aardvark Janitorial, would sponsor a voter's fair that he was arranging to be held at the county fairgrounds in Petoskey. We agreed, the first time we had ever made any sort of monetary donation to any political campaign or movement.

The voter's fair was a one day event. Occupying the nicely renovated building on the fairgrounds, it consisted of tables of information about every single candidate running for office. There was a lot of local radio advertising promoting the event. Brandon and I showed up to sit at the Ron Paul table and answer any questions that someone wandering up to the table may have. The turnout seemed to be reasonable as there were people walking through the door all day long, into the evening. A movie played at night, *Mr. Smith Goes to Washington*, to end the event. Here we met a woman running for office, also helping out at the Ron Paul table, who would later become our very good friend.

Linda Goldthorpe was running for Bart Stupak's U.S. Representative seat in Michigan's 1st congressional district. Linda was endorsed by Ron Paul and had the opportunity of meeting him on more than one occasion. Like most liberty minded folks, she wanted less government and more local control. We would talk off and on throughout that night while sitting at the table answering questions about Ron Paul. Eventually a couple of Mitt Romney's sons would walk into the voter's fair, I made sure they left with a 9/11 truth DVD, as Mitt Romney really seemed to have a high possibility of winning. Perhaps, I thought, if he was a good guy he would make some positive changes to this country.

We also began campaigning for Linda. We put up yard signs where we could or handed out one of her placards to random people walking around downtown Petoskey. First, however, there was another political meeting before we would all officially become good friends. Bill had asked that we show up to a town hall meeting that Bart Stupak was holding for his reelection campaign in Cheboygan, just northeast of Petoskey.

I had always been somewhat fond of Stupak, his familiar face had long been our U.S. Representative. He seemed like a gentleman and when I had a project assigned to me as a child in grade school in Alanson, to write about one of the candidates, it was his office that sent me a whole information packet, complete with a signed photo, though belated. I had never forgotten that out of all of the elected officials I had wrote to, he was the only one to respond. This would be my first time meeting him in person, though I was campaigning for Linda to take his position, I was still intrigued.

We wanted to know if Stupak would support bringing back our civil liberties, getting rid of the Patriot Act and other such legislation. We also wanted to know whether or not he would support a new, independent investigation into 9/11 and what he felt about other topics regarding the United Nations. As we walked into the meeting room Stupak told those who were in attendance that they should sign their name and put their contact information on the meeting attendance record by the door. He jokingly stated not to worry, he wouldn't give the list to the government. Sabrina and I declined, taking a seat behind Bill, with Linda and our friend Brandon.

I cannot recall exactly what was said in his opening speech, but my best friend Brandon rose up his hand to ask a question and was called upon. Whatever it was, Brandon being very constitutional minded, had asked him how these changes Stupak was going to introduce legislatively were in line with the Constitution. Stupak suddenly hollered for him to sit down and shut up. The crowd looked back and forth towards Brandon and Stupak, as Brandon blurted out that he had the right to free speech and would speak. Brandon briefly finished voicing his opinion and then sat quietly. This caused Bill to also speak out and at this time I went to turn on my video camera, walking to the back of the room to videotape the whole ordeal that was taking place. Stupak took note of me walking to the back of the room and told me to shut off my video camera, I refused, even though I hadn't begun to videotape. He then said to me that he wasn't going to have his speech put on Youtube, edited to make him look like a fool, the meeting ended early. We had nothing planned against Stupak and no video was ever taped to appear on Youtube or any other website. Afterwards all of us went to the local Big Boy restaurant and were talking about what had happened at the town hall meeting. It was here that Linda invited Sabrina and I, as well as Brandon, to her house for dinner.

After meeting with Linda at her humble home in Michigan's Upper Peninsula, our friendship was now well on its way. We were still busy business people though, our free time was limited. We enjoyed having dinner at her home, staying a bit into the evening, but we had to travel back to Petoskey, cleaning businesses the remainder of the night. It was now the spring of 2008, our business was booming.

Aardvark Janitorial continued to get new janitorial contracts and we kept the old ones we had. Sabrina was now contemplating quitting her job, but still holding onto it, just in case something went awry with our business. We were entering our busy summer season, cleaning the boat twice per day, a golf club nightly as well as a small fine dining restaurant in Boyne City, aside from our other weekly or multiple visit jobs per week. While Sabrina was at work I would get done some of those jobs and when she got off we would finish with the remainder of our work, oftentimes Brandon would either hang out with us or sometimes help out with the cleaning.

In 2008, there were big worries about the national economy in the news. I had been paying very close attention to the housing bubble and knew that this could not go on forever. Despite the fact that every single magazine and newspaper seemed to be promoting flipping houses, I knew this was a very dangerous game of musical chairs, eventually this bubble would burst. This artificial bubble couldn't last forever, we were already priced out of the housing market in Petoskey, which would get hit hard by the bubble as it burst. Petoskey had the most expensive housing in the state, with the exception of Harbor Springs that was smaller and located just across the bay. Why the television wouldn't stop promoting this ongoing insanity, with shows telling people how to get involved in flipping houses for a profit, with easy credit that was given out with hardly anything but a signature, was unknown to me. Didn't Americans understand that this would not work?

Aside from worries in the news about the national economy there was beginning to be all of this concern and panic about a potential Bird Flu pandemic. I researched this a lot and saw that the government could essentially declare martial law if such a thing actually happened. Due to knowing that a hit would come from the housing bubble to the national economy and seeing a potential Bird Flu pandemic that could happen around the same time, we began to wonder what we would do. These scenarios could indeed create so much civil unrest that the government would have to step in to keep order. If such a scenario did happen, having some extra food and a plan, just like Company X was trying to sell, didn't seem to be a bad idea.

We began to talk with a couple of our friends about what we would do should something happen to tank the economy. We had already witnessed what happened in New Orleans and took note of the gun confiscation that happened even in the dry affluent neighborhoods. Troops showing up at those people's doors, demanding them to turn in their firearms. What was wrong with our government? What were they doing? What about Second Amendment rights? There was no rioting in some of these affluent neighborhoods in New Orleans, those residents had food and generators, they were fine, able to take care of themselves. We decided to come up with a backup plan, Plan B, as it would come to be called.

Plan B

Prepping, as it is called, in and of itself is not a bad idea. If you live in Florida and know that hurricane season is coming soon, having a few extra cases of water, food and some additional batteries for your flashlights is a good idea. Why join the masses of panicking people waiting in lines at the local Costco store, scrambling to just get some cases of water? As Person Y would mention at the town hall meeting about Company X, most people had less than a weeks' worth of food in their cupboards. That was were Company X was going to step in for their clients. With a housing bubble looking to pop soon, we began slowly evolving a plan, our own Company X type plan.

Really this had been on our mind since early 2007. We would purchase throughout that year four firearms. One was a handgun for self defense and just plan old shooting fun. We often worked late at night cleaning businesses, even though Petoskey was not known for much crime, the gun was for a just in case scenario. We also purchased a .22 rifle at a yard sale, for small game, a 30.06 for deer hunting and a used AR-15 at a gun dealer, who had told us owning such a weapon would make lots of friends at the shooting range. In 2008 I would apply for a concealed carry permit and it would be approved by the local county board. This concealed carry permit was the only way to be able to legally carry a hand gun in a vehicle while working late at night.

Neither of us had a criminal background. I had gotten into some trouble with the law when I was a teenager, but I had wrote the judge when I was 19 years old that I was now married and running a business. He granted that my record be expunged and it was. We also decided to purchase several cases of canned food and kept them in our food pantry. Water was not an issue in Petoskey, as there were abundant sources including natural springs in the area to collect water. Prepping or preppers were starting to appear across the country.

Each family or individual that got involved in prepping had to decide what means of survival that they may need, how much they were willing to spend, how long they might need those resources, all to determine how much and what was needed. Finally they would have to decide where to go should there be a necessity to actually utilize the preparations that they made. We certainly had the resources, making over $75k per year at the time and living in a cheap rental with no debt. Just how bad did we think it could get in our country?

Our thoughts were that a crash of the economy could cause rioting, looting and eventually martial law. What about those watchlists, who were these enemies of the federal government and what would they do with them during martial law? Was it possible, like a couple of MTV commercials depicted, that those who were dissidents, during a time of total chaos from coast to coast, could simply disappear behind barbed wire somewhere in the middle of the night? Why had the government passed such laws that allowed for these watchlists to be made and infringed on the privacy rights of Americans? Why were videos all over online of law enforcement officers stepping on people's rights? What options would we have for a serious nationwide emergency? Our little group consisted of two others besides us. We would all prepare to go camping, short or long term if needed.

The plan was simple, if such a scenario happened, until order was restored, we would camp out in the woods, begin to hunt and fish, while waiting hopefully to one day return to a new normalcy in this country. Most of the items Sabrina and I would purchase for the group, though our friends would also slowly pay for some of their own camping and survival items. This was a backup plan, our Plan B, not what we intended on doing, but what we would do if needed to be. Then in August of 2008 the housing bubble starting to pop.

The chaos that would ensue from this idiotic idea of flipping houses, though it had generated much wealth in the short term, would end up changing, not only America, but much of the world. Even to this day the effects of this foolishness are still being felt, the economy may be on a slight rebound, but it is still not as sound as it once was, despite the stock market hitting record highs. We, as janitors, began to take big note of what was happening.

Like the rest of the nation, we listened to President Bush talk about restimulating the economy, we then heard President Obama, beginning in 2009, unveil a plan to pour billions into jump starting the economy, but we had an insight that most didn't, we cleaned those businesses that employed many people. Soon after the crash began, people began to cancel their pooper scooper service that we also provided and we were getting many late payments from our commercial cleaning customers, it would get worse.

In 2009, worrying about keeping our customers, we came up with an emergency plan. We would offer deep price discounts to customers in the short term, that customer would have to pay us prior for our work though. This was not advertised within our business, but would only be told to a customer when there were simply too many empty desks appearing to justify keeping the same contracted price that we had with them. Even though the economy was tanking nationwide, 2009 would be the year that Sabrina quit her job, our business began to boom.

Our reputation was well known in the area, especially in Petoskey, as our businesses had great references. As other businesses were letting go of employee after employee, they were also looking to save expenses on everything that was purchased by their business or services that were used by them. With our reputation the business phone began to ring more frequently and we received seven new customers within 2009, much between the late spring and early fall. Our janitorial service was better than what they had been used to and we gave them a price that allowed these businesses to save money at the same time. We were all about efficiency in running our janitorial service.

Using backpack vacuum cleaners, plus owning around a dozen vacuums, we stored some equipment on most job sites. We had extra mop buckets left at some sites and all of our equipment was well maintained and kept in good working order. Our clean uniforms and appearance, as well as professional attitude and paperwork, meant that almost every customer that called us would decide to go with our service. Price we knew was the deciding factor on whether or not we would get the prospective customer to sign. If the customer perceived we could do the work, had a good first impression, had a price that was within their budget and cheaper than most, if not all of the competition, then after they called our references a decision was made to use our service. This business philosophy proved very true.

We also knew preciously how to clean and how to cheat. We knew what customers looked for and what they thought they needed. We also understood the importance of telling the proper people of maintenance issues we noted while working in their buildings. With their chairs neatly pushed in after each visit, there was a consistency, these businesses would look the same each and every single time after our visit. Plus we went out of our way to avoid customers. As odd as this may seem, out of sight, out of mind, was one way to avoid complaints that the customer themselves didn't even know the origin of. If they saw us, they would think of something more we could be doing.

Often when an employee of a company we worked for ran into us we would receive a call from our contact with that company within a day or two afterwards, asking us to address an area of concern that had suddenly became known to them. As the economy grew much tighter, very quickly, many people came to realize that more was expected of them at work for the same pay or less, it had turned into an employer's market, this was also true with business to business contracts.

In 2009 Boyne USA gave us another golf clubhouse to clean in beautiful Bay Harbor. The whole ordeal of the economy crashing had lost us one good client, a quick care office in Petoskey and though they apologized for having to cancel, they simply had to make the cut due to a decrease in business. By the summer of 2009, our work load during the Memorial Day to Labor Day season would be seven days per week, 90 something hours each and every week. It was clock work to us. Every evening we would begin work and we would usually finish sometime during the early morning hours around sunrise. We still held bible studies at our home on Sunday, as that was the night that we had the least amount of work, we would wait until midnight on Sundays, before heading off to work.

Every Friday night, during 2009, there would be newly emptied desks at many businesses. One such business outside of Petoskey, that had literally made a fortune becoming the third biggest in their industry in the country, in terms of sales, started to shrink rapidly, their business being tied directly to the housing boom. They would continue with their shrinking in sales, until eventually the company would close their doors with only a job or two remaining offsite. One of our jobs we eventually received was cleaning for the local newspaper, the Petoskey News-Review. We had got hired about a year or so after new ownership took over. Even there, desk after desk was emptied on a monthly basis, though before our problem arose in 2012, many of the positions had been refilled, they had survived. Grey hair became a brief problem due to our own business.

Our past due accounts in our janitorial service suddenly rose to the point that we had over $12k in past due payments we hadn't received! Each month 30% of our customers would not pay their bills, our pooper scooper business was literally falling to pieces. Within a year we were already almost to the same amount of customers we had during the first summer that we began providing residents with a pooper scooper service. We had to cancel those people who were late on their pooper scooper payments and knock on their door to collect payments. Never once could we get ourselves to feel sorry for them. We were not the electricity company, if you couldn't afford a pooper scooper service, then cancel, it is not even close to being a necessity. With our janitorial service we kept working with our customers and would threaten to cancel some, but this would always seem to have them then send some money, not the full balance, so we continued on with these occasional threats. In the meantime we finalized our emergency plans.

Finding good gear that could be carried into the woods turned out to be very expensive. This also required a lot of research and some hard shopping. Things were going so fast at online stores, that anyone who bought such survival items, knew these high quality products would often be on backorder. The idea was, that if you can't have a lot with you, but may need to survive for up to a year, which was the plan, than you should have the highest quality and lightest weight gear, which also turned out to be the most expensive. As an example, Filson makes great quality clothing that is very expensive, much of it made in their facility in Seattle, Washington. A $200 pair of Filson pants would be on backorder for months, even Filson couldn't keep up with the new demand. When the bubble popped a lot of Americans quit spending money on junk they didn't need and began to sell things, plus purchase emergency items that could prove to be useful in the future.

While the true number of people who have actually became preppers is unknown, it has been estimated to be at just over 3 million people. Some hardened their houses, some purchased new houses in the middle of nowhere, off the grid, others even bought lavish underground bunkers and there were some who were digging in for a fight with the federal government. Everyone who participated or who still does participate, have their own thoughts on what will happen and their plan against that scenario, whether or not they are correct, remains to be determined. Armed with some Gregory Packs, a Titanium Goat tent, complete with a titanium heater system to provide for up to 8 people warmth of around 60 degrees, even in brutal winter, using only twigs to keep the fire going; and all of the proper clothing needed for all weather conditions, cooking gear, accessories, hunting knives, plus our weapons, we had a good plan going. Probably our biggest failure was outdoorsman skills, of which we had limited experience, with the exception of one of those who also prepared with us. Ammunition was also needed and we ended up purchasing several thousand rounds. Recalling that the government might consider this to be terrorist activity, all the ammo was bought with cash, slowly. Transportation of all of these survival items and being able to get back in the woods was also a problem of concern.

The solution was to get a Cabela's deer cart, with the double wheels, to haul everything back to a camping location. However, with the cart we also would have very durable plastic snow sleds, in case a scenario that required activation of this emergency plan played out during the winter season. We continued to live our lives normally, even though the economy was still in freefall. Fingers were being pointed as to who's fault this economic crash was, but in reality, Americans and their greed must also take part of the blame, it was everyone's fault.

With Company X still on our mind, plus remembering that possible FBI agent parked at the bottom of the hill from our apartment, we began to wonder if we were on a government watchlist. Was it possible? Perhaps too many books ordered or the wrong kind read? The wrong videos on Youtube watched? Certainly there were some ties between Person Y and the Pentagon, which could possibly allow for some influence by Company X? Where were we to keep all of these prepped items at?

A few stories began to surface of some preppers, though they had much more than we did, would be shown with guns and ammo, where it was now being called by federal agents an arsenal. These unlucky individuals were being charged with domestic terrorism, just for owning these things! Plus if there ever was a knock on the door late at night, what would we do? Even though the economy might have collapsed already, that didn't mean that we would have had to flee. If such a scenario played out we would have to wait and see what actually happened, we lived in Petoskey, not a major city, we had a lot of business income. Things would likely get worse in Petoskey under that scenario, but not necessarily cause someone to go camping in the woods. We wondered what would happen if we were wrong and couldn't get our camping gear out of our house? How would we know until it was too late? We decided to relocate all of our preparations to a storage unit in the middle of nowhere in the Upper Peninsula. We had already concluded that if we ever had to use these things, Michigan's Upper Peninsula (U.P.) was a much better place than the Lower Peninsula to go camping. Despite it's size, the U.P. of Michigan only has around 300k people, half of them living in small cities.

There was plenty of places where there was nothing for nearly miles in the U.P. A perfect place to go and camp out until whatever new society is back in play, once order had resumed. Then we assumed it would be safe to rejoin society, the chaos over. That storage unit would be rented in cash, never paid for with a check, so there would not be a financial record of the rental. In October of 2008, a few months after the financial crash, we drove these items up to their new home and went on with our life, working the janitorial service. As the economy continued to rescind during 2009, the purchase of this camping gear was beginning to seem more necessary. Then some information came across our way, information from a reliable source.

The Mackinaw Bridge the connected Michigan's lower and upper peninsula was being hardened. The Department of Homeland Security (DHS) was pouring tons of money into the mighty bridge and it could potentially cause the bridge to be used as an internal checkpoint, one to even round up and collect Americans attempting to flee to Canada, just miles to the north. Those Americans who were on the watchlist, though they wouldn't know it, some suspecting it, would have the greatest threat to themselves while trying to cross between Michigan's peninsulas. Some research was done independently to see if these sorts of things were going on across the nation, and indeed, as mentioned before, with the ITS systems, cameras, license plate reading technology, there was the chance of abuse by a government that had gone so far away from its original foundation on civil liberties and was bent on keeping a controlled society. The federal government appeared to be collecting the names of people who would likely resist and try and detain them, so that they could regain order out of chaos. How would we beat that system?

Having our stuff stored in a desirable location, hidden from the ever more watchful eyes of the federal government was certainly comforting, but of no necessity if we couldn't access it. Here was where some trust was put into God. We knew that if such a scenario played out, God would have to be our help. We really didn't have the proper skills, though we had the gear. We also wouldn't know necessarily when it was time to go. Perhaps we still had enough work and would manage just fine in Petoskey. We had money saved up anyway and could make it a year without earning a dime. After praying about the matter, we became resolute to put our trust in God, that He would tell us when or if such a time ever came to flee. We trusted in Him to deal with the problem of getting across the bridge. We also spoke with several others and determined that it was possible that during martial law, the Mackinaw Bridge would only allow people to cross over to the other peninsula if they were residents of those cities nearby or had a good enough explanation. Our decision would lead into committing our only crime, a misdemeanor.

In December of 2008, all four of us changed our address to that of an apartment complex in Manistique, Michigan. Situated about a hundred miles away from Petoskey, this small industrial and prison town had a couple of decent sized low income apartment communities. The apartment community was a place with frequent vacancies, it could never be proved without an actual investigation, that we did or had not lived there. We all kept a separate mailing address, ours a post office box in Petoskey that we had rented since moving back in 2003, to get any correspondence that the Secretary of State (SOS) might send about registration or driver license renewals. Until months after we disappeared, Michigan had always been as simple as telling the SOS your new address, they would simply print out a label, affix it to the back of your driver's license, no questions asked, no proof required, simple as that to update your address. The penalty for lying was a hefty fine and up to a year in jail. We didn't think anyone would figure it out, but knew that if we got caught we would have to hire an attorney and face the consequences of our actions. Things remained normal until one day I got a call from the Beaver Island Boat Company, where we had been contracted seasonally to clean.

With the 2009 contract just having been signed, I was told it would be mandatory to have a Transportation Workers Identification Card (TWIC) in order for us to clean the boat. The Department of Homeland Security required these radio frequency (RFID) identity cards, which were issued through the Transportation Security Administration (TSA), a sub department of the DHS. Over the years of cleaning the boat, the ship dock had become hardened through federal grants. A very tall iron fence was placed all around the docking area, the gates were always locked, the Coast Guard would occasionally send someone aboard during trips, carrying an automatic weapon, cameras were erected everywhere, Sabrina had to attend a special homeland security class on what to watch out for, part of the ridiculous See-Something, Say-Something campaign. The boat company was serious about security against domestic terrorist events, the federal government required them to be. The new regulations required that one person on the ship dock yard at all times have a TWIC card. With the boat company knowing how we would be there cleaning daily, usually by ourselves, I had to obtain one. All of this didn't make sense to me, sure you couldn't just walk up to the boat as you had been able to in the past, but the cargo door on the ship wasn't left locked. What about scuba divers or someone swimming? How would any of this stop a real terrorist? Who watched the video footage from the night before to see if someone jumped the fence and placed a bomb on the boat? With all of these things on my mind, Sabrina came home from the mandatory security class having been told to keep an eye out for dogs with wires hanging out their butt. This sort of logic was just as insane as the housing bubble, a supposed solution that really couldn't stop a determined terrorist. Were these things being setup to prevent supposed domestic terrorists or rather political dissidents the freedom of movement during a martial law incidence?

Needless to say, I wasn't happy about having to get a TWIC card, but I did. I went and got fingerprinted the second time in my life, the first having been for my concealed carry permit. I filled out their form and had a brief meeting in St. Ignace, Michigan, just on the other side of the Mackinaw Bridge as you cross over into the U.P.. There at the local office I applied for this security clearance credential. After filling it out, I took and turned in my application, they took a digital photograph of me, a copy of two pieces of my state and federal identification, one being the passport that I had never used, but got in 2006. Now I would await the TWIC card to come in the mail as the boat was getting ready for the season to begin and would need a copy of the card prior to our janitorial services being performed for them.

The boat company, though private, was also run through the Michigan Department of Transportation. This large passenger ferry boat was, aside from taking a chartered flight, the only means of getting supplies over to Beaver Island, which was several miles out into lake Michigan, off of more Emmet County than Charlevoix County, where it was originally claimed as part of. The agreement with the state of Michigan was that the state paid for the boat, but the boat company managed it. Tons and tons of tourists would flock to the island every summer and spend a day or two on a vacation enjoying the beaches and rich, odd history. Under this guise, being part of the Michigan Department of Transportation, they fell into DHS administrative decrees. As our contract start date was starting to close in, I gave TSA a phone call to see where my card was.

Knowing that I would have no problem getting the card, as I didn't have a criminal background or anything else that would prevent me, I didn't think anything was awry. Surprisingly, for being a federal government agency, it didn't take long to get a representative of the TSA on the phone. A friendly woman, another surprise, answered and asked how she could help me. I explained that I was wondering the status on my TWIC card and that I would need it soon to begin work. She collected my information over the phone and what happened next would be the second time in my life that it appeared we had a problem, one that we weren't fully aware of yet. With a surprised tone to her voice she exclaimed that she didn't know what was going on. My application had been denied before it was ever sent to even have a background check done on me. She had never once seen that scenario before. She worked on her computer to reopen my application and put a priority flag on it. A few days later I received the card in the mail in time to start our contract.

Once again life returned to normal. We had our emergency backup plan, but we focused on the tasks at hand, building a business, establishing ourselves and eventually purchasing a home. The only thing we did differently was to begin to spend the money out of our bank account, without replacing most of it; also when we would deposit business checks, we would take a decent amount of cash money from that deposit to take home. We began to store only smaller amounts of money in the bank and kept a decent portion of our earnings at home, hidden in a lock box. We also began to invest a little bit of money in gold and silver, seeing as how the gold bugs appeared to be right; and for years they were, those prices would continue to climb. It was our investment for retirement, we didn't have an IRA or stocks, we didn't have a pension and our bank only paid 0.10% interest, a joke.

There would be some big changes coming to our life, but they were all good. At the moment with housing prices beginning to crash we refused to purchase a home, but things were about to get to where we had always wanted to be in life, with the exception of working too much and we had a plan to fix that also.

Big Changes

Our apartment was starting to become smaller and smaller. Though we had a sufficiently large two bedroom apartment at a reasonable price, we also had a lot of expendable money. We cleverly placed newly purchased items here and there, but it was starting to look a bit packratted, especially the spare bedroom that we used for the office. In that room, cases upon cases of cleaners were kept. Prices were starting to climb so fast, seemingly starting with the toilet paper, that we would buy in bulk all of our commercial cleaning products before another potential price increase hit. The janitorial business began to have a lot of equity in supplies. Our income was growing and we were hoping that perhaps things would calm down with the economy and pricing on houses would become affordable.

With housing prices now in freefall, why buy a house? That same house, if still available, could literally be twenty or thirty thousand less dollars in a year. Even though we had the desire to find our perfect home for us, it just didn't make sense. For now we would rent and wait and see what happened to the market. Still the economy was showing the effects of the crash. Even in 2010, tons of restaurants were shutting down, other businesses were closing and even though there were not as many mass layoffs as the year before, we were many more times likely to clean up a desk from someone who lost their job, rather than clean the desk of a new employee who had just begun. Our landlord began to run into some financial trouble.

In the fall of 2010, with our business now earning over $100k per year, a pace at which it would maintain, the natural gas to our apartment building suddenly got shut off, due to non payment by the landlord. Quickly calling the landlord, we spent a night sleeping in a much cooler apartment, not too cold, but thinking of what would have happened if it were January. Then we would come home one day about a month later and there was a notice left on our door. The notice told us to call a county department, where we learned the apartment building might be lost, due to past due taxes owed by our landlord on the property.

After calling the county department we learned he still had several months to pay the taxes, the county just didn't know what to do. They hadn't yet run into a situation where they would take over a property, due to non-tax payment, that had five separate apartments in a house. I called the landlord and expressed my concern. He assured me that they would be paid, he knew about it. Still, we ran a business and couldn't just up and move on the spot, if it were summer we would be in trouble. We decided to find a new place to rent, we wanted to rent a house.

We had been living in apartments for most of our married life. Having to listen to partying, fighting, smelling weed or just the lack of privacy was not at all favorable to us. Though we were fortunate with most places we rented, there would on occasion be a bad apple. Usually they wouldn't last too long, as they usually got evicted for non-payment of rent. We had always held a philosophy that you shouldn't pay too much for rentals. We didn't want to move into a house and suddenly pay an extra $600 or $700 for rent and utilities, just to live larger. Rather, we would try to find a house in a good price range and we were willing to pay up to $300 more per month. The apartment that we rented only required that we pay electricity, that was it. With a house rental we would have to pay gas, water and sewer, plus garbage, so the base rent couldn't be too much more than what we were currently paying. In a very beautiful neighborhood, on a quiet street, we met up with a man named Don, he would become our new landlord.

This older home was decent. It had large windows, a big backyard, complete with a black raspberry patch. A good amount of trees in the yard, the home was in a middle class neighborhood. The house that we rented would be on Jefferson Avenue in Petoskey. The large two story white house had a typical Michigan basement. The dug out basement was complete with walls of dirt and large rocks, wooden beam supports, cylinder concrete blocks and of course spiders. The property had hedges in the front and side yards, they needed to be trimmed badly, but Don was an older man who needed some help with yard work.

We liked Don the second we met him. This retired man handed us the keys and told us to make it our home, do whatever we wished, just don't paint the stairs. Immediately we began trips to Lowe's and Home Depot to buy new window coverings, area rugs and planned where the office was going to be, as well as the child's room.

For years we had been thinking about having kids. Originally it would not have happened until after college. With the college option off the table and now finally the feeling of being settled, we began to discuss this over and over again. The economy had us worried, the couple of weird problems had us equally concerned. I just wasn't sure, but looking at pictures of people's children on their desks while cleaning businesses had started to become depressing. I turned to God for an answer.

Several times I prayed about whether or not we were able to have kids or if there was even a point of doing so in this current world. On one hand, we had plans should there be an emergency, on the other hand, one of the friends who was in our plan had backed out. He had a child on the way. Each time I prayed I felt it was alright, that God would provide for our family, He would keep us safe. We didn't know if the economy would get better or worse, we didn't know if something would trigger a freefall. Finally by the summer of 2010 we had decided to have a child. We hadn't actual set a time frame to try to do so, but we were resolute about our decision. In December of 2010 we moved into the house that we would stay at until 'they' came.

I had been keeping a close eye on truck prices. We were driving a 2008 Ford Ranger that had around 80k miles on it. Though the truck had long been paid off, we were always looking for base model vehicles, cheap, but new, as we drove around 30k miles per year for the business and needed reliable transportation, having to be a truck. With a child soon to be on the way, our vehicle didn't hold a car seat, it had no back seat. Our search began.

There was no rush, Sabrina wasn't even pregnant yet, but we knew that the very first deal we found would replace our Ford Ranger. We looked into every option, even Subaru Outbacks. Finally with the close of the year, both the GMC and Ford dealers in Petoskey had an absolutely great deal on new vehicles. Ford was offering $8,000 in incentives on a new F-150 and GMC was nearly equal. There was a catch though, we really didn't want OnStar or any other sort of satellite onboard system. Nearly all newer, high end trucks came with that service. We went to find out what rock bottom on pricing really was on these trucks. The GMC pickup, extended cab came out to $20,500 with our trade-in, the Ranger, the F-150 came out to $22,500. We are not terribly brand loyal, so we began to decide on which truck we should buy. Was it worth an extra $2,000 to buy the F-150 that didn't have satellite connectivity? Could we really just be paranoid or did we really have a problem? What about that FBI agent down the hill, what about the TWIC card originally being denied? Plus our business phone had just lit up late at night when we came into the office, this still being the apartment as we had not yet moved.

A couple of times prior in the past month, as I unlocked the office door and went to turn on the light, I could have sworn that I saw the phone have a quick red light flash. This Panasonic phone, old school and corded, had a built-in answering machine. Each time that it would ring there was a red light that would light up. If there was a message the red light would be flashing, likewise if you picked up the phone off the receiver, the red light would flash once. Finally determined to put an end to what was going on, I began to go into the office and look immediately at the phone before I hit the light. I had caught it, indeed it flashed red once. I wasn't seeing things, it was either a very overzealous government agency or the phone was on the blitz. Still, as we pondered the F-150, I decided to give our salesman friend at the Ford dealership, a former Weekly Scoop pooper scooper customer, a call. Is that really as low as you can go?

He called me back a few minutes later. Since our truck had always had the work done at the Ford dealership, oil changes, brakes, etc., the owner of the dealership decided to take off another thousand. I told him I would be right there, we bought our first luxury truck, an F-150 extended cab, with a lot of bells and whistles, but no satellite.

This satellite paranoia seemed odd to the people at the GMC dealership. Jon, the Ford salesman didn't mind, he also had his own opinions, but the people at the GMC dealer couldn't understand why we wouldn't want that option. They stated, "what if you are in a car accident and can't call?" and "there is no way the government could do that?" We knew better, yes the government could do that. When we went to our storage unit every couple of months or so to check up on it, we never brought our cell phone. Why would you? After all of the revelations that Snowden laid out I would hope that Americans would at least realize, that yes, the government can tap into onboard vehicle satellite systems and they will.

I made sure that Jon took the truck across the street and filled it up with gas before we took possession of it and exchanged keys for the vehicles. After our trade in, the rebates, etc., we found that in order to receive a thousand of the rebate we would have to keep a loan through Ford for three months, taking out a minimum loan of $7,000. I pulled out some cash to pay for the truck as well as my check book. Being the Petoskey area, for anyone who has ever been there, these dealerships are used to a lot of summer seasonal home owners buying new cars with cash all the time. We were well known at the dealership and often window shopped while our truck was getting worked on. The loan man asked me, as he is getting ready to do the paperwork, how much cash I was putting down. I told him $10k, at which he replied to make it $9,900, he didn't care to have to fill out government paperwork over a $100 bill. I did as he asked, paying the remainder of the balance, aside from the temporary loan, with a check. We were off to work to start our busy night in our new F-150, no time for joy riding.

The new truck was remarkable. Finally my lead foot had a V-8 engine. Sabrina would always complain that I was going to hurt our vehicle from my jackrabbit starts and my quick passing. Now with this truck I didn't even have to floor the gas pedal to get moving quickly, it just went. There is an oddity to this story that should be mentioned now. When we registered the title, we did so with our apartment address, our real address in Petoskey. We figured we would just pick up the title there, at the moment we were still living at the apartment with only some of our stuff in the new house.

The very next day after buying the truck, we would move out of that apartment into our rented house. While we would go back and forth a few more times to get the remainder of our things and clean the place, it is our belief, had we not been in the process of moving, our life would have had an unexpected turn for the worse, immediately. However, safely at our new house, we were unaware of any true problems going on, we just suspected one. They say time heals wounds, perhaps this is true, but God also heals them.

Even though the FBI had been parked at the bottom of the hill from our apartment, it had been years, it began to even be questionable, there must be another reasonable explanation, so we thought. The same rang true with the TWIC card phone call I had made to the TSA. It had been over a year and a half since that happened. Aside from the lighting up of the phone, there was no other reason to suspect that anything was going on. We were moving beyond these premises and forgetting what we had been so certain about.

In January of 2011, Sabrina got pregnant. We had determined that we would use a midwife for the pregnancy. We didn't want to use the local hospital and the fact is that we were anti-vaccine, not embarrassed to say so, we wanted a natural, healthy pregnancy. Some might consider it too far, but we knew how to research online. There would be no ultrasounds the next nine months, the prenatal vitamins would be organic food and expensive vitamin powder drinks. We were in the process of changing.

In 2010, after being overweight for years and years, we determined that despite the fact that we were busy, we were no longer going to eat out. We had tried this before, but this time we would succeed. We went on a no sugar, all organic diet. We cut out all of the food that we had read could cause bad health problems, could make us sick or just simply had ingredients that we wouldn't have in our cupboard. With the exception of Mrs.

Renfro's habanero sauce, we were done. No more pop, no more donuts, nothing. We did allow a cheat day once per month though.

On those days we would usually meet up with friends. They had missed not dining out with us and we would spend the better part of the day, getting up early, eating. We would start off with a donut from Johan's bakery in Petoskey for breakfast, then eat lunch out and finally dinner, often at our favorite place La Senorita, where we would feast on appetizers and fajitas or burritos. To finish it off we would always find a dessert somewhere. Doing this only seemed to cause a one or two day weight gain and then in three days we would actually be lower in weight than before we pigged out. Our theory behind that was that the body was kicked into overdrive and actually speed up the metabolic rate due to this temporary increase in calories, if only done once in awhile, it appeared this would actually cause you to lose weight. With our diet starting in May of 2010, we were down to the ideal weight by October of that same year.

This might not sound possible, but it is true, so I will relate the story. Our diet consisted of two sandwiches per day, some potato chips, string cheese, a power snack pack (a nut mixture with one bit of real dark chocolate), fresh fruit and vegetables, all organic. On Sunday, our slow day, we would cook a meal, usually spaghetti, pizza or burritos, all organic, with the exception of that great salsa! This was enough food to consume and though there was hunger, the weight came off quickly. I lost nearly 100 pounds and Sabrina lost nearly 50, all in six months. A total change of diet, not a diet.

In the fall of 2010, Concord Academy, a charter school in Petoskey, called for a cleaning estimate. We did a walk-through and I came up with a bid. We were to cover the current employee doing the cleaning, vacation. We did so and found the school was a bit tougher than we thought, we had underbid. The school was mostly carpet, did not have a gym or a lunch room; the school did have about 20 classrooms, plus a couple of dance and art rooms. Without having a cafeteria we figured it would be easy, we didn't want to deal with the hassle of a gym floor, we had bid on a couple of different schools in the area to know that gymnasiums were trouble. Redoing a gym floor was too much liability, too much unknown, too much expense, essentially just too big of a hassle for us to bother with. This charter school was different. Here was something that was manageable, though it took us three hours each, per night, to clean the school.

Finally after we covered the employee's vacation, the director of the school asked us to finish out the school year. In Michigan, schools all over were making major budget cuts. The amount of state funding per student had been lowered and there was constant threatening to lower it even more. These cutbacks were still a side effect going on after the housing bubble burst. I declined and told him that I was sorry, I fulfilled our one week service, but I accidentally gave him too low of a price. He asked what I should have bid and I told him. A little later he called back and accepted the new price, I signed.

The school would work out better with Sabrina being pregnant. I emailed both managers of the clubhouses and told them that we were going to take a year off because Sabrina was pregnant. They understood and I realized that the decision not to clean the clubhouses during that year meant we might never get them back. Remembering that we had plans to trim down the business, we also had considered plans to hire people, both of these were in the works. The whole economical situation had made us think to hold onto all of our business work, but with it now being 2011 and us moving forward with having a child, we decided that now was the time to have a child, we had money, our place and could take a decent economic hit, if we had too. With the school we would have a very steady year round work schedule. When the school wasn't operating we would have a seasonal restaurant in Boyne City to clean, as well as the boat, when those were done we would be back at the school again. Plus the pooper scooper still earned around $600 a month, even though we had finally hit less customers than we originally had.

We began to realize years prior, that our pooper scooper customers either had the money or they didn't. Seeing as how a lot of the wealthy lived in homes outside of town, we decided to jump the price, completely double, for those who lived outside of town. The locals living in town could still get their one dog yard scooped for $8.50 per week, but it would start at $16.00 for those on the outside. Those customers who we had at older prices would get a slight increase in price every other year. We kept with this same philosophy in Aardvark Janitorial. We didn't usually increase price, unless space or responsibilities were increased, except every other year. With the current economic downturn we only raised prices around that time to weed out customers, as we were going to cut back on work due to Sabrina's pregnancy anyway. Surprisingly no one cancelled after the modest price increases.

The school was a hard job, but as with any janitorial job, once you get the hang of it and figure out some shortcuts, plus buy the necessary equipment, such as a 100' extension cord for places like the school, the time spent cleaning the building normally comes way down. By fall of the 2011 school year, we were already cleaning the school in less than two hours each. Despite our not taking the golf clubhouses, we still picked up another very good bi-weekly account that paid top dollar. We didn't even want the work and they required a vetted company that would follow their confidentiality policies. In case there is a question, this small office didn't have anything to do with what will be told on the following pages. This place was in operation due to an environmental concern in the local area.

With our extra weight off we would eat tons of food per day. I had placed an estimate, to the best of my ability, on the amount of calories that I ate per day at around 5,000. Even with this, I would end up buying some organic cookies a few times a week at the Grain Train in downtown Petoskey. The Grain Train was a great store to purchase lots of delicious foods and had an excellent deli with a limited lunch menu and good soup. The calories didn't seem to matter, we certainly worked them off. In 2011 we averaged 70 hours per week, for the most part, year round.

After our weight loss in the fall of 2010, we began to go to a gym in downtown Petoskey. I remember Sabrina not wanting to use our membership cards to sign in with the bar code reader before our workout. The argument was that if something ever did come of that address they would be able to prove we were here, so most of the time we didn't, though at least once the owner asked us to not forget. We managed to eat right, but going to the gym was a chore for us and after a few months after moving into the house, we stopped.

There was a prize for all of this weight loss. We had been planning a vacation to Chicago and did so in early November of 2010. With the seven day a week contracts done for the season, we managed to call a few customers and rearrange our schedule for an upcoming week. We would get three days off in a row! With that, we would immediately head down to Chicago and visit with family and friends. For two nights we would stay at the Congress Plaza Hotel in downtown Chicago.

The economic downturn had taken and cut the cost of hotel rooms in downtown Chicago in half. A $300 room, such as where we stayed, was now only $149 a night. We went down there and had a blast, eating at our favorite place Arnie's, right away. When we arrived, we took and met up with some friends. We left our truck in their driveway, so we didn't have to pay for parking in downtown Chicago. All of us spent the day at the Navy Pier and we had pizza at Giordano's in downtown Chicago, quite possibly the best pizza. From there we said our goodbyes for the day and retired to our room.

The next day we enjoyed the waterfront park, visited the Shedd Aquarium and peeked at the Field Museum, a place where we had already been to. After spending much time window shopping and trying some more excellent food in the downtown area, we made our way to the Chicago Bulls game where we had purchased a couple of tickets. Finally getting back to the hotel room late that night, we rested and began our journey, very slowly, back to Petoskey. We knew we couldn't head back up north until Arnies hot dog stand in Whiting was opened. The next day at work I was up 9 pounds from before we went on our trip, Sabrina an equal proportion, but within a week it was gone, most of it having only been temporary, due to excessive drinking from the sodium content of the food anyway. When we arrived back, our business life would continue, things would be relatively the same, despite the fact that we were about to move, starting to cleaning a school and purchase a new truck. For the meantime, we were looking forward to our new member of the family that we would have.

We had purchased some pregnancy tests, the early result ones, keeping a box of them in the bathroom. Early one morning, in January 2011, before Sabrina had went to bed for the night, she decided to take one of the tests, as I was in the process of dosing off. She comes in the room and exclaims that there appears to be a very faint line. I put on my glasses and take and put the test up under the light. Staring hard under a light, I could barely see a line. Now wide awake, I rushed downstairs and hopped on the computer in the office. Sure enough, after googling it, even a very faint line is usually an indicator that she is pregnant. We rush off and purchase two more early types of pregnancy tests. One of them comes up as positive, one of them negative. Two out of three, we now know she is pregnant and plans begin to fill our mind on the child's room, business work and everything else.

Our desire was to have as many natural or organic products for our soon to be born child. After having changed our diet, we felt the additional energy that we had from it at work, seen the effects of healthy living on our bodies, we also felt it was also necessary to take and do the same for our child. We would not know, until he was born, whether or not it was a boy or girl. By May of 2011 we had already furnished the child's room, complete with a crib, bed, dresser, night stand, some toys and some neutral colored clothing all the way through size 2T. We also had our car seat and stroller, everything that would be needed in the near future. In the meantime we continued to work, anxiously awaiting the birth of our child.

Names had already been picked out for the child a year prior. If it were a boy, it would be Joshua, if it were a girl, it would be Abigail. We wanted to use names found in the bible and thought that Joshua was a great example of obedience to God, as well as Abigail. We did have a backup plan in case Sabrina had twins. Twins ran in her family, even though we knew that the chances were low for her to have twins. We were prepared with a second name. In the meantime I began to do a little bit of work, writing articles on a new website, Northern Michigan Truth Out.

Originally my handle had been NMTO (Northern Michigan Truth Out) on the Northern Michigan Update forum website. That website had been taken down for some time now. Kyle, the site owner, had gotten sick and tired of the fighting going on back and forth between members. After the Company X ordeal, the website had less and less people going to it. I began to only visit every few days, then once per week and finally every once in awhile. We were busy doing our business work and we had decided that it was better to focus on the things of God, rather than political things. I got a phone call from a mutual friend, Ken, in the beginning of 2011, that Kyle had just been diagnosed with lung cancer. At only 38 years old he would succumb to cancer a few weeks later. Any hopes I would have had to get involved in restarting Northern Michigan Update was gone, still Brandon had decided that he wanted to get his own website up and running and NMTO was born.

That handle, NMTO, had been used by me for awhile. Originally I had thought to actually run a 9/11 truth group using Northern Michigan Truth Out and attempted to do so, but no one, aside from my friends, ever cared to get involved. With it being nearly ten years after the event, I gave up that desire and will that I had to be involved in trying to explain to people what really happened on 9/11. With a backup plan in place, a successful business and life going good, despite a lackluster economy, our only political stance was against Obamacare.

On the day the Senate voted to pass Obamacare, we held signs next to the highway in Petoskey with a couple of friends for around two hours, against Obamacare. My sign read simply, Screw Obama Death Care, that was it. Aside from those who wrote the bill, we knew more about what this new health care system in the United States would cause. There was eugenics, police state measures, economical problems, control from the health insurers about making our own choices through preventive care and a host of other problems. Once the bill passed the Senate we looked at each other and simply said that the country was gone, there was no saving it. The last nail was put in the coffin, this would eventually unravel and cause mass problems. The desire to save the country ended that day while holding those signs, we said no more to further political activities, our hope was gone. We would live our lives and wait to see what would come out of all of these problems in this country. We are still waiting.

Brandon wanted to get more involved. He figured that he would design a great website with a forum. Eventually he did and the forum even had chat software. The website took him nearly a year to develop and he had the help of a friend who professionally built websites out west. I reluctantly agreed that I would write an article every once in awhile. He needed content to generate interest in the website, for it to grow. The website was complete with a mailing list, using Mail Chimp, and a photo album. On the website Brandon prominently posted his contact information. He had even talked about buying a van and making it a truth van with a loud speaker on top. That I actually thought was funny and just because the whole situation with the United States made me mad, I would have actually rode around in it, even though our passion for being politically active had went as fast as it had come.

With much badgering from Brandon I started to write an article approximately once per month, plus I would proofread articles that he had written, editing them and sending them back to him to post online. My articles turned from exposing government lies to writing about how it was more important to follow Christ, than it was to be politically involved. I wasn't against those who took a political stance against a tyrannical government, it was just no longer our thing. Still, there came a point where I was asked by Brandon to write an article on Obamacare, I knew so much, shouldn't I share it with the world?

The website never really seemed to pick up much steam. Even though it was a nice looking, professional site, the only people who signed up to the mailing list were people who we personally knew. The forum never had much activity, even though it actually had premium chat software installed, complete with free video games. Brandon finally wrote a masterpiece article. He wrote about the birther movement that was going on across the country at that time.

Late 2016 Edit

After years of not ever checking what was left of the website emails and Mailchimp email list, Brandon finally logged in. Google mail was used to access the NMTO emails and despite the fact that the website was long gone, the gmail accounts were still there. We wanted to see if perhaps a federal agent had signed up to the email list that we didn't notice. Indeed Brandon would find that there was only one person who we didn't know that had signed up to receive emails.

Upon searching this person out, it was found that they had lived locally, in Emmet County, Michigan. The man had some tea party postings and seemed to advocate for rights of fathers and their children. Last year this man who had signed up to our mailings ran, without any known reason, from deputies while driving late at night. He ended up hitting some trees near Pellston and was pronounced dead at the scene. What, if anything, that suggests is not known, but a very strange oddity. After Brandon got that information and missed emails, which was not much, he suddenly had what appears to be a keylogger software on his computer.

Trying two different keyboards, he could not get them to fully work. Discussing the situation with two separate senior tech workers, both told him that they thought he had keylogger software on his computer. He wiped his computer clean and reinstalled everything. In 2016 he met with one of these tech workers, which was his friend, who wanted to update Brandon's contact information on his smart phone. He had several phone numbers for Brandon and as they are meeting up, he goes to delete the one that hasn't been used in years, associated with the NMTO website. For some reason his phone would not delete it after several attempts. Finally he was able to delete the number. While that in and of itself does not provide proof of anything, it certainly adds to the number of abnormalities associated with the whole NMTO ordeal.

End Edit

While there are different opinions out there, we were ones who also felt that President Obama was not eligible to be the President of the United States. We saw the evidence that his supposed birth certificate from Hawaii looked to be a photoshopped piece of work. We had our reasons and Brandon, enjoying the study of law, wrote what would be his best article ever. All of the reasons why President Obama could not possibly be eligible were all contained in his article. In my opinion it was the very best single article ever written on the subject, the most comprehensive, the most well researched. The article had taken him nearly forty hours to complete. My article about Obamacare would go up next, with Brandon writing the reasons it was unconstitutional in the second part of the article.

A few months before the article would be written, Brandon and I decided to try and start a web design business. We formed a partnership, got a phone line and were prepared to get going. The business was named Northern Michigan Geeks. We would never have a client and it would be short lived, I would sign the business over to him, he would repartner with another friend. Our son Joshua had just been born, it was October 30th, 2011. Within a few days, my priorities of business would change, our focus was more on our family than trying to start another business we didn't have time for, nor the proper skills to do so.

Our Little Guy

"Behold, children are a heritage from Jehovah, the fruit of the womb is a reward."
Psalms 127:3

Joshua was instantly a blessing to us. We were overjoyed holding this little man in our arms. There is no way to even describe the excitement that came after he was born. I imagine that only those who have experienced this would understand. We had heard about the joy of having a child, but until we experienced it would not have understood it.

Late one night while cleaning the school Sabrina thought she was having labor pains. She sat in a chair as I finished up the school, the last job of the night. With it being the end of October our work load was lighter. I had hired an employee, Dan, a few months prior. He would work at many of our job sites, particularly the larger ones. We knew we would need help to get our work done and Sabrina was going to take a little bit of time off after the child was born.

There were also plans for the next year, to either hire several people and expand the business or cancel customers and keep it within our ability. We were pushing towards the expansion and had already paid for additional phone book advertising to also provide residential housecleaning, lawn service, promote the pooper scooper service more and do window cleaning. Boyne USA expressed its desire to go with our service the following golf season and we had purchased some additional equipment and supplies to staff people. The idea was to hire through a temp agency, in order to relieve ourselves of the hassle of having to do all of the payroll paperwork and in case we had to lay people off due to loss of work. We even picked up worker's compensation insurance, whereas, we had a state worker's compensation exemption prior and I bonded the business. The plans were there, we had enough business lined up by the next spring to hire a few people, assuming no one cancelled throughout the winter. We would never get to that point.

Sabrina had gone into labor and the midwife was called. We were thinking that she would rush over immediately, but she asked Sabrina a few questions and had her check a couple of things and told her to call back a bit later. A few hours later we called her again and she agreed to come out immediately with her bag for a nights stay. Things wouldn't go as we planned though.

The midwife tried everything she could think of, with Sabrina now ready to have the child, but it just wasn't coming. A warm bath was drawn, different positions were tried, in the meantime I had to go to work and had all sorts of family and friends helping clean all of these buildings. We were very quick about cleaning them, as I was expecting to leave from a job site the very second the phone rang. I stayed very near in Petoskey working only a couple of miles away. Finally with all of the work done I came home to see Sabrina struggling to keep awake and no baby. The midwife stated that we could wait a bit longer. Pulling her aside, I spoke to Sabrina, something didn't seem right, we were off to the hospital.

Prior to going, I had called the hospital in Petoskey and told them that we would be coming in. Before we even arrived we had told them that we were bringing our midwife and would want no vaccinations, no vitamin K shot, nothing. When we arrived they were waiting for us outside. We had a Blue Cross Blue Shield insurance plan for Sabrina, but were rushed to a delivery room before I could even register her. There laying on the hospital bed, as she was hooked up to a monitor, the doctor was already suggesting a C-Section, something neither of us wanted, but we were willing to do, if it were absolutely necessary. To our surprise the hospital staff were completely accommodating.

They agreed not to do any shots, nothing. We did allow them to do an ultrasound, using a Doppler, as it was in the best interest of everyone. By the doctor's accord everything appeared to be normal and healthy, but she had to have this baby now. She had been in labor too long and it could cause problems. They decided to give her Pitocin through an IV to speed up the process. That was still taking too long and the doctor ordered the dosage increased. If Sabrina was not going to be able to push out this child soon, even with all of the coaching, she would have to undergo an emergency C-Section. With that time now nearing, the doctor suddenly had to deal with another emergency, someone else needed a C-Section.

If that emergency hadn't come up, the time would have been up. Sabrina could go no longer, but with the doctor now gone for nearly a half an hour, by time he would come back the baby was being born. With much coaching from all of us, a few minutes later appeared Joshua Joseph Medsker. With the nurses washing him up right in front of us, they would return him to his loving mom's arms and we would be put into another room to spend the night. We slept well that night and the next morning the doctor came in to see how things were going. Everything was fine and we were ready to go, he promised to try and get us out of their by noon.

After filling out the birth certificate information they gave us our discharge paperwork, shortly after noon. Her family was on their way to tend to Sabrina for the next several days, while I was ready to tackle the business using prearranged friends and family to help with the cleaning, giving Sabrina rest with our new son. We had been warned that because of the delivery being so rough, Joshua was a likely candidate for jaundice. We knew what to look for and kept a close eye on him.

Everything seemed to be going well until two days later we noticed a yellow tint to his skin and eyes. Concerned we immediately took him to a quick care facility. Here the doctor, who also served as a pediatric physician, looked over Joshua and didn't see the signs of jaundice, yet he had us go to the hospital and have blood drawn to see if he did have jaundice. We went back home awaiting a phone call once the results from the blood test were completed. The phone call came.

Joshua had jaundice and should seek immediate medical attention. We told them that we wished to avoid the hospital in Petoskey, for personal reasons, not due to their great care when we were there and instead would be going to the emergency room a few miles away in Charlevoix. It was already after hours for quick care facilities so we had no choice, but to use a hospital.

After checking into the hospital in Charlevoix, we waited for what was over an hour before a doctor finally came to see Joshua. He had the test results and with it being so late in the evening he decided it would be best for Sabrina to just stay the night in the hospital as they treated Joshua with a special light. That night they would take blood sample after blood sample, his bilirubin levels in his blood were rising, our new doctor, who was assigned to Sabrina's room, was getting concerned. I had met up with a friend and began to clean our nightly businesses with the cell phone in my pocket, awaiting a call.

The levels began to get worse and worse and now there was talk about rushing Joshua to the emergency room in Traverse City by ambulance where he might have to go through a blood transfusion. There was a big problem with this. Sabrina and I, as Christians, were completely against blood transfusions. We were willing, if necessary, to give our blood to Joshua, but were completely against anything else. We are not of the Jehovah Witness crowd, but agreed with them on this point. I began to pray about this situation, as I did prior to going to the hospital.

My assurance, before Joshua was born, was that God would take care of us, that we would be fine adding an additional family member, regardless of what occurred in our lives or the world. Here, with the doctor threatening to take immediate action, I didn't know what to do. The doctor had told me that Joshua was already to the point where he should go to Traverse City, I explained that we were against blood transfusions. As we went back and forth on the phone she agreed to wait another hour, take one more test, however, she would also call the hospital in Traverse City to have them begin to make preparations for our arrival. I stood outside a business in Boyne City, walking back and forth, praying and wondering what was going on, as a friend cleaned the building. An hour would go by and I would call the doctor back.

The test that she took had a problem. For some reason the blood sample hadn't given them any results, she ordered another blood test and we would have to wait for that one to come in. Now I was on my way back to the hospital in Charlevoix to meet up with Sabrina and Joshua. As we all sat there awaiting the test results we put our trust in Him who Created everything anyway. A few minutes later the doctor would walk in, the test results were in. Joshua's bilirubin levels had dropped significantly, he no longer needed to go to Traverse City.

Each hour the results were getting better and better, even the doctor was surprised at how fast of a recovery that Joshua was having. By late afternoon the next day, we would be released from Charlevoix hospital on our way back home. Awaiting us were some phone messages from the hospital in Petoskey.

Someone had called from the hospital in Petoskey telling us to urgently seek medical attention immediately. Somewhere the line of communication had broken down between the quick care that we went to and the hospital. We had told the quick care that we were going to go to Charlevoix instead, but the message never got across to the hospital in Petoskey. On top of that, there were business cards from Child Protective Services (CPS) left in the cracks of our doors. We went to sleep that night and Sabrina got up early the next morning to take Joshua to the pediatrician appointment that we setup after leaving the hospital, to double check to make sure everything was still going fine with him. Sabrina's mom, Kathy, had arrived the day before and was going to stay for a few more days to help out. Myself, still sleeping, was suddenly awakened to some of the loudest pounding on a door I have ever heard.

I ran downstairs, still in my pajamas and opened the door to this younger woman. She handed me her card, she was from CPS and yelled at me that I needed to get Joshua to the emergency room right now. Angry from having been woken up and thinking of how ridiculous this situation was, I told her one moment and closed the door. I came back with the discharge paperwork, angrily telling her that his jaundice was already resolved, it was not my problem that communication had broken down. She demanded to come inside to have me answer some questions and to see Joshua before she left. I told her that I owed her nothing and everything was fine, Joshua was in the process of seeing a doctor at the moment. With my refusal, she headed off promising to get a court order if I didn't comply. Sabrina came back with her mom and Joshua a few minutes later.

After explaining what had happened in their absence, Sabrina's mom, Kathy, convinced me to just call her and let her come over. Kathy was as displeased with the CPS situation as me. I called back and told the CPS worker that we were all here, to head back over. This time when she arrived, she was nicer than before, but still insistent on gathering all of the information on her form. After she saw Joshua, had a bit of yelling done at her, courtesy of Kathy, the CPS woman proceeded up the stairs to look at Joshua's room. Everything appeared to be proper and she was pleased to see our setup. She walked down the stairs and told us she was satisfied with what she saw and for us to continue to follow up with our current pediatrician and left. This whole incidence, an invasion of our privacy, had caused me to make a decision.

For years we had entertained the idea of a video camera system. I had even picked them out online, but never ordered them. Spending the nearly $500 for a system seemed unnecessary in our safe neighborhood, but with the prospect of hiring employees and doing interviews in the upcoming months, it was still an idea. Now with the CPS worker having left her business cards, we were convinced to take and order the entire setup, an all-in-one package, complete with 4 color cameras, a small monitor and a DVR system. The system was independent and not hooked up to the internet. Knowing the potential for abuse by the government, we didn't want one that was integrated with the internet and computer, streaming to a website somewhere. The idea was that if CPS returned and left a card, we would then call an attorney and also document any harassment. We were doing nothing wrong just because we didn't follow every recommendation made by the medical profession. Joshua was a healthy baby when he was born, in the 90th percentile.

CPS never harassed us again, there was no follow up phone calls, no visits, nothing. The camera system was wired, not wireless, and I had quickly ran cables around the house, along with our other ethernet cables for internet and aimed the cameras looking out the windows. Out of respect and ethics, our cameras never pointed at our neighbor's houses. They were hidden behind the curtains, near the top of the windows and if we didn't tell someone we had a system, most people would never have even noticed. One camera watched our back door in the back yard, another watched the porch, another pointed out to the intersection of the street and another was pointed to the same direction, but focused more on our driveway, without being able to see the intersection. Unlike we thought when we purchased the camera system, the cameras couldn't see anything at night time, they would just reflect the windows. This meant that the blinds were always closed at nighttime, as usual, because there was nothing to see due to the infrared lighting on the cameras causing a reflection on the window panes. Only once or twice did we even view the cameras during the day out of boredom. The big activity would be the mailman delivering the mail. We had no time to waste watching video footage. We thought the camera system was a waste of money, as it didn't work at night when we were gone, we had no reason to have them running during the day when we were home. Yet the DVR was always clicking away, keeping up to 5 full days of video, running 24/7. We already bought the system, why not use it? Life was turning to normal once again, our new normal with baby Joshua.

Sabrina went back to work around a week or so after Joshua got out of the hospital. We would take Joshua with us to work, late at night. Our schedule worked where Sabrina would help clean a few buildings several nights per week. Dan, our employee, would help with the school, I would take care of the Petoskey News-Review and smaller accounts, using Dan on the harder accounts. Brandon would sometimes work at a job site during the week also. Sabrina was now to be permanently part time. Our plan was to remain this way until spring when she would take over managing employees, working a bit and doing all of the office paperwork responsibility. With everything settled, we continued on as planned, everything in our business going well.

One a warm spring-like Sunday morning in January of 2012, we had been looking at a used sports car for sale online on Craigslist. We pondered buying this car, as we always regretted selling Sabrina's Camaro. We had the room in our drive way for another vehicle, we didn't want a project car, but this car being less than $10,000 appeared to be good enough to drive around for fun, once in awhile. Until we began to hire more employees we had no use for the extra money we were earning.

In 2011 there was quite a good tax incentive for small businesses, part of the stimulus package passed by Congress. With that incentive, we had taken and purchased an additional backpack vacuum cleaner, a new high end custom designed gaming computer, as I was a nerd, for our business, as well as overstocked by the end of the 2011 fiscal year on tons of supplies, including mops, cleaners, garbage bags, gloves and everything else we used in both businesses. We couldn't pass up the incentive, so now we had essentially very little business expenses per month. We had enough supplies to run the business for 8-9 months without having to buy anything.

We would finish out the 2011 year with things running smoothly, still continuing to meet up with one or two people at our house on Sunday for a weekly bible study. Usually, with extra expendable money, we would go to dinner at La Senorita or make some good food, like pizza, at home and often go the bowling alley afterwards, as they were open quite late. During the winter we never usually worked at all on Sundays. There were a couple of signs that trouble was brewing, but with having had a few weird things over the years, we didn't give it much thought, nothing had ever come of those oddities.

In January of 2012, after around 40 hours of work on my masterpiece for Brandon's website, a serious critique of Obamacare and what was really in the bill, how it could work and the dangers of it complete, I called Brandon and placed it on the website for the world to see. This would be my final political move, I told Brandon that I was no longer going to write for the website, I was done, I had written the article at his behest, as he had made some valid points for doing so. I placed links to the article on a couple of other websites that discussed politics, hoping to generate traffic to Brandon's website. There had been a small issue noted again though.

One night a few weeks prior, I walked into our office to put the backpack vacuum back in there for the night and thought I saw the phone flash again. The old phone had indeed finally broke and this one was the replacement, at least we thought it broke. When we moved into the house we had our business lines transferred. The utility worker from AT&T came out in the evening and told us how bad our wiring was in the house, the house did need to have a total update with electricity and everything, it was old. He would spend nearly three hours on the telephone poles outside, working on making sure that we had a good drop. Indeed he replaced the drop line going to our house. We had thought it was odd when the cable company would install our internet service for our house and likewise would spend hours, working well into the evening, rewiring everything. Now, a year later, the phone began to have some serious static.

The static began in December of 2011 and was only on the Aardvark Janitorial business line, the Weekly Scoop phone line worked fine. Sometimes the phone line would be nearly static free, but finally it took a turn for the worse. People were now saying they were having a hard time hearing me. Sabrina and I, after the few problems in the past, began to look at the phone box attached to our house, everything looked normal. We looked up at the poles to see if we noted anything suspicious, but we did not. Finally, not wanting to have to pay for repair service, if the problem was on our end, we replaced that phone. We even switched the lines on the outside box afterwards and then at that point we realized it wasn't our equipment, the line had gone bad. I called AT&T's small business services technical support line and told them of the problems we were having.

The following day a worker came out and fixed the phone line as we were still sleeping in the morning, from having worked the prior night. Within about an hour, as we are now awake, he came back, checked the phone, having fixed the problem. The line was now crystal clear again. Bored, we put our camera system to use and noted that he looked in a window on our garage. The old garage, an unattached two story building at the end of our very long driveway, did not have a regular door to it, only the garage door. We stored a few things in it, usually boxes and a punching bag, but it was for the use by the landlord for storage. A short time afterwards, I saw the red flash on the phone or thought I saw the flash when I put away that backpack vacuum cleaner in the office. The next day as we came home I remembered to look directly at the phone, indeed it did flash. I had caught the phone, it wasn't my imagination. Not really knowing what to think, we added that to our oddities list that had slowly grown over the years. What else could we do?

With the Obamacare article up online, Brandon had his portion done also. I proofread it, edited it and emailed it back to him. My article went up in late January, Brandon's portion of the Obamacare mini series was about the constitutional aspect. As I was cleaning a building we were on the phone speaking about the articles and how it seemed to have the potential, if it went viral, to make people really question this new legislation. Those articles, in our opinion, were very good and to this day I still think mine was the very best ever written on the subject against Obamacare. As we were talking on our cell phones that evening and he is joking about releasing a huge info bomb, suddenly the phone goes silent on my end.

I look down at my cell phone and the timer is still going, I put it back up to my ear, doing the annoying, "hello, helloooo?" and hang up. He calls me back a minute later. On his end the phone suddenly began to play music and then had a dead silence, he had perhaps heard something like people talking in the background. Now the connection between our cell phones was once again completely clear and normal. We joked about the dangers of releasing those articles, but ended with the statement of "screw them." We wouldn't be stopped, the second article written by Brandon, would be posted on January 26th, 2012, just three days after mine. It was too late for the government, we had released it, I took and published it on a couple of more websites, linking to Brandon's site, Northern Michigan Truth Out. Little did we know that in a few days our lives would completely change.

Of Missing Persons

Life was about to change drastically. There were a lot of little things that in the five years proceeding this incident were signs there was trouble brewing. Though we would never once have imagined such a scenario happening, it did, and with detail we will explain exactly how it happened.

Sunday, January 29th, 2012

On Sunday January 29th, 2012, we did our usual grocery store shopping at the Grain Train. We were big spenders, perhaps their biggest. We didn't usually eat out, we ate high end organic food and we ate a lot, despite having proper BMI's. Our food budget would always run a thousand or more per month, a little bit of that was in our back stock supply of food that we would rotate out. We always kept an emergency supply of food that could last up to three months.

We had extra butter kept in the fridge, a chest freezer full of buffalo, elk and free range chickens, plus our leftover blackberries, picked from our secret spot, and fish; we stored extra cans of tuna, jars of mayonnaise and dried beans. We also had regular canned goods stored that had not worked too well for us. We would replace these relatively inexpensive canned goods, that we usually bought during the annual truck load sale and would end up donating them when they were within a year of expiration to the local food pantry. Our emergency supply of canned food was not organic, it was whatever was cheap at the grocery stores and had a decent amount of calories. For a few years we did this and finally we decided to order an entire one person, one year supply of food from E-Foods Direct, after Joshua was born. That food came in a nice stack of boxes, with some barrels of wheat and we placed them in our food pantry, found underneath our stairwell at our house. Sick and tired of dealing with all of the canned food rotation, we placed it in the back of our truck and dropped it off at the local food pantry. Now we owned a supply of freeze dried food that would last ten years or more, rotating no longer an issue to deal with. Our rotating pantry of three months worth of organic food was kept running as usual.

The Grain Train had constantly been trying to ask us to become coop members. We always paid cash for our groceries. In fact all local purchases were paid only in cash, we would only use a credit card online for purchases, sometimes amounting to thousands of dollars per month. These online purchases were for business supplies, a new computer, Joshua's room, new bedding, whatever. We had learned a lot of the things we liked to buy were not even available in places like Walmart or Kmart. Plus being busy, able to read reviews, not buying things that broke, online just seemed smarter to us. We knew a lot of the staff at the Grain Train, but this one constantly rode us about not being a coop member. We knew we would save money, but we had been against all of the rewards or membership cards that many stores were now offering. We liked cash, always used it, and why give anyone all of our information to build up in their databases about us?

One day while shopping at the Grain Train this same cashier kept badgering us to become coop members. "What would it take to get us to sign up as a member?," he asked. I explained to him briefly about how stores had used the information in the past and our objection to it. Finally he walked back up to us and asked for us to just use a fictitious name. We thought about it and as we came to the checkout, he once again pressured us and we finally agreed.

What name would be used? I figured I would use my real first name, but the last name should be different. Both the cashier and I sat there at the checkout coming up with different last names, when I finally decided on Bourne, Tim Bourne it would be. We both liked the Bourne movies and thought using that last name was quite hilarious. From then on when we would go shopping, this cashier would address us as Mr. & Mrs. Bourne. It had become a joke, we paid for the coop membership and it was coming up on a year of having our card, the membership having paid for itself. We were now indeed saving money on our groceries. On that Sunday, January 29th, 2012, all seemed normal.

We had a quick bible study, ate at La Senorita and then headed out to the bowling alley to play some pool and video games. Aside from a couple of people in the bar area of the bowling alley, it was empty. No one else was there, but they would still stay open until 1am for the couple of customers that they had in the bar. Joshua was looking around, being held by Sabrina, at all of the arcade games and their flashing lights. It would be a ticket night, to see how many we could win and what prizes we would get. Pool was fun and we all played a few games of it. Eventually the night employee would come out and talk with us for a bit.

He knew we came in often and asked what we did for a living. I told him and he had been interested and looking for another part time job. Late nights, a couple days per week, would work for him. While I wasn't yet ready to hire, I took his name and phone number, intending to give him a call. We had watched him vacuum the bowling alley, collect the garbage and do some other tasks. He seemed like a nice guy and that was exactly how we had met our other employee, from a business that we frequented. To us it seemed like a good approach, rather than just placing a help wanted ad in the classifieds section of the local newspaper. Get to know someone, somewhat, and if they are interested in work, give them a try. We knew that people wouldn't be as fast as us and usually would take training to get that eye for detail, but they were usually sufficient for the work that we did. Our employee we already had did what we would expect any employee at a business to do, whether we managed it or we owned it. Little did we know, armed with a phone number of a new friend, that our life would change that night.

Just after 1am, at the bowling alley between Harbor Springs and Petoskey, we left. Brandon had his car and we were in our truck, Joshua now long asleep. On a relatively warm winter's night, we proceeded to go down the bowling alley's very long driveway towards M-119, the state highway that connected Petoskey to Harbor Springs. As we go down the driveway, towards the highway, I briefly see a state trooper that had been sitting at the entrance of the driveway, with their headlights turned off, drive off into the night, still with no lights on.

We approach the end of the driveway making a left towards Petoskey, with Brandon following close behind. He is planning on heading back to his home in Topinabee, Michigan, about a half an hour or so away, where he lived with his family. As we are now on the highway and quite a bit ahead of Brandon, who drives like a grandmother, we see a car in our rear view mirror quickly approaching his car. Knowing that a Michigan state trooper was just sitting outside of the driveway to the bowling alley and seeing the speed of approach, plus the look of the headlights, I am certain it is that same trooper. He must be looking for drunk drivers, Brandon could be in for trouble, he often doesn't have his seatbelt on.

Picking up our cell phone, I call Brandon and tell him to put on his seatbelt. Sure enough, his seatbelt wasn't on and he assured me that it now was. We told him once again to have a good night and continued. About a half a mile later, I see something that would shock me. The trooper had suddenly passed Brandon, turned on his flashing red bubble light on his cruiser and was now quickly approaching the back of our truck. We pulled off to the side of the road and Brandon pulled over behind the state trooper car.

Immediately I'm angry, as I am a very safe driver who obeys all the laws, with the exception of speeding on occasion. I'm frustrated for this infringement on our rights. I know that he probably is wondering if I am drunk or had been drinking, but I flip on my interior light as I wait for the trooper to approach my window. Out of respect for having a concealed carry permit, my light goes on, despite the fact I had not been carrying my 9mm handgun that night. Most nights I never carried the gun. I couldn't have it on the school property where we cleaned, so it stayed at home. The officer walks up to my window and I already have my paperwork ready for him.

He takes a quick glance at Sabrina and I, seemingly not noticing Joshua sleeping in the back seat and asks if I had anything to drink that night. Bingo! I knew it, but I figured it was better to remain calm, not to stir up trouble. I knew he would let me go with a warning for the crime he would soon tell me about, that I hadn't committed. I responded that I had not been drinking and asked him why I was being pulled over.

The officer told me that I had crossed over the fog line 4 or 5 times and he wondered if perhaps I was too tired to drive, now that he knew I hadn't been drinking. That would be one of those nights where I was glad I hadn't ordered a beer. Once in awhile I would get one beer while bowling, though not illegal, the smell on my breath could have led to a field sobriety test. The trooper then looked at Sabrina and asked her what was wrong. He stated that she appeared to be nervous, asked if we had been fighting and what she was nervous about. She told the officer she was just angry with having been pulled over and he once again turned his attention to me.

Then the officer asked a question, that I thought was very odd.

"Do you smoke?"

"Yes, I do." I did smoke, I struggled to stay quit, though Sabrina had been quit for years. I had been supposed to be quit before Joshua was born, but still hadn't done so. There were plans to quit, eventually.

He finally asked if the address was correct on our driver's license. We replied that it was, even though it wasn't, we had been talking recently about changing it to our real address. There was some legitimate concerns that 2012 would still bring trouble, so we weren't sure. No, we were never of the attitude that life would cease on the 21st of December, but we thought perhaps some major event would happen during the year. He asked where we were staying, as it was already late and he must of assumed we would not drive a hundred or so miles that night back to our supposed home in Manistique. I looked at him and told him I was going to be staying at my mom's house. He seemed satisfied and took my information with him back to his patrol car.

We talked as he was back in the police cruiser for a few minutes. This was ridiculous, being pulled over for crossing the fog lines. I was always a conscious driver and knew not to cross those fog lines, in fact I usually drove closer to the yellow line, rather than the white. I felt that was the safer way to drive. We both told ourselves that if he wrote us a ticket, we would fight it. He came back with my driver's license and registration, plus proof of car insurance in his hand. There was no ticket and once again he asked me a couple of questions.

"So you are staying at your mom's house tonight?"

"Yes, I am," I replied.

"You're mom lives in Petoskey?"

"Yes, she does," was my response.

Then he told us to be more cautious while driving and not to cross the white lines. I kept my mouth shut and he bid us farewell and to drive safely. We began to head back home, mad, but letting it go. Brandon had decided to follow us so we pulled into Glen's north parking lot where we chatted for a couple of minutes about the situation.

The other trooper in the car had gotten out after Brandon pulled over behind him. The state trooper asked Brandon who he was and told him that he wasn't used to people pulling over behind him. For some reason the trooper thought he was my brother, despite the fact that Brandon told him he was my friend. The officer glanced at his driver's license, also with a Manistique address and went back to the patrol car. We sat in Glen's parking lot for a few minutes, discussing how once again I had been pulled over for no reason and finally, for the last time of the night, parted ways.

Doing a late night janitorial service we had a few experiences with the police. By late 2010, the local city of Petoskey boys knew who we were and didn't bother us. Bay Harbor always had an extra patrol and they would wave as they drove by. We would have to drive through much of Bay Harbor, to clean the restrooms found on the golf courses, there were three separate sets of restrooms that were cleaned twice per day, in addition to the actual clubhouse building. These restrooms were an add on by Boyne USA that actually earned us a good deal of money for relatively easy work that only took around a half an hour or so per cleaning. There was one time when the city of Petoskey police had found a way into the Bay Harbor clubhouse from a door left unlocked.

We were only responsible for checking the door we came in and out of, Boyne USA had their own security service, who would usually stop by the clubhouse before we were finished cleaning the building to check all of the doors. In this instance, we were surprised to see the police walking out the front of the building, as we were loading our truck with the business equipment.

That night, the city of Petoskey officers demanded that I give them my identification and I began to have an exchange of words with them about being harassed and not having to show identification. We were in uniform, had the keys, loading cleaning supplies, what was the problem? Finally one of the officers hollered that I had an attitude problem, which I probably did, as I had stated that this was not Nazi Germany and I didn't have to show my papers, so I flashed them my driver's license and then told them I knew the acting chief of police. I did know the acting chief of police from my high school years. He had a son around my age and we both went to the same church for years in Petoskey. After I told these officers that, they suddenly apologized sincerely, shook my hand and drove off.

Another time in Bay Harbor I was driving around late at night and suddenly had red and blue lights from a city of Petoskey patrol SUV lighting me up. The officer, who turned out to be the officer that I knew, walked up, saw it was me, greeted me with a hello and went back to his SUV, continuing his patrol. For years the residents in Bay Harbor had been asking for more patrols. The million or more dollar homes that littered this gated community had sometimes been robbed. A lot of times the homes had no occupants, the owners were busy in their lives in some major city.

The gate system at Bay Harbor was well secured. Bay Harbor also had their own security patrol cars that would drive around throughout the night. We were the only or one of the only contractors, that had access to nearly all of Bay Harbor, 24 hours a day, 7 days a week. We had a pass that allowed us to beep into the gate system ourselves, just as a resident did. They didn't want to give us a pass, as it was not allowed, but they were pressured by the clubhouse because we came into Bay Harbor twice per day, we needed access. A few times we were also stopped by the police in Charlevoix county.

In Boyne City, which was located in Charlevoix county, while cleaning the library, a couple of times different officers approached us as we were leaving, inquiring what we were doing. One of them was extremely nice, the other a young punk who demanded to know what we were drinking, at the time it was Cherry Coke. He asked if he could smell it and Sabrina told him he could have a sip, he literally, in youth like fashion, drove the patrol car to the end of the lot and had a mini burn out. After that the Boyne City police knew who we were and never messed with us again. A couple of Charlevoix County sheriff deputies had also stopped us a couple of times, with one we did have an incidence, the other just checked up on the restaurant we were cleaning on Boyne City/Charlevoix Road. He asked what we were doing and then left, apparently satisfied with my answer.

The other time we were sitting in a park, not too far from the restaurant. We had arrived to clean the restaurant, but as happened sometimes they still had customers. If a big group came in with money and decided to start drinking, they would serve them until they were done. We knew that was their policy and would have to wait to clean the restaurant. As we waited in the park, a sheriff's deputy pulled in front of our parked truck. This happened in the late summer of 2010. As we sat in our Ford Ranger, completely packed out with our food cooler and window cleaning equipment up front, as it was that time of the month to also clean some windows, he walked over to the passenger side and started to talk with Sabrina.

She was told the park was closed and she responded that we would leave. He then requested to see both of our driver's license. Sabrina refused, knowing that she wasn't driving and wasn't even required to have a license on her. He thought that was odd, but went with it. I handed him my license and he radioed it in. At this time another man, who had been riding with the deputy, steps up to my window. This man is dressed in plain street clothes, a big city looking man. I begin a small conversation with him and he tells me he is training up here from downstate, part of a special team. I asked if he was actually law enforcement, but he wouldn't give a straight answer. It seemed so, but we didn't know. In a minute or so the deputy once again approaches Sabrina's window.

As the deputy approaches he asks Sabrina whether or not he has permission to search the truck. She tells him no and then he begins with asking what we have to hide and we could be selling drugs or guns as far as he knows. I respond with the fact that we have a Fourth Amendment right and he will need a warrant. We are outside of Boyne City, Michigan, where hardly anything criminal takes place. The deputy promises me he will get a warrant and grabs his cell phone, walking several feet away from our truck so that we can not hear his conversation. For the next ten minutes he stands off talking on the phone. The other supposed officer, the deputy's passenger, is asking where we are from. Having to stick with the story of where we live, we talk about Manistique and he has a few questions about the U.P. of Michigan, about fishing and relays a story about his buddies having done that once. Finally as I am getting angry from waiting for so long, the deputy returns to our truck, this time at my window.

"How come you didn't tell me you had a CPL (Concealed Pistol License)?"

"Sir, I am not carrying a gun right now, that's why," I replied as the reason I didn't declare it.

"Yes, you do have to tell me, it is the law, can I see your concealed weapons permit?"

Even though I had the CCW on me, I told him it was at home, that I didn't carry it on me unless I was carrying a gun. He told me that I had to carry it on me at all times and I could lose my permit for not declaring that I had one. In fact, he had told me that he was now concerned that he could have walked up to my truck and been shot. At this point I realized this deputy was going too far. There is a limit of how much arguing to do, regardless of rights, with any police officer. So I apologized that I did not know the law required me to do so and would take and carry it from now on, telling any other officer that pulled me over immediately that I had one. He then proceeded to ask a few questions about Manistique.

He wondered if we drove all the way from there to do work. He also wondered how long it took to drive there. He seemed satisfied with our answers and once again told me about how I could have been wrote a ticket for not having my CCW license on me. The deputy told me he was now being nice and giving me a verbal warning. This deputy just seemed to be on a power trip, but we always took note of a brief discussion about trying to take away my CCW on the spot and the mentioning of Manistique. After what would take nearly a half an hour, we would leave, they were finally gone at the restaurant and we began our work.

A year and a half later, that night after bowling, in late January of 2012, sitting on the side of the highway, with the red flash from the bubble on top of the Michigan state police cruiser, this was the first time that I had been pulled over by a state trooper in nearly a decade and the second time in my life. The only other incident was over a loud muffler when I was very young driving a station wagon around. To me, the incident was no different that other times I had been pulled over. Something would happen the next day that would change our lives for ever.

Monday, January 30th, 2012

On Monday, January 30th, 2012, our day is running normally. Sabrina is getting caught up on the laundry and I am working on the end of the month billing for all of our customers. We are both cleaning up the house and enjoying ourselves before I head off to work at around 5pm. Then a text message comes across our cell phone.

At this point in our story, we must note that we had our own cell phone service for years, but in 2009, the cellular company we were with got bought out by AT&T. Our unlimited plan was going to nearly double in cost. Brandon was a Verizon wireless customer. He had a very good reputation with the company. He offered to add us to his friends and family program, where we would be able to use our cell phone the same amount, but would end up paying him $25 per month towards being on his plan. We agreed and as we were no longer in a contract with our old company, we got rid of that phone and picked out a new one with him at Verizon. We had been on Brandon's cellular plan for just over two and a half years, the phone never having been in our name.

The text message from my sister came around 2pm in the afternoon. She had gotten a weird phone call asking for me. I texted her back to give me the caller ID information and she did. The information led me to a woman's name out of Manton, Michigan. I gave my sister a call and found out the following information.

A man had called to ask for me, Timothy Medsker. Kelly, my sister, stated that he had the wrong number. He then asked her if she knew me, to which she once again told him that he had the wrong number and hung up. There was no more phone calls, he didn't call back, however, she felt it was strange as no one had ever called for me at her house. Kelly is a married woman with a different last name. They had called her on her home phone, not her cell phone. There was a catch though, my mom, Laura, lived with my sister.

Kelly's basement is essentially an apartment, my mom's apartment. Those two get along great and my mom acts as the nanny for her grandchildren, which helps Kelly and her busy husband. Just the night before we had a state trooper ask us where we were staying. I told him my mom's house in Petoskey and now my sister is getting a phone call asking for me. Nothing at all at Kelly's house is in my mom's name, the only exception is my mom's driver's license address is listed correctly at Kelly's home. Sabrina and I began to talk about this phone call Kelly received.

Could it really be linked? That was crazy thinking! Perhaps it is an old high school friend's mom or something. I would spend the next hour searching that phone number online. There were no complaints from the phone number, nothing, just a name and an address. We continued our conversation in the kitchen, could it be related to last night's incidence? Pestered by the whole situation, I went outside and smoked a cigarette thinking about it. A few minutes later I would reemerge into the house and tell Sabrina that I am just going to call back the phone number. I am going to end this nonsense conspiratorial thinking!

Walking into the office, I go to grab my cell phone and suddenly think twice. No, I will call from the business line, Aardvark Janitorial. I pick up the phone and dial the phone number. The message on the other end of the line shocks me. I immediately hang up and holler for Sabrina.

"Get in here now! What the #$@% is going on. Listen to this!!!"

Now I place the phone on the speaker phone option and dial the number.

"This investigative agency does not accept voicemail," I then hang up.

We both calmly get up and walk to the kitchen, once again sitting at the dining room table. What is going on, what are the odds? I hop into the office once again and beginning deeply searching on the web to find the source of this. Nothing. All I can find is an address and a name, even the address takes awhile to search out. I called Kelly back and asked her about the phone call again, the only additional information I got was that the man sounded very professional. Kelly knows what professional sounds like, she has held professional jobs and her husband is the vice president of a local family owned factory in the area. I never tell her what I heard when I called the number back, I didn't want to sound like a nut. The address that I find online shows the owner of the phone number coming from a low income housing apartment community in Manton.

Manton is just over an hour and a half drive south of Petoskey. Located a few miles away from Cadillac, it is a very small town, but has enough things to be considered a working community. I search online for any law enforcement, state or federal, that have locations in Manton. No one does, it is too small, there isn't even a state police post there. We knew about the fusion centers. We knew that only the state troopers were connected to such a system. What we didn't know about at the time was the Terrorist Screening Center (TSC).

Rushing through the business work that night, I return home and give Brandon a call, who decides to hang out with us. Searching and searching the internet, I come across the TSC. Could it be that I was on the terrorist watchlist and that officer made a phone call regarding me, thus the call to my mom? Why did he ask whether or not I smoked? What was going on, why did Kyle, the owner of Northern Michigan Update, die so young at the age of 38 from lung cancer? Questions were running through our mind and finally with the night still young and our work done, we decided to take a road trip down to Manton. We wanted to see if there was any clue of the originator to the phone call there.

All of us hopped in the F-150 and arrived in Manton at just after 3am. The town was asleep, there was no life. Sabrina stayed in the truck with Joshua, who was sound asleep, and Brandon and I walked around the community, finding the apartment number. There was nothing unusual to look at, nothing at all. We looked at the roof for satellite dishes or special communication devices and checked to see if there was anything different at all. The only thing we discovered was that the apartment listed as the owner to that phone number had a different, separate lock on the apartment style mailbox. We walked across a field, covered with snow, to see a neighboring building next to this apartment community.

This county department looking building had no name on it. There were very few windows and it was a newly built building. This building did have some satellite dishes and dome cameras keeping a careful eye on the property. To this day we have never figured out what that building is, whether or not it is part of the story, we simply don't know. As Brandon and I are heading back up to the apartment community parking lot, Sabrina hollers at us to get in the truck. This black, clean Cadillac has pulled into the parking lot, at now 3:30am in the morning, with no headlights on.

I hop into the truck with Brandon and we sit there watching them as they creep up towards the corner or the lot. They sit in the car for several minutes and finally a woman emerges. She grabs some paperwork out of her car and we decide to leave right then. She appears to be getting in one of the apartments, standing by the front door with keys, though we left before she opened the door. How can she have such a nice clean car on a night when the salt spray was terrible? Where did she come from, the car wash? We drive down and check out that odd building, speculating what it could be and wondering if it has anything to do with the phone call. We wanted answers, but tonight we would get more questions and no answers. For the next couple of days we all hang out quite a bit, Brandon tagging along chatting with us, while Dan is busy cleaning the businesses. We still don't have any more answers, we refuse to call back that phone number. Suddenly, as I am cleaning the school, a thought comes across.

We had all been wondering why we would have trouble. What if someone had found the storage unit?! What if someone broke into it and the police recovered part of it? Two of the guns were registered in my name. Could this be the problem, they found it, didn't know how to contact us? We had already double checked to make sure no crimes had happened in Manistique that could tie us into trouble with our address, nothing had.

All of us raced to finish the school, though Dan was never part of the conversation, but vacuumed with his ear buds playing music from his phone. A second mini road trip in just a few nights. Finally after a couple of hours of driving we arrived in Manistique, a few miles from where we stored our things. Sabrina thought it was best to check our post office box there, to see if the storage company had tried to contact us, before we went and visited the storage area, just in case someone was looking out.

While we understand that sounds paranoid, in fact I lashed out against her when she suggested checking the mail first. Sure we had a phone call and we were trying to get to the bottom of it, but I had my limits. Now with Brandon pressing me to heed Sabrina's advice, I decided it seemed reasonable to check our post office box up there first. We had all heard of a few stories were a neighbor complained or the police had found weapons, ammo and survival gear, sending the innocent person to jail or even prison for a perceived crime that hadn't even been committed. This was about survival, a backup plan, not taking on the government, as some think to do so, but a getaway plan. My purpose in going up to Manistique area was not to stay up all night long and wait for the post office to be opened, as their lobby was always locked at night. Instead I wanted to go up, check on things and go right back home. Then the conversation turned even worse.

Both of them didn't think I should be driving around Manistique, but rather to go and park somewhere. What if the state troopers were looking for us there? They did have a post in town. Sick of arguing, I pulled next to some semi-trucks sitting for the night in a lot near the end of town. It was already nearly 6am, we wouldn't have to wait that long. An explanation is needed here for the post office box in Manistique.

When one of those who was in on the backup plan with us backed out due to having a child, we knew we needed to change our storage unit. Even though we totally trusted him, it was out of abundance precaution. A few people had been locked away on domestic terrorism charges for essentially the same thing. Though they had more guns and ammo, we had enough that could warrant an investigation and some serious questioning. One day while we were at the storage facility, we picked up an application that was left in an empty unit. The owners were not on site, as the unit was in the middle of nowhere. However, it was a normal sized complex, complete with a few different buildings and never very busy. Every couple of months we would come up and check on things. This time we decided that it would get out of my name, we would rent another unit in a fictitious name, but how to do that, without a mailing address.

Knowing a lot about business, we decided to take and buy a Doing Business As (DBA) name in Manistique. We purchased the name Cleaned U.P., it had sounded nice and we thought it was something that could actually make money. A few times we had pondered moving to the U.P., but up towards the Houghton area, near Copper Harbor. The housing was incredibly cheap to purchase, as there had been no housing boom in the U.P.; in reality, the U.P. was a dying area with more people leaving than coming in. We always assumed that potentially a janitorial service could be run anywhere in a town big enough, like Houghton. Each business needs someone to clean. With our new DBA in hand, we opened up a business post office box, using both of our real names. There we also added to the list two other people who could receive mail through that business box, those names were fictitious. We then mailed a money order for an empty storage unit, requesting a pallet be placed in there, that way we would know for sure they received it. The newly rented unit was no longer in my name, but rather a fictitious name.

The storage unit company didn't send any bills, you were to simply send a payment to them, simple as that. There was usually no correspondence back and forth. The next course of action was that Sabrina and I were going to change our address to another place. We found a vacant foreclosed home that was for sale and used that address, still in Manistique. We also changed our mailing address to our new post office box. This took place a year and a half or so prior to the phone call, sometime in the summer of 2010. After doing all of that, we waited a few more days to move all of our items from one storage unit to the other, what we saw when we arrived at the storage complex that day shocked us.

Our storage unit had been hit by a car. The car had pushed in the door quite a bit so that the contents were partially revealed. To anyone who saw inside the storage unit, it looked just like a bunch of backpacks, a game cart, a few bags, as the ammo cans were covered with trash bags to keep bugs and moisture out, still, in the corner of the unit, you could see a few rifles, in cases, standing up. We quickly slid underneath the broken unit door and in a matter of fifteen minutes or so had our stuff in the new unit around the corner that we had arranged, under a different name. In the meantime we tried to get a hold of the owners.

Finally we did get a hold of the owners, we wanted to know what happened, at the time we just knew our unit garage door was seriously damaged. The actual owner had been out of town, but one of his friends who oversaw the property happened to be in the area when the car accident occurred. An old man, just a few hours prior to the very day we came to move our emergency camping gear, had accidentally placed his car in reverse and backed into the door. Aside from the storage complex owners having to repair a garage door to our unit, nothing was amiss. The owner asked where I placed all of our stuff from the damaged unit, to which I had replied a friends house. Since I still had a credit, as we paid usually six months at a time, he strongly insisted that I move into an empty unit, though larger and store our stuff there. His persistence was very heavy, so I agreed, at least till the funds were used up. All we really did was place a lock on the new unit he assigned us, it was left empty. We did purchase another high quality lock that was different than the one we originally had on the unit that was involved on the accident. We had that new lock with us the day that we went to move it, it was already purchased out of abundance precaution. Daylight had finally hit in Manistique, now sitting in a parking lot with the semi-trucks, the time to check the post office box had come.

There was nothing in the mail box that suggested anything. The usual advertisements and local free newspapers that we received were in there. The women behind the counter would only leave so much in the box, as they knew we didn't check it very often. They had asked permission to throw away some of the newspaper style advertisements, of which I agreed. I also didn't want to wait in line to pick up junk. Aside from the Secretary of State and the storage unit, we had no real use for the address. Next we went to check on the storage unit. Could someone have broken into it? Was that the reason for the phone call?

With the nagging still going on, I once again listened to the other two talk about hiking in via the few acres of woods, verses driving in through the main gated entrance. Brandon and I did hike in as Sabrina sat in the truck, attending to Joshua who was now awake. We came through the several acres of woods into the storage complex and viewed the contents of our unit. We did not note anything out of the ordinary, everything was just as it should be. I drove home a bit frustrated with having taken all of this extra time to do something that could have been taken care of in 5 minutes, but as they told me, just in case. Now I was out of ideas of what could be the source of this phone call. On our way back Brandon got out at a casino in Saint Ignace, just before the Mackinaw Bridge, borrowing their phone to call that strange phone number. He listened to the whole message and came back outside to where we were sitting in the parking lot. Nothing had changed, still no answers. Brandon resumed his normal life and we just thought it was perhaps one of those weird incidences again.

Friday, February 3rd, 2012

On February 3rd, 2012, on a sunny afternoon, before we headed out to work we decided to pay a visit to the Secretary of State (SOS). If we were in some sort of trouble and the only address that they knew was my sisters home, where my mom also lived, we didn't want them to think we were there. She has kids, so we came to the conclusion, almost immediately, that we were going to update our address to our real address, something we were ready to do anyway. Though we had bought some baby prep items, the warmest clothing and highest quality that money could buy, all the way through 2T and even had an infant boiled wool sleeping bag we had finally just received, it was all but impossible to even try this emergency plan, even if necessary, with a baby. While we didn't officially call it quits with the one other person involved, as we had originally committed to waiting until the end of 2012 and then forgetting about it, we knew, that without God it would be impossible anyways, even with the heated tent. We headed to the SOS where another surprise would be awaiting us.

Walking into the SOS we grabbed our number and took a seat. It wouldn't be long, surprising for a Friday, for our number to be called. We walked up to the counter seeing the woman worker whom we knew and began to make an address change. This woman rented a small house that was in the yard of one of our pooper scooper clients. She also had a dog and appreciated the service too, as her dog waste would also be cleaned up once per week. We had run across her a few times while servicing the yard. There she updated our addresses to our correct address, at the house we rented in Petoskey and the mailing address to our post office box in Petoskey. She completed Sabrina's first and then began on mine. After she completed it and handed me my driver's license with the new sticker on back, she suddenly had an odd look come across her face while reading the computer screen in front of her.

"You don't have an enhanced driver's license, do you?" I responded that I did not.

"Why does it say you do, you don't do you? Wait, I know you don't, I just had your license. I've never seen this before. Let me just check your license again."

I gave her back my license and then she proceeded to attempt to fix the computer from saying that I had an enhanced drivers license. She remarked that it was very strange, she had never seen that before. We said our goodbyes, walking out the door heading to work. Now we were even more confused, what was going on? The memory of the TWIC card incident immediately became a talking point, what are the odds? We decided that for the next week we would not park in our driveway. We had recently given out our real address to one other federal agency in early December.

After Joshua was born we decided to get him a passport. Walking into the post office in Boyne City, where they had it setup to do passports, including pictures, we went through the process. Our home address was given, we did not want to commit a crime, a federal crime, so we just put it down. Why not? We were almost to the point of changing our address. We had already received the passport in early January and nothing seemed to come out of it.

If someone were to try to keep tabs on us, it would be hard. If a federal or state investigator even suspected that we lived in Petoskey, having an address, they could drive by several times late in the evening hours and early morning hours. For much of the year we would simply be at work. To an investigator, it could appear that we didn't live there. For much of the year we only ate and slept at home, we spent the rest of our time at work, shopping or doing something fun. Now we would wait and see what would happen, our address had been changed.

We knew our nighttime neighborhood well. Nothing happened, we lived on a slow block with very little traffic, except for a bit of a rush of cars right when school got out with people trying to take a short cut to avoid traffic, there wasn't a problem. The city of

Petoskey police would drive by once per night, usually around 3am or so. This was routine as they went up and down every street, every night, at least once. At night there was never any traffic, never anyone walking down the street, nothing. With the exception of our one neighbor who would leave for work at 3:45am, most people would take and go to work on the day shift. We had a teacher across the street, a city worker next to them, a rental house next to us, a empty house not too far away, with some retirees also living on the block. There was nothing at all out of the ordinary, we were the only night owls. If we were still up around 5:30am, a man would drive up, dropping off a newspaper to the house up the street. Happen to stay up later than that, the kids would walk to school, the neighbors would head off to work, the city of Petoskey police would drive by again. Nothing noteworthy, it was a nice neighborhood tucked into the heart of Petoskey, a few blocks from downtown, not too far from the local community college.

For the next week we left a couple of night lights on in the home and didn't turn on any lights at night. With so little to do sitting in the dark, we sat actually realizing how we suddenly had all of this spare time. Our truck was left a few blocks away, parked on the side of a street near other vehicles, by someone's oversized lot. We would load and unload the truck at our house quickly. After work I would drop off Sabrina and Joshua, park the truck and walk home. Now we were putting our camera system into use, reviewing what happened as we slept during the morning hours.

For an entire week there was nothing that we noted at all. Light traffic drove by and there seemed to be nothing out of the ordinary, with the exception of one man who walked down the street and slowly walked back. For this we were home and saw it in person. He seemed out of place, but he didn't see us, our truck wasn't in the driveway and we watched out the window as he walked up to that vacant house across the street from ours and knocked on the door. The only other thing was a very slow driving black Cadillac. Old people often drive Caddies around and them driving slow is not unheard of! At night we noticed a new truck hanging around town.

This truck would hang out at 7-Eleven for a bit and then drive around. We knew the night life around town. The traffic in the middle of the night in Petoskey was usually extremely light. Stopping at a gas station for a cup of coffee would lead to small conversations from others who worked the same shift. Nothing happened in Petoskey, usually. We made note that one time the man in the truck was talking with someone from the city of Petoskey police department, but other than that, it was just something noted. After giving it a full week, as we had discussed, I once again parked in our driveway. It was now February 11th, 2012.

Saturday, February 11th, 2012

The phone call had happened nearly two weeks ago. We thought about it, looked into it as much as we could and finally we put our real address on our driver's licenses. Aside from the phone call, there was nothing going on out of the ordinary. We would just resume our life as we had. Perhaps the phone call was some sort of odd coincidence, a scam or something. They just happened to call my sister's and mom's home the day after we had gotten pulled over by the Michigan state trooper. Ready to write ourselves off as having actually become paranoid, we readied ourselves to go on, trying to forget about it. We still thought it would be smart to watch the cameras for one more week, just to make sure.

Monday, February 13th, 2012

On Monday, February 13th, 2012, while parked in our driveway an incident would be seen on the camera that would make us suspect that there was a serious issue going on, though we still wouldn't know it yet. We got up around our usual time of 11:30am in the morning. Drinking coffee, I began to watch the surveillance video to see what had happened during those early morning hours. An older model gold Volvo had parked across the street from us. The door swung open and it appeared that he dumped coffee out on the ground or something and looked like he could have taken a picture of our truck!

Our camera system was not the best. It had no zoom capabilities, no crystal clear digital image, it was a basic camera system, that while decent, was for general use. Even though we could blow up the screen a bit, the bigger it was made, the less clear the image became. However, the camera system did allow frame by frame replay. Here we watched over and over again, but couldn't be sure what the man was doing. There was no flash seen, but did he take a picture? Was there a camera in his hand? We really couldn't tell.

That gold Volvo had drove by our house a few times after that incident the same day while we were still sleeping. He had parked across the street just up the road once, he had also parked on our side of the road. The final time he had went in front of our house and before we have him on camera again, he sat there for a minute. If he was an investigator he would have spotted the camera system. We didn't have a camera pointed directly out in front of our house, as we did not want to have it pointed at our neighbors, the camera shot down the street as far as it could see, the angle being aimed towards the middle of our street with full view of our front porch. Each time he drove by, in the course of two hours, he came from or went a different direction.

I went and parked the truck back away from the house, right then and there and we continued to wonder what a reasonable explanation for such behavior could be. The only thing we could think of was that the man was bored, driving around as his wife got her hair done in downtown Petoskey. The next day that same gold Volvo drove by once, this time at a normal speed and not stopping, but our truck was no longer there. We began to go back reviewing footage from the previous Thursday afternoon, that was as far back as the DVR saved.

As we reviewed the video footage, we noted that the gold Volvo had drove by once the prior Thursday afternoon and would not be seen again till that Monday, when it appeared that the driver took a picture. One thing we had overlooked, the first day we parked in the driveway that Saturday, a white very clean full size pickup truck had pulled across the street from us. We could see the front end of the truck on one camera. He sat there for a couple of minutes before driving off. That day I had backed into the driveway, the license plate, as Michigan only requires one in the rear of the vehicle, was not visible. Now Wednesday we watched the tape for that morning and saw nothing, no more gold Volvo, nothing going on. Now we were getting frustrated, did we have a problem or not?

I had been praying about whether or not we had a problem, for God to make the matter known to me. For nearly two weeks I had asked God, but nothing changed. With incidences like the SOS, things got weirder, but still not enough concrete evidence to know we had a problem. The night before Brandon was over at our house, he also parked up near my truck a few blocks away, when he walked back to his car there was a city of Petoskey police vehicle sitting near our truck with their headlights off, but it didn't mean anything. Brandon left with no incidence. The city of Petoskey police department often would wait here or there around town for the unsuspecting speeder, late at night. There was evidence of trouble brewing, but not enough to say it wasn't all a bunch of coincidences.

Wednesday, February 15th, 2012

Finally late on that Wednesday, February 15th, 2012, we would now have enough evidence to suspect we had a real problem and something had to be done. We hadn't seen anything out of the ordinary that morning on the camera footage. I went to clean the Petoskey News-Review by myself, as usual. Afterwards I went to pickup Sabrina and Joshua to continue our nightly cleaning jobs. Wednesday's were busy and aside from Saturday we had the most businesses to clean that night than other days. It was at around 8pm in the evening when I arrived back home from the Petoskey News-Review.

Sabrina was almost ready to get going, she was grabbing a couple of last minute things for Joshua. The portable crib was already loaded in the truck. I decided to have a cigarette on the front porch while waiting. Right next to the porch was a bush, the leaves long gone as the winter was well set in. Not paying attention, my cigarette accidentally bumped the bush causing hots to go everywhere. When I looked at the hots falling to make sure they didn't burn a hole in my jacket, I caught a glimpse of Jennings Avenue, the busy street that was at the other end of our street, there was a white undercover patrol car sitting in the middle of the road, where our truck could be viewed sitting in the end of our driveway.

Traffic built up quickly behind the undercover patrol car and he was forced to move on. Usually in the evening there is always an influx of traffic on Jennings Avenue as around that time college students are coming and going to the campus that is just blocks away. The white undercover patrol car turned immediately into someone's driveway, with his reverse lights on, trying to back up and come back towards our street. I watched, telling Sabrina to get in the truck now, we had to leave. With all of the traffic he was unsuccessful at backing up to head back towards our street, but rather found a slim opening to slip out continuing on in the same direction he had been heading originally. We shot into action, what was the cause of all of this trouble?

With the engine racing I took off going completely around the block, I wanted a plate number, I wanted answers! If someone was looking for us and willing to call my sister, why didn't they just leave a business card at the door. We could talk, if it was a serious allegation, we could talk at an attorney's office. That never happened. At the moment we took off trying to catch this white undercover car, trying to get to the bottom of this situation. Unfortunately our trip around the block didn't find the white undercover car. Disappointed we continued off to work.

That night our business accounts were dirtier than normal. Despite the fact we were trying to move along as quickly as possible, taking every shortcut we could get away with, we ended up not getting home until 4am. Dropping off our business equipment, I left Sabrina and Joshua at the house, driving a few blocks away to park and walk back home. We had tried some serious investigation tactics, but we still had no answers.

On Tuesday night of that week we had drove around to all of the parking lots of the hotels in the area. We were looking for a gold Volvo, to see if we could get answers. There was none to be found, so after hours of driving around we simply returned home. Now, after doing our Wednesday job sites it was early Thursday morning, we would finally get some more answers. Realizing that the video cameras didn't work at night through the windows, we had taken and cracked our upstairs window before we went to work so that a camera could view outside. Even though the camera didn't produce the best video footage at night, things could be made out. When we would get home from work we would once again close that window. We certainly didn't want to scare our neighbors or cause alarm, so we were very careful about doing that. It wasn't that having a video surveillance system was illegal, it was the fact that in our neighborhood someone might have one pointed to a garage door or something, but it wasn't common. So the first thing we did when we got home that night was to review the tape from the time we left.

Less than a minute after I hit the gas on the F-150 and tried to find this undercover car he was apparently doing the same thing. He drove by my house almost immediately after I left. The remainder of the night he would not drive by the house, but would drive, 5 minutes to the hour, every hour, on the adjacent Pearl Street that was readily viewable from the front of the house and where that camera was pointed at. Just a few minutes prior to us arriving back, he had drove by. However, that next hour we never saw him once. I called Brandon to meet up with me and discuss what was going on and what we would do.

Our backup plan, Plan B, was never for such a scenario. It was not meant for an outlaw type scenario as society remained normal. We hadn't planned for anything like that, though our plans would have some benefits in the next several weeks, we really didn't know what to do. Brandon arrived around 5:30am in the morning.

After he arrived, Brandon and I left Sabrina and Joshua, who was asleep at the house and decided to go for a drive. Petoskey was a small town, there were not yet many places opened for business. This undercover car had to be around the area somewhere, but where? We didn't have to look far, riding in Brandon's car we went to Mitchell Street in downtown Petoskey and there was the white undercover patrol car. The gym across the street was open and one of those people inside, working out, was this agent. Brandon parked his car a half of a block away so that we could get some information from the undercover car.

Walking up the sidewalk we came up to the front of the undercover car. No one in the gym was paying attention or looking outside, so we looked at the undercover car. Inside the front grill were hidden red and blue police lights. On the backside was a Michigan license plate, municipal. We now knew that indeed law enforcement was after us, but we didn't know why or what they wanted. We decided to go back and get Sabrina. In what I would regret to this day, we did not jot down the plate number. The feeling that night was to verify it was an undercover police car, not one of those used ones people drive around, we did not overstay our welcome while inspecting that car. This plate number would have been very valuable information afterwards.

After picking up Sabrina we decided to ride in Brandon's car to Big Boy. It was just after 6am and they were open for breakfast. What happened next would not have significance at that moment for us, the only explanation we have for it is God allowed us to see this and hid us from those who were trying to find us. We sat in the very corner of the front part of the restaurant, all ordering a large breakfast. Joshua started to cry so Sabrina walked with him to the rear of the restaurant, near the restrooms, sitting by a table.

At that time, a professionally dressed woman strolled down to use the restroom. She gave Sabrina an awkward smile, as Sabrina stated that very day, *"it was as if she didn't notice me, just Joshua,"* and used the restroom. Sabrina took note that she was carrying a Michigan State Police bag. We were informed of that when Sabrina came back to our table. Off the main dining room there is a small meeting room that can be rented out for a few dollars, where people can hold meetings and dine at the same time.

There were already a few people in the meeting room when we arrived, but more were coming. That woman with the state police bag entered the room, as well as some men with shirts and ties. John Calabrese, the chief of police from Petoskey and Pete Wallin, the acting Sheriff at the time, also joined this group, as well as the Michigan State Police. They held a meeting about something and we joked that it was about us. Little did we know that our lives would continue to get worse and never be the same. They had found us.

We finished our breakfast, paid the tab and left. We never thought to check the parking lot to try and identify some cars, we really didn't think the meeting was about us, but we saw Calabrese's white SUV that we knew he drove around. Hopping into Brandon's car we decided to find this white undercover car again.

Riding around with Brandon can be interesting, though sometimes scary. We also joke that by the grace of God he is still alive. That day Brandon was driving all around Petoskey as we kept an eye out for this car. Finally we spot it at Tom and Dick's party store parking lot, a few blocks away from our house. We pull over and park around the corner as Brandon goes inside the party store. In there is a man dressed in plain clothes with a beard, he is the driver of the car. He's at the counter talking with the clerk, apparently not in a rush, purchasing some junk food. Brandon comes back around the corner, where we are viewing through a closed down business window that has a view to Tom and Dick's parking lot. Out this man comes and gets in the white undercover car, we decide to follow.

From there our house is not that far and sure enough he once again drives by the side street, where our house is viewable, not actually going down our street. He then continues going the back way up towards the south area of Petoskey. We follow, several cars behind. As he turns onto the highway, we continue to follow him. The trip eventually leads us to Walmart, where he gets out and goes into the store. Dead tired and not sure what to do about this situation we head back, it is now nearly 11am, we need some sleep. Brandon returns to his home to also get some rest. One thing for sure is that we came up with a plan while talking at Big Boy.

Sabrina and I are planning on renting an apartment in the area, we are going to rent something in cash that includes utilities. Living there, we will still operate our business, but we are going to place the business for sale. If the business doesn't sell, God willing within two weeks, we are going to give a 30 day notice and relocate to the U.P., rent a place with cash and restart a business. At the table in Big Boy, not knowing everything that will happen, we exclaim that we will be leaving the area in anywhere from 1 to 45 days, depending on how severe the situation appears to be. Some additional explaining needs to be done. How come they couldn't find us?

This is something that we pondered right after the whole incident finally hit a flash point. How come they couldn't find us? Here is what we came up with. We hadn't had gas through Michcon in years, only when we rented that house did we finally have to get gas in our name again. Had they been looking for awhile and checked several times they probably would have given up on that lead. Likewise the city of Petoskey has a coop electricity deal. While I don't know how it completely works, it is different that going with electricity elsewhere in the area. We were also a city of Petoskey customer and we did have electricity in my name, but if someone was checking the databases down in Lansing or Washington, DC, they would likely not have been able to get access to it back in 2011 or before, as things are now only progressing to be all digital records. Our phones were both in business names, they were business lines. If you had searched AT&T databases for us by name, they may not have been able to find us that way. We NEVER used a credit card in Petoskey, at least not since 2006. Everything was paid for with cash, except our online purchases. We never updated the information of our address to our credit card company because the post office box was the same mailing address we had since we moved back in 2003. Our cell phone was underneath Brandon's plan, so here, a choice tool of law enforcement, was not available. We didn't make monthly payments on anything, everything was paid off. There are two other points of interest here.

When we opened up our bank accounts back in 2003 we used our friend's, Shannon's address, which was where we were living at the time and our Indiana driver's license, which is what we then possessed, as we had just moved back to Michigan. We banked with a small local bank chain, plus had another account that we didn't use at a local credit union. That credit union account was opened because we refinanced our Chevy S-10, that we had bought in Indiana before moving back in 2003. However, we had currently been having problems with our regular bank in the proceeding month or two prior to getting pulled over by the state police.

The branch that we did all of our business at had asked for an updated driver's license. While this shouldn't be a big deal, the couple of times it happened we simply stated we didn't have our license on us at the moment. Sometimes the way someone asks for something can say more than they are speaking. This perhaps was the case or it was nothing at all, but policy of the bank. Every other branch we went to never said a single thing, just the one we had frequented for years. When it happened a third time, we stopped going to that branch. The image from our check had our phone number on it, which would have led to our address. There are certain things we just don't understand, perhaps no one requested information from them or the person was simply not that sleuth to put the pieces together. Perhaps they only had a warrant on our personal accounts. We never used them, we had closed our personal savings and only held onto the checking account that was very drained. Everything we wrote a check for, utilities, rent or some other oddity, was paid for out of business checking, not personal checking. Law enforcement would have had to have a warrant for both, not just one. If they weren't aware that we were running a business, then they wouldn't know to look. Then there was our cable internet.

We used Charter, they were the only provider in the Petoskey area. That was in my name, had our real address as it had to. We have speculated that God allowed something to happen to this. Between July and August of 2011, without our noticing until after the whole ordeal happened, our phone number on our Charter account changed to an Illinois number. Why this happened we will never know, but it is not something we did. We gave these companies real information, we just never kept them up to date when our information changed.

Only the passport, through the Department of State, had a current up to date address, this passport was for Joshua, we were obviously listed as his parents. It is possible that had the trooper who turned over the information he collected that night, not pulled us over, that this passport would have eventually led to the same thing, with no warning via a phone call.

Perhaps God blinded their eyes to finding information we left behind during our daily lives? We were hard to find, but not impossible. Though we had cancelled our social media page due to privacy concerns years ago, we had just launched websites for our businesses in November of 2011. These had our names, a photo of us and our business phone number on them. Prior a search online for us came up empty, only in very late 2011, a search for our names on Google came up with those new business websites. Information was out there, at least to some extent.

Now we were back at home that morning after following the white undercover car up to Walmart, with the truck once again left several blocks away. We were tired, ready for bed, ready to think more about this when we woke up. Before we went to sleep we began to watch the camera footage to see what had happened in the nearly six hours since our absence. What we were about to see would surprise us.

The entire morning was normal, we noticed a couple of new joggers going by and a few unfamiliar faces walking dogs. At the time we hadn't really given it much thought, this would be something we wouldn't realize until later was actually a problem, so we weren't looking at it with suspicion. We really didn't think things could be that bad. Around 10:30am on the video footage we see the gold Volvo drive by, parking for a minute across the street. Then a few minutes go by and here comes the gold Volvo again, this time parking on our side of the street near the end of our driveway, sitting for a minute and slowly driving off. We are still watching in horror and here comes the gold Volvo driving by again and this time stopping in front of our house, sitting for a minute, before reappearing on the camera, leaving. There was a big problem, we were at the house when this last incident happened, we had caught up with the recorded footage and were now watching events unfold on the DVR that had occurred since we were home. Each time prior that our truck wasn't there the gold Volvo just drove by, only that one day that we were parked at home, the driver would stop and appear to take a picture. Did he know we were sitting inside the house, despite the fact that our truck was blocks away?

At the time we didn't realize that the FBI and other federal law enforcement agencies can carry around with them portable thermal imaging devices. These devices can help them see if their suspect is in a house or an apartment and what part of the house they are in. We didn't realize that this was a standard issue with many FBI agents until much later. In a few minutes we would be on the run.

Documentation

STATE OF MICHIGAN
DEPARTMENT OF STATE POLICE
LANSING

RICK SNYDER
GOVERNOR

COL. KRISTE KIBBEY ETUE
DIRECTOR

December 2, 2013

Mr. Timothy Joseph Medsker

Re: CR-78529-14

Dear Mr. Medsker:

The Department has received your November 16, 2013, correspondence appealing the Department's November 8, 2012, written notice denying your request for information under the Freedom of Information Act (FOIA), MCL 15.231 et seq. You requested a copy of files which contain information pertaining to you. Specifically, you referred to an investigation conducted by Lt. Brown in Marquette, any multi-agency investigations, and any information about you "entered into the Michigan Fusion Center, also known as MIOC."

After review, our original determination is upheld.

Section 13(1)(d) of the Act exempts "records or information specifically described and exempted from disclosure by statute." As such, any information which may be in the possession of the Department would be exempt from disclosure under 28 CFR Part 23. The federal statute prohibits dissemination of information outside of law enforcement and defines dissemination to include disclosure of the existence or non-existence of such records. Therefore, the Department cannot confirm or deny whether there is information about you contained in records maintained by the Michigan Fusion Center, or the MIOC.

Under section 10 of the FOIA, the Department is obligated to inform you that you may file an action in circuit court within 180 days after the date of the final determination to deny your request. If you prevail in such an action, the court is to award reasonable attorney fees, costs, and disbursements. Further, if the court finds the denial to be arbitrary and capricious, you may receive punitive damages of $500.00.

Sincerely,

Lori M. Hinkley
FOIA Coordinator
Michigan State Police

MICHIGAN STATE POLICE HEADQUARTERS • 333 SOUTH GRAND AVENUE • P.O. BOX 30634 • LANSING, MICHIGAN 48909
www.michigan.gov/msp • (517) 241-0606

Michigan legislation regarding FOIA requests does not allow for
a Glomar Response. A Glomar Response is "cannot confirm or deny"
as listed above. 28 CFR Part 23 is federal legislation, not state.

RICK SNYDER
GOVERNOR

COL. KRISTE KIBBEY ETUE
DIRECTOR

August 12, 2015

TIMOTHY MEDSKER
704C E 13TH STE 221
WHITEFISH, MT 59937

Paid
$ 9.19
8/25/15

Subject: CR-2001399

Dear TIMOTHY MEDSKER:

The Michigan Department of State Police has received your request for public records and has processed it under the provisions of the Michigan Freedom of Information Act (FOIA), MCL 15.231 et seq.

Your request has been:

    [   ] Granted.

    [X] Granted in part and denied in part. Portions of your request are exempt from disclosure based on provisions set forth in the Act. (See comments on the back of this letter.) Under the FOIA, Section 10 (a copy of which is enclosed), you have the right to appeal to the head of this public body or to a judicial review of the denial.

    [   ] Denied. (See comments on the back of this letter.) Under the FOIA, Section 10 (a copy of which is enclosed), you have the right to appeal to the head of this public body or to a judicial review of the denial.

    [   ] The documents you requested are enclosed. Please pay the amount of $—. Under the FOIA, Section 10a (a copy of which is enclosed), you have the right to appeal the fee to the head of this public body.

    [X] Please pay the amount of $9.19. Once payment is received the documents will be mailed to you. Under the FOIA, Section 10a (a copy of which is enclosed), you have the right to appeal the fee to the head of this public body.

You may pay the amount due online at www.michigan.gov/mspfoiapayments using a credit card or check. You will need to provide your name and the reference number listed above. Please note, there is a $2.00 processing fee for using this service. If you prefer, you can submit a check or money order made payable to the STATE OF MICHIGAN and mail to P.O. Box 30266, Lansing, MI 48909. To ensure proper credit, please enclose a copy of this letter with your payment.

If you have any questions concerning this matter, please feel free to contact our office at (517) 241-   or email MSP-FOIA@michigan.gov. You may also write to us at the address listed below and enclose a copy of this letter.

To review a copy of the Department's written public summary, procedures, and guidelines, go to www.michigan.gov/msp.

Sincerely,

ERIC ▮▮▮▮▮▮▮▮
Freedom of Information Unit
Michigan State Police

Page 1 of a 2015 FOIA request to Michigan State Police.

DENIAL OF RECORDS:
Denial is based on the following provision(s) of the Freedom of Information Act. MCL 15.243, Sec. 13(1). (All that apply will be checked.)

[X] (a)   Information of a personal nature where the public disclosure of the information would constitute a clearly unwarranted invasion of an individual's privacy.
     □ telephone number(s)   X address(es)   □ date(s) of birth   X physical characteristics   □ driver license number(s)
     X other _account #_

□ (b)   Investigating records compiled for law enforcement purposes, but only to the extent that disclosure would do any of the following:
     □ (i)   Interfere with law enforcement proceedings.
     □ (ii)   Deprive a person of the right to a fair trial or impartial administrative adjudication.
     □ (iii)   Constitute an unwarranted invasion of personal privacy.
     □ (iv)   Disclose the identity of a confidential source, or if the record is compiled by a law enforcement agency in the course of a criminal investigation, disclose confidential information furnished only by a confidential source.
     □ (v)   Disclose law enforcement investigative techniques or procedures.
     □ (vi)   Endanger the life or physical safety of law enforcement personnel.

□ (d)   Records or information specifically described and exempted from disclosure by statute.
     Statute:
     □ MCL 780.758 William Van Regenmorter Crime Victim's Rights Act   □ MCL 28.421b Firearms
     □ MCL 28.214 C.J.I.S. Policy Council Act (LEIN information)

□ (m)   Communications and notes within a public body or between public bodies of an advisory nature to the extent that they cover other than purely factual materials and are preliminary to a final agency determination of policy or action.

□ (n)   Records of law enforcement communication codes, or plans for deployment of law enforcement personnel, that if disclosed would prejudice a public body's ability to protect the public safety.

[X] (s)   Unless the public interest in disclosure outweighs the public interest in nondisclosure in the particular instance, public records of a law enforcement agency, the release of which would do any of the following:
     □ (i)   Identify or provide a means of identifying an informant.
     X (iii)   Identify or provide a means of identifying a law enforcement undercover officer or agent or a plain clothes officer as a law enforcement officer or agent.
     □ (v)   Disclose operation instructions for law enforcement officers or agents.
     □ (vi)   Endanger the life or safety of law enforcement officers or agents or their families, relatives, children, parents or those who furnish information to law enforcement departments or agencies.
     X (viii)   Identify or provide a means of identifying a person as a law enforcement officer, agent, or informant.
     □ (ix)   Disclose personnel records of law enforcement agencies.

□ (u)   Records of a public body's security measures, including security plans, security codes and combinations, passwords, passes, keys, and security procedures, to the extent that the records relate to the ongoing security of the public body.

[X] (w)   Information or records that would disclose the social security number of any individual.

[X]   To the best of the Department's knowledge, information, and belief, under the information provided by you or by any other description reasonably known to the Department, the public records do not exist within the Department.
     MICC files

□   Based on the information you provided, we are unable to locate any records pertaining to the incident you described. Please resubmit a request with additional information. The following information, if available, is suggested:
     □   Specific location (i.e. city, county.)
     □   Michigan State Police incident number
     □   Names of those involved in the incident
     □   Specific dates (i.e., date of incident)
     □   Name of driver and their birth date or driver license number
     □   Date of birth

□   The report you have requested has not yet been completed and filed. Please resubmit your request in 30 days.

Additional Comments:

Page 2 of a 2015 Michigan State Police FOIA request. Note the following denial of records including the use of an undercover officer and informant.

90

MICHIGAN STATE POLICE
FIELD SERVICES BUREAU AUTOMATED DAILY

COREY L	983	01/29/2012 Sunday	TASER 16 X00-368874 (TPR RUTHIG)	Meter No: N002205
GENERAL	8:00 PM - 6:00 AM	1301 (8G* SERV/A)	SHOTGUN 15 V679418V (TPR WERNER) RIFLE 15 LE025569 (TPR NADEAU)	OUT IN
		37940 37275 62		Display Segment Check Y Y
				Internal Verification Y Y
				Range Test Y Y
			KIT ITEMS 02 Petoskey	Audio Test Y Y
				Patrol Speed Test Y Y

Start	Clear	Activity	Code	Location	Activity Description / Notes
				Assignment #1 GENERAL DISTRICT 7 GAYLORD POST 1/29/2012 9:00 PM HEBNER	
8:00 PM		ON			ON-DUTY
8:00 PM	12:30 AM	SUPP	54002	POST	MC73-0000498-/2 COMPLETED AICS REPORT; LEIN WORK; WARRANT REQUESTS
12:45 AM	12:50 AM	PI		HARBOR HALL	ATL WARRANT
1:10 AM		BTOP	8141	M-119 / KONLE	2010 FORD BXC0869/MI, TIMOTHY JOSEPH MEDSKER, W/M, P1 - FRONT DRIVER
	1:15 AM	VW	8141		TIMOTHY JOSEPH MEDSKER, W/M, 4/1 9/
1:15 AM		STOP	8212	M-119 / KONLE RD	2002 OLDS 1ECA24/MI, BRANDON EVERETT SCHUCKARDT, - FRONT DRIVER
		VI			1ECA24/MI; 2002 OLDS, LEFT FRONT HL
	1:18 AM	VW	8212		BRANDON EVERETT SCHUCKARDT
1:30 AM	1:35 AM	CI		LUCE ST	BAC0425/MI 1996 TOYT 4D
1:36 AM	1:38 AM	CI		LUCE ST	CJJ484/MI 1989 FORD 2D
1:42 AM		BTOP	8061	HATHAWAY RD / HEDRICK	2002 BUIC TAN CEA/MI, JAMISON DANIEL
		PIV			JAMISON DANIEL
		VW	9061		CEA/MI 2002 BUIC TAN
	1:52 AM	VI			CEA/MI 2002 BUIC TAN
2:20 AM	2:23 AM	CI		US 31 / CITY	BAC0965/MI 2007 FORD
2:40 AM	3:00 AM	R		NEXT DOOR FOOD	COFFEE SNACK
3:20 AM	3:25 AM	CI		HOME DEPOT	BAJ5764/MI 1998 FORD 4D, STORE MANAGER RIDING AROUND STORE
3:30 AM	3:40 AM	PI		BAYVIEW	PROPERTY INSPECTION
3:55 AM	6:00 AM	SUPP	24001	POST	#078-00C2156-11
5:00 AM	6:00 AM	OA	50000	POST	REVIEW WARRANT LIST SUPPLEMENTAL INCIDENT
6:00 AM		OFF			OFF DUTY

This is from the officer that pulled us over and the event that
started this whole ordeal. Note Brandon is also noted as he pulled
over behind the Michigan State Police trooper.

MICHIGAN STATE POLICE
FIELD SERVICES BUREAU DAILY REPORT

COREY L	Tpr.	983		GAYLORD POST	Reg3	2000 - 0600	01/29/2012
GENERAL	2000 - 0600						
JOHN A	JR	Tpr.	918			Reg3	0030 - 0600
10.00		BRETT E					

HOURS WORKED	hr	ss.
Obligated		
Administrative		
Enforcement	1.30	
Incident	5.67	
Investigative	0.86	
Other	2.16	
TOTAL	0.00	10.00

PATROL/BULK/V MILES	BKTIME	MILES	ENGTIME	MILES
Freeway			1.00	30
Trunkline			1.25	32
County				
Traffic				
Other				
TOTAL	0.00	0	2.25	62

CRIM NATION/IDEN HOURS	HA CASE	DC-INV NUMBER	JA	BL
OPERATING UNDER THE INFLUENCE OF LIQUOR OR DRUGS	54002	073-0D90498-12		4.50
MOTOR VEHICLE THEFT	24001	078-0002158-11		1.17
OBSTRUCTING JUSTICE	50000			1.00

ADMIN. (ERATIVE		
Operational Support		
Court		
Desk		
Training		
Recruiting		
Sergeant Duties		
Public Relations		
Report Writing		
Subpoena Service		

SCHEDULED		
Contacts Per Hour		2.35
Original Traffic Stops		
Traffic Stops	0.30	3
Citations (Non-Driver)		
Verbal Warnings (Non-Driver)		
Car Assists		
Person(s) Investigated		1

INSPECTIONS		
Vehicles Inspected		2
Cars Investigated	0.27	4
Property Inspections	0.58	3
Liquor Inspections		
Background Investigation		
Address Check		

ENFORCEMENT		
Citations (Driver)		3
Verbal Warnings (Driver)		
Vehicles Towed		
Officer Assists	1.00	1
SOR - Address Check		

INCIDENTS		
AT POST		
DISPATCHED		
OTHER AGENCY		
PATROL		
Supplementals	5.67	2

FUGITIVE FELONY		
FUGITIVE MISDEMEANOR		
ORIGINAL FELONY		
ORIGINAL MISDEMEANOR		

Second page of the same ordeal. Interesting to note the 50000 code
and Obstructing Justice, though uncertain whether that has anything
to do with us.

The City of Petoskey police knew that we had left on our own accord. Not only were they aware that a family member had our cat, that our rent had been paid via money orders, but they also knew that we had taken several thousands of dollars in cash out of the bank. This information was not disclosed to the media, throughout the entire ordeal.

One of the Customs and Border Protection documents that we received. Note that they blacked out the Result (RSLT) line with a (b) (7) (E) Exemption. This was when we reentered the United States from Mexico, on our way back from Panama.

```
                           ------ QUERY  -----   LNE       TERM/
       NAME           DOB   DATE  TIME AGN RSLT  TYP  REF  LANE  API
MEDSKER, TIMOTHY JOSEPH  041578 050914 2136 CUS        PED       SH61  N
L25C-CBP-SAN YSIDRO, PED LAN DOC: 219              US P  INSP:
```

TECS RECORD ID   :

CARRIER CODE   :
FLT/VES NUMBER   :

Key:
*A - (b) (7) (E)
*B - (b) (6) , (b) (7) (C)
*C - (b) (7) (E)
*D - (b) (7) (E)
*E - (b) (6) , (b) (7) (C)

Another document from the Customs and Border Protection showing that there is a Result (RSLT) with my entering back into the United States from Mexico. We had entered on foot back into the United States to give them no heads up.

12:28   PQH API/HIT DATA   082615

```
                           ------ QUERY  -----   LNE       TERM/
       NAME           DOB   DATE  TIME AGN RSLT  TYP  REF  LANE  API
MEDSKER, TIMOTHY JOSEPH  041578 101413 0047 CUS        VEH       EI01  N
L337-CBP-ROOSVILLE, BORDER X DOC: 219            US P  INSP:
```

TECS RECORD ID   :

CARRIER CODE   :
FLT/VES NUMBER   :

Key:
*A - (b) (7) (E)
*B - (b) (6) , (b) (7) (C)
*C - (b) (7) (E)
*D - (b) (6) , (b) (7) (C)

Finally a document from the Customs and Border Protection showing one of our crossing into Canada from Montana. Note that there is no Result (RSLT).

Charter

Security Code: 7064

Statement of Service

July 27, 2010

TIM MEDSKER
PO BOX 1714
PETOSKEY MI 49770-1714

TIM MEDSKER
Account   8245 12 233 0039066
Phone Number (231) 348-7688
For Service at 138 E SHERIDAN ST APT 1
              PETOSKEY MI 49770-2952

Account Information

Thank you for choosing Charter. We appreciate your prompt payment and value you as a customer.

Contact Us   For Billing or Service inquiries
             visit us at www.charter.com or call
             1-888-GET-CHARTER (1-888-438-2427)

Charter News

Summary details on following pages
Service from 06/08/10 through 09/08/10

Previous Balance	39.99
Payments Received	-39.99
Remaining Balance	0.00
Charter Internet Services	39.99
Total Due by 08/17/10	**$39.99**

A copy of our Charter bill showing our real phone number.

93

A month later our Charter bill had another phone number listed, that was
not our own. We did not make this change and didn't realize that this had
happened until after the whole ordeal. We could figure out how they couldn't
find us with all of our other bills, but Charter was one that we originally
didn't have an answer to. This appeared to be the answer.

Central Intelligence Agency

Washington, D.C. 20505

18 February 2016

Mr. Timothy J. Medsker
704C E. 13th Street, Suite 221
Whitefish, MT 59937

Reference: P-2015-00743

Dear Mr. Medsker:

This is a final response to your 4 September 2015 administrative appeal under the
Privacy Act (PA) and Freedom of Information Act (FOIA), which was processed under the
referenced case identification number by the office of the Information and Privacy
Coordinator and our 26 December 2015 status request. As a reminder, you are appealing
our failure to locate records that would reveal an openly acknowledged Agency affiliation
with yourself and our determination that we are unable to confirm or deny the existence or
nonexistence of records that would reveal a classified connection between the CIA and
yourself.

*The Agency Release Panel (ARP) carefully considered your petition and
determined that your administrative appeal should be denied in full in accordance with
Agency regulations set forth in Parts 1900 and 1901 of Title 32 of the Code of Federal
Regulations.* In reaching this determination, the ARP concluded that with respect to
records that might reflect an open or otherwise acknowledged relationship between you
and the CIA, the Agency conducted a reasonable search calculated to uncover material
responsive to the request and was unable to locate any responsive records. With respect to
any records that may reveal a classified connection between yourself and the CIA, the ARP
determined that, in accordance with section 3.6(a) of Executive Order 13526, the CIA can
neither confirm nor deny the existence or nonexistence of records responsive to your
request. The fact of the existence or nonexistence of such records is itself currently and
properly classified and is intelligence sources and methods information protected from
disclosure by Section 6 of the CIA Act of 1949, as amended, and Section 102A(i)(l) of the
National Security Act of 1947, as amended. Therefore, your request is denied pursuant to
FOIA exemptions (b)(1) and (b)(3) and PA exemptions (j)(1) and(k)(1). As the panel's
Executive Secretary, I am the CIA official responsible for informing you of the appellate
determination.

Page 1 of a letter received from the CIA about an FOIA Appeal.

In accordance with the provisions of the FOIA, you have the right to seek judicial review of this determination in a United States district court. Alternatively, the Office of Government Information Services (OGIS) offers mediation services to resolve disputes between FOIA requesters and federal agencies. Using services offered by OGIS does not affect your right to pursue litigation. For more information, including how to contact OGIS, please consult its website, http://ogis/archives.gov.

Sincerely,

Michael Lavergne

Michael Lavergne
Executive Secretary
Agency Release Panel

Page 2 of a letter received from the CIA about an FOIA Appeal. I received a Glomar Response, as well as other Exemptions.

Petoskey Department of Public Safety
100 W. Lake St.
Petoskey, MI. 49770

Received 9.29.15 gc

Timothy Joseph Medsker
704C E. 13th St.; Suite 221
Whitefish, Montana 59937

Re: Freedom of Information Act Request

September 24th, 2015

Dear Petoskey Department of Public Safety,

This is a request under the Freedom of Information Act. I request that a search pertaining of the following documents be provided to me at the above listed address:

In my former request I asked for:

Police Activity Logs from February 16th - 18th, 2012. Police Vehicle Logs from February 16th-18th.

Upon further review, I have noted that the morning of February 16th logs are missing (generally seeming to be 6AM-6PM), as well as the evening of the 18th, generally seeming to be 6pm-6am. I am once again requesting these logs.

Please include logs from all of your vehicles that were active those following times. I am willing to pay up to $100 towards any expense regarding this request. If the dollar amount exceeds that amount, please notify me.

I declare under penalty of perjury under the laws of the United States of America that the foregoing is true and correct, and that I am the person named above, and I understand that any falsification of this statement is punishable under the provisions of 18 U.S.C. Section 1001 by a fine of not more than $10,000 or by imprisonment of not more than five years or both, and that requesting or obtaining any record(s) under false pretenses is punishable under the provisions of 5 U.S.C. 552a(i)(3) by a fine of not more than $5,000.

Signature: _Timothy J Medsker_   Date: _9/24/15_

A 2015 request to the Petoskey Department of Public Safety regarding receiving logs that would show that we had justification for having fled on the 16th of February, 2012, from our home.

City of Petoskey
Department of Public Safety
101 East Lake Street, Petoskey, Michigan 49770 • 231 347-2500 • Fax 231 347-2471

September 29, 2015

Timothy Joseph Medsker
704C E. 13ᵗʰ St.; Suite 221
Whitefish, Montana 59937

Dear Mr. Medsker,

This correspondence is in answer to your letter dated September 24ᵗʰ, 2015, regarding your previous FOIA request.

As far as the request for Police Activity Logs from February 16ᵗʰ-18ᵗʰ, 2012, I have provided you with all the existing documents. No other logs are in our records.

Please feel free to contact me if you have any questions or concerns regarding this.

Sincerely,

John Calabrese
Director of Public Safety

My response to my appeal request to Petoskey's Department of

Public Safety. We left the range for three days (16th - 18th) though it was the 16th that we were really after, as that was were the logs would show collusion with another Agency.

City of Petoskey
Department of Public Safety
101 East Lake Street, Petoskey, Michigan 49770 • 231-347-2500 • Fax 231-447-2751

September 27, 2016

Timothy Joseph Medsker
704C E. 13th St. Suite 721
Whitefish, MT 59937

Re: Freedom of Information Request

Dear Mr. Medsker,

We have received your Freedom of Information Act Appeal dated September 22, 2016. In your original request you were asking for all EMCD, Police Logs, and Police vehicle logs from 12:00am, February 16th 2012, thru February 18th, 2012 at 11:59pm. In your appeal you stated that we failed to fulfill your request, this statement is inaccurate. Attached please find all the information requested in your original request, this should be consistent with what you have in your possession from your original request. If there are no officer's daily logs then that log does not exist. We have had some issues over the years with the daily programs we use and have had issues with trying to save those dailies. EMCD is generated through dispatch and if it shows this department having no activity from midnight to 7am on a February night I would find that unusual but certainly understandable. We do not generate patrol vehicle logs.

Over the years you have filed multiple FOIA requests with this department in reference to the same incident. This incident is closed and as such we have provided you with all the information, logs and photographs you have requested. If there is something specific that you are looking for please let me know and I may be able to assist you. If there is nothing specific please refrain from filing FOIA requests for information we have already provided to you, this takes up valuable time of our office staff. If you would like to discuss this matter please call me.

Sincerely,

Matthew Breed, Director
Petoskey Department of Public Safety
101 E. Lake St.
Petoskey, MI 49770
(231) 347-2500

With a new Director of Petoskey's Department of Public Safety, I once again made another attempt to get those same records. Prior I had requested a large swath of time and had numerous records from the entire time we were "missing", but always had not received records from the 16th of February, 2012, as well as when search warrants were done, etc. Oddly the one date that I really needed, the 2/16/12, was the date that it appears there was a software problem and the records were not saved, according to the new Director. This was the date that I needed to provide absolute proof of our arguments.

96

REPORTING OFFICER NARRATIVE

Petoskey Public Safety

Victim	Offense	Date / Time Reported
MEDSKER, TIMOTHY JOSEPH	MISSING PERSONS	Thu 02/23/2012 11:03

OCA 2012-000826

EXECUTION OF SEARCH WARRANT: On March 5, 2012 myself, Lt. Weston, and Chief Calabrese made our way to ███ Jefferson Street. The key was used once again to enter the front door. During that time photographs were taken. An itemized inventory sheet of items collected from the home is attached to this report. In all there were 17 items of evidence seized from the home. That itemized list was left at the home and the return and tabulation was filed with the court. Some of the items taken from the home were ammunition, firearms, computers, hard drives, and paperwork. More detailed photographs were taken of the home, including some of the books and literature that the Medsker's had been reading, these will be attached to this report.

ASSISTING AGENCIES: It had been almost three weeks since the Medsker's had made any contact with any family members, and we still had not received any response. We began to make contact with other agencies to assist in getting the word out on the disappearance, specifically we made contact with MSP MIOC Intelligence Center. I made contact with DHS Child Protection. I made contact with Magloclen Intelligence Agency, which is part of the RISSNET. I made contact with the FBI out of Traverse City. I made contact with the Department of Homeland Security, Agent Brown. I made contact with the National Center for Missing and Exploited Children. I made contact with several national news media outlets. They picked up the story and began running segments on the news about the disappearance of the family.

Reporting Officer: SCHULTZ ███
Printed by: LT-02, PtPD01   07/18/2014 11:57

Page 6

Submitted as evidence of Petoskey's Department of Public Safety having worked with "the Department of Homeland Security, Agent Brown."

County of Emmet
Office of Civil Counsel
200 Division Street, Suite G70
Petoskey, Michigan 49770

September 11, 2015

Timothy Joseph Medsker
704C E. 13th St., Suite 221
Whitefish, Montana 59937

Re: Freedom of Information Act "Appeal" Received September 9, 2015

Dear Mr. Medsker:

You have requested a second search of records pertaining to yourself after Emmet County responded to your July 24, 2015 request indicating that the County had no records and advising that you may want to check with other local law enforcement agencies.

The County's August 3, 2015 response was accurate. Emmet County has no such records. Again, you may wish to submit your request to other area law enforcement agencies, including, but not limited to, the Petoskey Department of Public Safety and/or Michigan State Police.

In addition, the County has no records regarding a meeting at Petoskey's Big Boy on February 16, 2012 that may have been attended by the Emmet County Sheriff. If a record was made of the meeting, it was neither created by nor is maintained by Emmet County.

Please be advised that you can access Emmet County's FOIA Procedures and Guidelines and Emmet County's Public Summary of FOIA Procedures and Guidelines on Emmet County's website at www.emmetcounty.org.

If your request is denied, in whole or in part, under the Michigan Freedom of Information Act, you have the right to seek review of the decision by either (1) submitting to the Emmet County Board of Commissioners a written appeal that specifically states the word "appeal" and identifies the reason or reasons for reversal of the denial, or (2) seeking judicial review of the denial under section 10 of the Act. You may have the right to receive attorneys' fees and damages if, after judicial review, the court determines that the County has not complied with the Act and orders disclosure of all or a portion of a record

Sincerely,

Kathleen M. ███
Civil Counsel
231-348-███

pc   Sheriff Pete Wallin
      Priscilla

I had seen the Sheriff with my own eyes at the Big Boy meeting, as well as the Director or Chief of the Petoskey Department of Public Safety, with Michigan State Police and men with shirts and ties. This was on 2/16/2012, both agencies had no documentation regarding this meeting.

Pictures of our house while we were "missing". Top Left: Stairway leading to the upstairs, note the guns. Top Right: Our living room with bags of items packed up and ready to go. Bottom Left and Right: Still living room, with storable foods packed up and ready to be hauled out of the home.

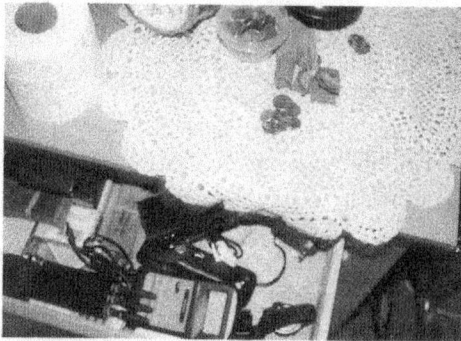

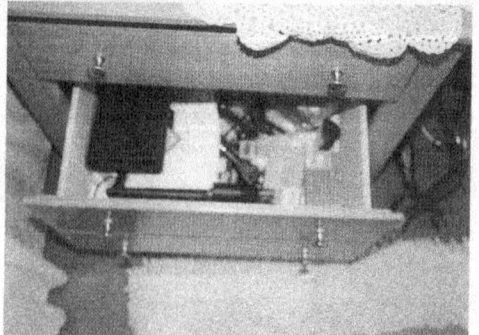

More picture from when we were "missing". Top Left and Right: Some gear that we had to use should a necessity ever arise, including: EMF detector, jammers for cell phones, cameras, bug detector. Bottom Left: The back of our Tribulation packet, with additional documentation added in the form of a supplemental letter. Bottom Right: Ammo, shooting targets and miscellaneous drawer from a nerd of chargers, cables, etc.

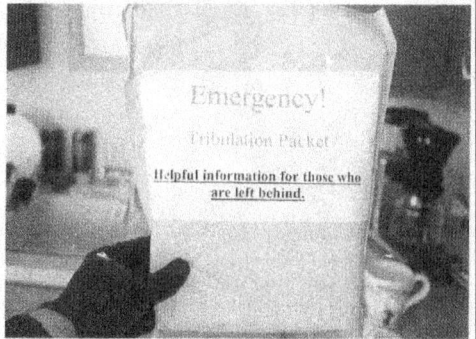

More pictures from when we were "missing". Top Left: Back of my old computer that was left in our room upstairs. Top Right: An officer holds up one of the two Tribulation packets that were in our home. They only found one. Bottom Left: A picture of a screen shot showing the date of 2/15/2012 on Yahoo!. Bottom Right: Our router that connected our home computers to our home network, as well as internet.

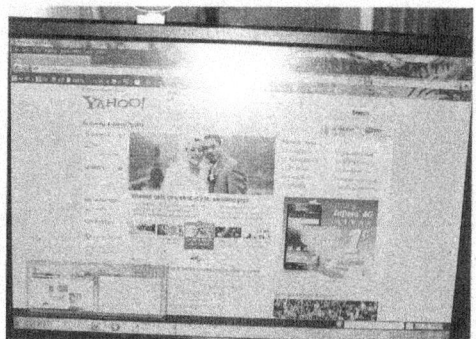

More pictures from when we were "missing". Top Left: Books on our main shelf. Top Right: Another screen shot of the other computer in our living room, with a date of 2/15/2012. Bottom Left: More books on our shelf. Bottom Right: On the table is a book for our weekly bible study held at our house, as well as Sabrina's life insurance policy and a letter to change the beneficiary. This should have set off alarm bells with Petoskey's "missing person" investigation, but it did not.

More pictures from when we were "missing". All Photos: Books on our main shelf.

More pictures from when we were "missing". All Photos: Apparently the Petoskey Department of Public Safety found great interest in our book collection. Note a large amount of these books are well known books on history, including world war and the Soviet Union.

More pictures from when we were "missing". All Photos: Note the dividers on the shelves that place the books into categories. We did have a lot of books that the government does not like. Under the Patriot Act federal investigators are allowed to see which books someone has checked out at their local library. What do you want to bet that these are the ones that would set off bells and whistles, adding the innocent reader who is looking for truth to a federal watchlist.

More pictures from when we were "missing". Top Left: Our monitor to our CCTV security camera system. Next to it are surveillance notes jotted down from happenings prior to us fleeing. Top Right and Bottom Right: More of our books that are displeasing the federal government. Bottom Left: Our DVR to our CCTV security camera system. This was a local system, not hooked up to the internet.

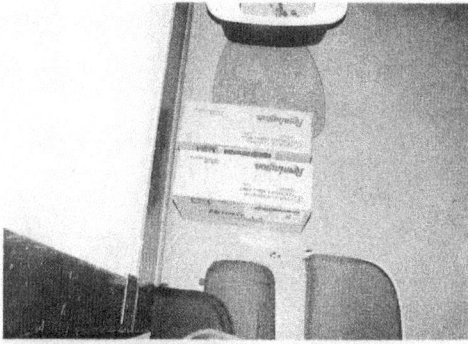

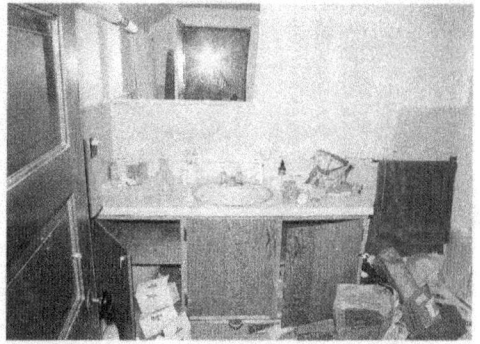

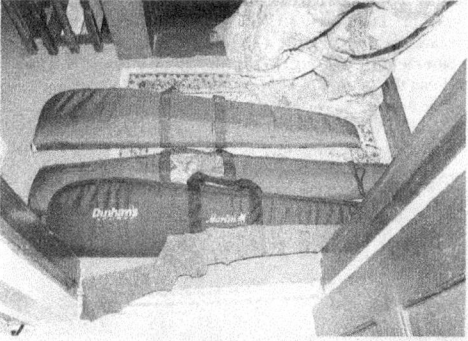

More pictures from when we were "missing". Top Left and Bottom Left: Guns and ammo found at the top of our staircase. They were supposed to have been taken out of the home, once we realized we had a problem. Top Right and Bottom Right: Our bathroom in disarray from having packed in hast. We had to flee out of the house, after sneaking in the early morning hours of 2/18/12. Our home was being surrounded by police and at least one undercover agent. We escaped our home at around 2:45 in the morning, over the backyard fence and into the snowstorm.

More pictures from when we were "missing". Top Left: A clear picture of our surveillance notes that Petoskey's Department of Public Safety took during the execution of a second search warrant. Top Right: A view into our office of Aardvark Janitorial LLC and The Weekly Scoop LLC, both of our service businesses. Bottom Left: A view of our living room, with our other bookshelves in the background, as well as our personal computer and CCTV security system. Bottom Right: Another picture of our office in disarray. Note the phone, that was the old phone that we had replaced after the static on the line, just weeks prior to the whole ordeal.

More pictures from when we were "missing". Left: Picture of our birds left in the hallway, they were supposed to be taken out of the home. Right: Our bedroom in disarray from packing in haste. The trash bags were over the window to keep the draft down as we had to point a camera directly out the window to prevent a glare and have one camera that could see into the overnight hours.

Endangered Missing

Joshua Medsker	Timothy Medsker	Sabrina Medsker

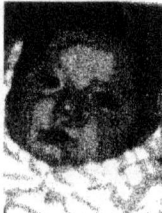

Birth: Race: White	Companion	Companion
Missing: 02/16/2012 Ht: 2'00" Wt: 13 lbs	Birth Race: White	Birth Race: White
Eyes: Brown Hair: Lt. Brown Sex: Male	Ht: 5'07" Wt: 200 lbs Sex: Male	Ht: 5'02" Wt: 130 lbs Sex: Female
Missing From: Petoskey , MI	Eyes: Hazel Hair: Brown	Eyes: Hazel Hair: Auburn
Age Now 0 Yrs United States		

Joshua was last seen on February 16, 2012. He may be in the company of his father, Timothy Medsker, and his mother, Sabrina Medsker. They may be traveling in a 2010 silver Ford pickup truck with Michigan license plates BXC0359.

ANYONE HAVING INFORMATION SHOULD CONTACT
The National Center for Missing and Exploited Children
1-800-843-5678 (1-800-THE-LOST) OR
Petoskey Police Department (Michigan) 1-231-

A poster faxed to a buddy's work place, just outside of the city of Chicago.

104

DENIAL OF RECORDS:
Denial is based on the following provision(s) of the Freedom of Information Act. MCL 15.243, Sec. 13(1). (All that apply will be checked.)

☒ (a)   Information of a personal nature where the public disclosure of the information would constitute a clearly unwarranted invasion of an individual's privacy. ☒ telephone number(s) ☒ address(es) ☒ date(s) of birth ☒ physical characteristics ☒ driver license number(s) ☒ other _account #, FBI #_

☐ (b)   Investigating records compiled for law enforcement purposes, but only to the extent that disclosure would do any of the following:
     ☐ (i)   Interfere with law enforcement proceedings.
     ☐ (ii)   Deprive a person of the right to a fair trial or impartial administrative adjudication
     ☐ (iii)   Constitute an unwarranted invasion of personal privacy.
     ☐ (iv)   Disclose the identity of a confidential source, or if the record is compiled by a law enforcement agency in the course of a criminal investigation, disclose confidential information furnished only by a confidential source.
     ☐ (vi)   Endanger the life or physical safety of law enforcement personnel.

☐ (d)   Records or information specifically described and exempted from disclosure by statute.
     Statute: _____

☐ (m)   Communications and notes within a public body or between public bodies of an advisory nature to the extent that they cover other than purely factual materials and are preliminary to a final agency determination of policy or action.

☐ (n)   Records of law enforcement communication codes, or plans for deployment of law enforcement personnel, that if disclosed would prejudice a public body's ability to protect the public.

☐ (s)   Unless the public interest in disclosure outweighs the public interest in nondisclosure in the particular instance, public records of a law enforcement agency, the release of which would do any of the following:
     ☐ (i)   Identify or provide a means of identifying an informer.
     ☐ (ii)   Identify or provide a means of identifying a law enforcement undercover officer or agent or a plain clothes officer as a law enforcement officer or agent.
     ☐ (viii)   Identify or provide a means of identifying a person as a law enforcement officer, agent, or informer.
     ☐ (ix)   Disclose personnel records of law enforcement agencies.

☐ (u)   Records of a public body's security measures, including security plans, security codes and combinations, passwords, passes, keys, and security procedures, to the extent that the records relate to the ongoing security of the public body.

☒ (w)   Information or records that would disclose the social security number of any individual.

☐   Your request is denied under the authority of Section 13(1)(a) above. However, if you provide a notarized, signed release of information from the individual to whom the records pertain, you will receive that information to which the individual signing the release is entitled.

☒   To the best of the Department's knowledge, information, and belief, under the information provided by you or by any other description reasonably known to the Department, the public records do not exist within the Department.

The missing person report was handled by Petoskey Dept. of Public Safety

☐   Based on the information you provided, we are unable to locate any records pertaining to the incident you described. In order for us to continue processing your request, please comply with the following items. To ensure proper handling of your request, please include a copy of this letter with your response.
     ☐   Specific location (i.e. city, county.)
     ☐   Michigan State Police incident number
     ☐   Names of those involved in the incident
     ☐   Specific dates (i.e., date of incident)
     ☐   Name of driver and their birth date or driver license number
     ☐   Date of birth

☐   The report you have requested has not yet been completed and filed. Please resubmit your request in 30 days.

Additional Comments: _This request is also responsive to CR-60530-13 that was mailed to MIOC_

This was the first FOIA ever sent to the Michigan State Police in late 2012. Note the following: one of our denials is an FBI #. Only this one time did they acknowledge that, subsequent requests never mentioned the FBI number again.

NOV 0 8 2013

MR TIMOTHY MEDSKER

RE: OR-79529-14,

Dear MR MEDSKER:

The department has received your request for certain records and has processed it under the provisions of the Michigan Freedom of Information Act (FOIA), MCL 15.231 et seq.

The records you have requested have been:

☐ Granted

☐ Granted in part and denied in part. Portions of your request are exempt from disclosure based on provisions set forth in the Act. (See comments on the back of this letter.) Under the FOIA Section 10 (a copy of which is enclosed), you have the right to appeal to the head of this public body or to a judicial review of this denial.

☑ Denied (See comments on the back of this letter.) Under the FOIA, Section 10 (a copy of which is enclosed), you have the right to appeal to the head of this public body or to a judicial review of the denial.

☐ The documents you requested are enclosed. Please pay the amount of $_____.

☐ Please pay the amount of $_____. Once we receive payment the documents will be mailed to you.

Checks or money orders should be made payable to the STATE OF MICHIGAN and mailed to P.O. Box 30266 Lansing, MI 48909. To ensure proper credit, please enclose a copy of this letter with your payment.

If you have questions concerning this matter, please feel free to contact our office at the address below, and enclose a copy of this correspondence.

Sincerely,

Bethany Godwin
Assistant FOIA Coordinator
Michigan State Police

Page 1 from a 2013 FOIA request to the Michigan State Police denying access to our records.

Page 2 from a 2013 FOIA request to the Michigan State Police that used 28 CFR Part 23 to deny us. This is a federal statue, not state of Michigan.

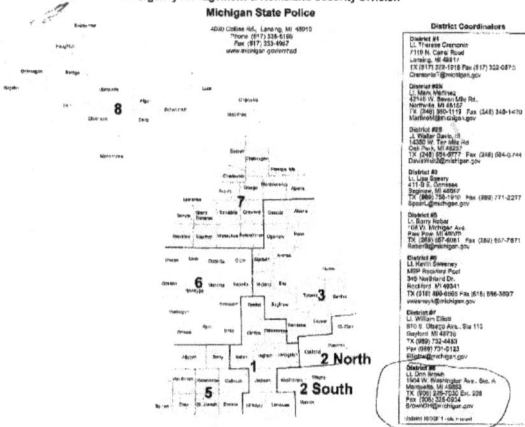

Michigan State Police

4000 Collins Rd., Lansing, MI 48910
Phone (517) 336-6198
Fax (517) 333-4987
www.michigan.gov/msp

District Coordinators

District #1
Lt. Therese Cremonini
7119 N. Canal Road
Lansing, MI 48917
TX (517) 322-1910 Fax (517) 322-0875
Cremonini@michigan.gov

District #2N
Lt. Mark Martinez
42146 W. Seven Mile Rd.
Northville MI 48167
TX (248) 380-1119 Fax (248) 348-1470
MartinezM@michigan.gov

District #2S
J. Walter Banks, III
14380 W. Ten Mile Rd
Oak Park, MI 48237
TX (248) 691-6777 Fax (248) 584-0744
DavidWall@michigan.gov

District #3
Lt. Lisa Sperry
411-B S. Grinnell
Saginaw, MI 48607
TX (989) 758-1910 Fax (989) 771-2277
SperryL@michigan.gov

District #5
Lt. Barry Rebel
120 W. Michigan Ave
Paw Paw MI 49079
TX (269) 657-6081 Fax (269) 657-7871
RebelB@michigan.gov

District #6
Lt. Harold Sweeney
MSP Rockford Post
349 Northland Dr.
Rockford MI 49341
TX (616) 890-6565 Fax (616) 866-3897
sweeneyh@michigan.gov

District #7
Lt. William Elliott
810 S. Otsego Ave., Ste 112
Gaylord MI 49735
TX (989) 732-4483
Fax (989) 731-0193
ElliottW@michigan.gov

District #8
Lt. Don Brown
1504 W. Washington Ave., Ste. A
Marquette, MI 49855
TX (906) 228-7230 Ext. 226
Fax (906) 226-6954
BrownDH@michigan.gov

A map of the Michigan State Police's Emergency Management and Homeland Security
Division. We had a listed address in the Upper Peninsula in Michigan. Lt. Brown (Agent
Brown?) was in charge of that region.

```
--- Original Message ---
Date: 5/6/2014
From: ███████████████████@parksidefcu.com>
Subject: RE: Re: Medsker Banking


Tim,
This has the most difficult wire I have ever worked with - I
would go to
your Bank in the Panama and start there, take your emails and
determine
with them what is happening - NO where on your wire instructions
was
there a "Payment Order" so we did not put that on the wire out to
B of
A -now they need one? You will need to go back to the banker that
gave
you the wire instructions and get the Payment Order number and I
will
forward that on to the Bank of America wire department - please
provide
a payment order for all the wires in question - I at this point
do not
even know which wires you have not received - we sent one for
$17000.00,
one for $8500.00 and one for $8500.00 do all three need a payment
order?
Please provide this new information (only the bank in the Panama
can
provide this) and I will work on getting the funds released at
Bank of
America
███████
Back Office Coordinator
Ph: 406.███████
Fax: 406.862.4891

We like to say YES.

ATTENTION: This e-mail is intended for the use of the party to
whom it is
addressed. It may contain confidential information. If you are
not the
intended recipient or an agent of the recipient, any use of this
e-mail
is prohibited. If you have received this in error, please notify
this
office immediately at 406-862-2652.
```

A copy of an email received regarding the wired money not being received. Note that
the veteran banker says "this has to be the most difficult wire I have ever
worked with".

```
--- Original Message ---
Date: 5/23/2014
From:                        @parksidefcu.com>
Subject: RE: Wires
```

Never even got notice of any activity from them - all that I
found out
about their inquiry into the missing wires was from you - thank
you for
being persistent and patient.

███████

Back Office Coordinator
Ph: 406.862.████
Fax: 406.862.4891

We like to say YES.

ATTENTION: This e-mail is intended for the use of the party to
whom it is
addressed. It may contain confidential information. If you are
not the
intended recipient or an agent of the recipient, any use of this
e-mail
is prohibited. If you have received this in error, please notify
this
office immediately at 406-862-2652.

```
-----Original Message-----
From: 70tsjme@pt-net.net [mailto:70tsjme@pt-net.net]
Sent: Friday, May 23, 2014 3:09 AM
To: ███████
Subject: Wires
```

███████

I see the wire is now back in the account. Finally, this ordeal
is
settled! Did BOA ever give a reason for their actions?

Regards,

Tim

**Another email regarding the money wire. Apparently Bank of America never once
responded to their inquiries regarding the wires.**

City of Petoskey
Department of Public Safety
101 East Lake Street, Petoskey, Michigan 49770 • 231 347-2500 • Fax 231 347-2471

March 7, 2012

Peter O'Rourke,

The Petoskey Department of Public Safety has no pending criminal investigation related
to Timothy Medsker or Sabrina Medsker. We have submitted no warrant request(s) to
the Emmet County Prosecutor's Office. To my knowledge there are no wants or
warrants for Timothy or Sabrina Medsker.

John Calabrese
Director of Public Safety
City of Petoskey

**A copy of the letter from Petoskey's Department of Public Safety regarding no warrants for
myself. Please note that the language "to my knowledge" is used by then director John
Calabrese. The Michigan State Police refused to give my attorney a similar letter.**

SEARCH WARRANT RETURN AND TABULATION

PETOSKEY PUBLIC SAFETY

INCIDENT NUMBER: _826-12_ PAGE _2_ OF ___.

OFFICER: _3436_ DATE: _3-5-12_
OFFICER: _3415_ DATE: _____

Item #16

Location of Item Found: _Upstairs Bedroom_
Found By: _____ Seized By: _3415_
Description of Item: _Dell Tower Computer_
_S/N 6143591_

#17

Location of Item Found: _____
Found By: _____ Seized By: _____
Description of Item: _____
Notes of surveillance.

Location of Item Found: _____
Found By: _____ Seized By: _____
Description of Item: _____

Location of Item Found: _____
Found By: _____ Seized By: _____
Description of Item: _____

Location of Item Found: _____
Found By: _____ Seized By: _____
Description of Item: _____

One of the itemizing sheets from items taken from our home during the execution of a search warrant on 3/5/2012. They seized our surveillance notes, yet never once had any concern for our wellbeing. This after my sister had reported to the detective on numerous occasions that she had received a weird phone call asking for me. Why didn't they search out the source of that call, instead simply disregarding it? Our response: because they knew who it was.

5.104.178.134

April 11th, 2015 Right as we entered Kalispell.

ofmissingpersons.com/f█████y█

An oddity that happened. We had went and visited family in Michigan for the first and only time since we went "missing".
We were cautious about not leaving any trails that we were heading there or back. Finally upon arriving back in Kalispell,
out of spite, I used my credit card to buy some coffee and headed home. At that moment someone visited the website using
that web address. The IP number goes to Burgas, Bulgaria, a place where the CIA is known to house a rendition center.

OGIS
OFFICE of GOVERNMENT INFORMATION SERVICES

January 19, 2016 - Sent via U.S. Mail

Mr. Timothy Joseph Medsker
704C E. 13th St.
Suite 221
Whitefish, MT 59937

NATIONAL
ARCHIVES
and RECORDS
ADMINISTRATION

In Re: Case No.: 201600048
NG: HK

Dear Mr. Medsker:

8601 ADELPHI ROAD
OGIS
COLLEGE PARK, MD
20740-6001

web www.ogis.archives.gov
e-mail ogis@nara.gov
phone 202-741-5770
toll-free 1-877-684-6448
fax 202-741-5769

This responds to your October 7, 2015, submission to the Office of Government
Information Services (OGIS). Your request for assistance pertains to your records
request (FBI FOIA tracking number 1333485-000) to the Federal Bureau of
Investigation (FBI).

As you are aware, Congress created OGIS to complement existing Freedom of
Information Act (FOIA) practice and procedure; we strive to work in conjunction
with the existing request and appeal process. The goal is for OGIS to allow,
whenever practical, the requester to exhaust his or her remedies within the agency,
including the appeal process. OGIS has no investigatory or enforcement power, nor
can we compel an agency to release documents. OGIS serves as the Federal FOIA
Ombudsman and our jurisdiction is limited to assisting with the FOIA process.

You submitted a request for copies of any files about you or records mentioning
your name. In your request to the FBI, you specifically ask that the agency conduct
a search of several specific databases in addition to a "cross-reference" search of
your name.

From the background information you submitted, it appears FBI's response to your
request informed you that the agency conducted a search of its Central Records
System and was unable to identify main file records responsive to your request. You
subsequently appealed the FBI's decision to the Office of Information Policy (OIP).
OIP upheld the FBI's decision on its search and stated that you may provide
additional information for a cross-reference search. In your submission to OGIS, you
ask for an explanation of the FBI's response and request assistance with asking the
FBI to search for responses and cross-references in several specific databases.

NATIONAL
ARCHIVES

In response to your submission, we contacted the FBI to discuss your request and
concern about the agency's search. FBI's FOIA Public Liaison, Mr. Dennis Argall,
explained that in response to your request for "cross-reference" search, FBI
conducted a subsequent "cross-reference" search and located 8 pages which were
reviewed under FOIA and released to you on December 11, 2015.

**Page 1 of an OGIS request to get assistance regarding the DOJ's FBI
FOIA process.**

In your submission to OGIS, you explain that you dispute the FBI's and OIP's responses to your request and appeal. Specifically, you assert that you directed the FBI to search its National Name Check Program (NNCP) and its Record/Information Dissemination Section (RIDS), which is the FBI's Freedom of Information Act Unit. The OGIS facilitator working on your case asked Mr. Argall for an explanation of its response concerning FBI's search of the National Name Check Program. Mr. Argall declined to provide a response, other than stating that all of the records responsive to your FOIA request(s) have been provided to you.

With regard to the RIDS database, Mr. Argall explained that their FOIA database is used for logging FOIA and Privacy Act requests. While the agency did not see any reason to do a search of its FOIA/PA database, in response to our inquiry, Mr. Argall conducted a search of its FOIA/PA database and found there were other FOIA requests logged in your name, all of which had been responded to previously.

Finally, with regard to the FBI's action to neither confirm nor deny the existence of records that would reveal your name on any watch list under FOIA Exemption 7(E), 5 U.S.C. § 552(b)(7)(E), this exemption authorizes an agency to withhold information compiled for law enforcement purposes that "would disclose techniques and procedures for law enforcement investigations or prosecutions, or would disclose guidelines for law enforcement investigations or prosecutions if such disclosure could reasonably be expected to risk circumvention of the law." In the case of watch lists, confirmation that an individual is or is not included on such a list may reveal information that could assist a terrorist organization in circumventing the law by determining which of its members are likely to be questioned or detained. Federal courts have consistently held that records pertaining to terrorism watch lists are appropriately withheld under Exemption 7(E). The FBI routinely informs *all* FOIA requesters that it can neither confirm nor deny that their names are on a watch list. As OIP informed you in its September 25, 2015 response to your appeal, the FBI's response is standard and you should not take it as an indication that watch list records pertaining to you do or do not exist.

In our role as FOIA ombudsman, we observe FOIA best practices and offer feedback to requesters and agencies. If you make a future request for records about yourself, you may wish to provide information as to why you believe that the agency may have records about you; this information can help an agency determine the correct program office to search. It is also helpful to include a daytime telephone number or an email address so that the agency can more easily contact you to discuss your request.

I hope you find this information useful in understanding why the FBI responded to your request as it did. At this time, there is no further assistance OGIS can offer and we will close your case. Thank you for bringing this matter to OGIS.

Sincerely,

for JAMES V.M.L. HOLZER
Director

cc: Dennis Argall, FOIA Public Liaison, Federal Bureau of Investigation

Page 2 of an OGIS request to get assistance regarding the DOJ's FBI FOIA process. OGIS had tried to figure out why the FBI would not run my name through the NNCP. The FBI declined to give a reason. This is currently being looked into by both Senator Daines and U.S. Representative Zinke, both of Montana.

Tim and Sabrina Medsker

704C E. 13th Street

Suite 221

Whitefish, Mt 59937

November 7, 2014

Dear Tim and Sabrina

Yesterday, I received, and was nicely surprised to find in a US Postal package, your book "OF MISSING PERSONS". In that the experiences surrounding the times when the "Missing Persons" events in which I was involved were so news-worthy and remain vivid in my mind, I opened the book and found the reading to be both interesting and captivating.

The dedication pages, which included me as one who was acknowledged, was sincerely appreciated.

It is an honor, indeed!

I look forward to continuing to read the book. You are to be commended for sharing your story with the world. Keep up a positive approach to life. Enjoy each sunrise and sunset, and your time together.

Yours Truly,

Peter O'Rourke

A letter from our attorney after having received a copy of our book.

-----Original Message-----
From: DOCUSEARCH.COM SUPPORT <███████████@docusearch.com>
To: tjmed20 <tjmed20@aol.com>
Sent: Wed, Nov 28, 2012 10:04 am
Subject: Re: Support Request

Tim,

Thank you for your support questions. Let's start with your previous searches. You stated that this was the third time you have searched this number. Please advise who the previous searches were conducted by. This may help us answer many of your questions.

Best regards,

Your Docusearch.com Client Support Team

DOCUSEARCH.COM
EMAIL US
OR CALL US AT (800) 474-5350

We hate spam as much as you do!
Your email address will not be shared with anyone else, for any reason

On Tue, Nov 27, 2012 at 4:37 PM, <tjmed20@aol.com> wrote:
Support Request
████████████locusearch.com
Tim Medsker
tjmed20@aol.com
231-555-5555
12110505
This is the third time I have had this number searched. It involves fact-finding for a civil litigation case. You are the only one who has tracked it to magicJack.

I am wondering how you came to that conclusion?

Page 1 from an email to another private investigator looking into that phone call that started the whole ordeal.

From: DOCUSEARCH.COM SUPPORT ████████████@Docusearch.com>
To: TJ Med <tjmed20@aol.com>
Subject: Re: Support Request
Date: Wed, Nov 28, 2012 12:26 pm

We've listened to the recording and it appears to be a trap line, often used in collections and skip tracing. Regarding your previous searches, we cannot be sure what method was used to determine subscriber information. You first have to understand that numbers can be ported (and re-ported) to any carrier and any time. We have access to the database (updated hourly) which informs us the most recent carrier ported to any given number. Once determined, we reach out to resources we have within the carrier to secure the recorded billing name and address.

Unfortunately, with VOIP numbers, no verification of identity is required to subscribe, therefore, as long as the invoice is paid, no attention is paid to the real identity of the subscriber. I hope this helps in some way.

Best regards,

Your Docusearch.com Client Support Team

DOCUSEARCH.COM
EMAIL US
OR CALL US AT (800) 474-5350

We hate spam as much as you do!
Your email address will not be shared with anyone else, for any reason

On Wed, Nov 28, 2012 at 12:52 PM, TJ Med <tjmed20@aol.com> wrote:
Docusearch.com,

One search was done using a database format via the internet. The other was done with a private investigator in Michigan. The private investigator was able to rule out that ████████████ lived in the area. In fact the family had lived in the area years past, but now lives in Illinois. So there really is no question that ████████████ s bogus. The phone number used to say 'this investigative agency does not accept voicemail' then switched to 'this department of investigation does not accept voicemail'. After having filed several FOIA recently, it just rings busy.

As an example...865-512-██████...will say the same thing (no one will answer), except it is a man's voice, verses a woman. There are actually 5 other phone number like the one you searched that are now ringing busy and had all said the exact same thing.

Tim

112

Page 2 of the same email regarding a private investigator looking into that phone number. Note that there conclusion is that it appears to be a 'trap line'. This was the first time I had ever heard that term, of which I am now very aware.

FedPayments Manager℠ -- Funds

Environment:	Prod	ABA:	████████
Mode:	Prod	Service Unit:	29297800
Cycle Date:	04/16/2014	System Date/Time:	04/16/2014 14:57:06

Status:	Completed	Message Type:	Standard
Create Time:	04/16/2014 14:56:31	Test/Prod:	Prod
IMAD:	20140416 QMSFT004 001710 04161454		
OMAD:	20140416 B6B7EO2B 000066 04161454		

BASIC INFORMATION
Sender ABA {3100}:   ████████ PARK SIDE CU
Receiver ABA {3400}:   026009593 Bank of America
Amount {2000}:   8,500.00
Type Code {1510}:   1000 - Transfer of Funds
Business Function {3600}:   CTR - Customer Transfer
ORIGINATOR INFORMATION
Originator {5000}
  ID Code: D - DDA Account Number
  Identifier: ████████
  Name: Sabrina Medaker
  Address: 6477 Highway 93 S 221
                                        Whitefish MT 59937
Originator to Beneficiary Information {6000}
  Text: final credit: ████████
                                        Sabrina Lynn Medaker
BENEFICIARY INFORMATION
Beneficiary {4200}
  ID Code: D - DDA Account Number
  Identifier: ████████
  Name:
  Address: SWIFT: ████████

04/16/2014 14:57:06   Page 1 of 1

One of three wires being sent to Panama. Note that the status is: Completed. We should have soon thereafter received the wire.

FedPayments Manager℠ -- Funds

Environment:	Prod	ABA:	████████
Mode:	Prod	Service Unit:	29297800
Cycle Date:	04/16/2014	System Date/Time:	04/16/2014 14:57:25

Status:	Completed	Message Type:	Standard
Create Time:	04/16/2014 14:54:35	Test/Prod:	Prod
IMAD:	20140416 QMSFT004 001674 04161454		
OMAD:	20140416 B6B7EO2B 008000 04161454		

BASIC INFORMATION
Sender ABA {3100}:   ████████ PARK SIDE CU
Receiver ABA {3400}:   026009593 Bank of America
Amount {2000}:   8,500.00
Type Code {1510}:   1000 - Transfer of Funds
Business Function {3600}:   CTR - Customer Transfer
ORIGINATOR INFORMATION
Originator {5000}
  ID Code: D - DDA Account Number
  Identifier: ████████
  Name: Timothy Medaker
  Address: 6477 Highway 93 S 221
                                        Whitefish MT 59937
Originator to Beneficiary Information {6000}
  Text: final credit: ████████
                                        Timothy J Medaker
BENEFICIARY INFORMATION
Beneficiary {4200}
  ID Code: D - DDA Account Number
  Identifier: ████████
  Name:
  Address: SWIFT: ████████

04/16/2014 14:57:25   Page 1 of 1

The second wire out of three, going to Panama. Note that it is also: Completed.
Panama is NOT behind in banking. In many ways the banking in Panama is
more secure and effective than the United States. Panama is known to be the "Swiss"

of Central and South America.

```
FedPayments Manager℠ -- Funds
Environment:   Prod                          ABA:             ████████
Mode:          Prod                          Service Unit:    25357800
Cycle Date:    04/16/2014                    System Date/Time: 04/16/2014 13:31:29

─────────────────────────────────────────────────────────────────────────────
Status:        Completed                     Message Type:    Standard
Create Time:   04/16/2014 13:31:15           Test/Prod:       Prod
IMAD:          20140416 QMGFT004 001213 04161331
OMAD:          20140416 B6B7MU3R 006393 04161331

BASIC INFORMATION
Sender ABA {3100}:                     ████████ PARK SIDE CU
Receiver ABA {3400}:                   026009593 BANK OF AMERICA NA
Amount {2000}:                         17,000.00
Type Code {1510}:                      1000 - Transfer of Funds
Business Function {3600}:              CTR - Customer Transfer
ORIGINATOR INFORMATION
Originator {5000}
   ID Code:                            D - DDA Account Number
   Identifier:                         ████████
   Name:                               TIMOTHY MUDSKER
   Address:                            6477 HWY 93 SOUTH SUITE 221
                                       WHITEFISH, MT 59937
Originator to Beneficiary Information {6000}
   Text:                               FOR FURTHER CREDIT TO:
                                       ACCT ████████
                                       TIMOTHY JOSEPH MUDSKER
BENEFICIARY INFORMATION
Beneficiary {4200}
   ID Code:                            B - SWIFT Bank Identifier Code
   Identifier:                         ████████
   Name:                               ████████
```

04/16/2014 13:31:29   Page 1 of 1

The third and final of three wires being sent to Panama, also marked as completed. When we wired the money back, of which this one eventually did land in Panama, it took a few hours for the money to show up from Panama to our bank account in Montana.

Monday, March 5, 2012 4:04 PM

apparently you're "missing"

From: "A Voice in the Wilderness" ▇▇▇@a-voice.org>

To: "Tim Medsker" <tjmedsker@yahoo.com>

Tim...

Don't know if you've gone "camping", but apparently your family filed a "missing" persons report with the police. And since your home had "materials" from vw, the Petosky PD detective e-mailed me. Anyway, they asked, if I had a way of contacting you (they though of chat room/message board) to put the word out, that your family is worried about you....to call and let them know you're OK. I'll paste below the correspondence with the detective. And the one about the "rapture" was an added note from him.

PB

~~~~~~~~~~~~~~~~~paste~~~~~~~~~~~~~~~~~~

Tim and Sabina medsker appear to have been planning for the rapture and left suddenly for know apparent reason. Family and close friends are worried and filed a missing person report with Petoskey pd. This can be verified by reviewing the Petoskey news review and read the article written by the paper and the local cbs and nbc affiliates in northern Michigan.

Just wondering if you operate a chat room or message board to put a message out to tim and Sabrina to contact their family and let them know if they are ok. So this investigation can be closed and I can move on.

-----Original Message-----
From: A Voice in the Wilderness [mailto:▇▇▇@a-voice.org]
Sent: Monday, March 05, 2012 3:01 PM
To: ▇▇▇ Schultz
Subject: RE: tim and sabrina medsker

Go ahead and ask your questions.

At 3/5/2012   07:48 PM, you wrote:
>Detective ▇▇▇ Schultz

An email that a friend received while we were "missing". Detective Shultz had seen that we had material from A Voice in the Wilderness (a-voice.org) and decided to email the contact to try and find us. We had already been accused of being religious extremist, but now we "appear to have been planning for the rapture"! The only plan needed for the Rapture is Salvation through Jesus Christ our Lord and Savior.

STATE OF MICHIGAN JUDICIAL DISTRICT	SEARCH WARRANT	CASE NO.

TO THE SHERIFF OR ANY PEACE OFFICER: Police Agency
Report Number: _Petoskey DPS / 826-2012_

_____ Detective David Schultz _____ , has sworn to the attached affidavit regarding the following:
1. The person, place, or thing to be searched is described as and is located at:

1014 Jefferson Street, Petoskey, Michigan and more particularly described as being a white two-story, stick-built residential structure with a white detatched single vehicle garage located to the rear of the residential. The residence has a covered front porch which faces Jefferson Street. The structure is located on the west side of Jefferson Street and is the third house south of the Pearl Street intersection. The number ▮▮▮▮ mounted or attached to the facia board of the covered porch.

2. The PROPERTY to be searched for and seized, if found, is specifically described as:

Tim Medsker (DOB: ▮▮▮▮), Sabrina Medsker (DOB: unknown), and/or Joshua Medsker (DOB: ▮▮▮▮ or evidence of the whereabouts/location.

IN THE NAME OF THE PEOPLE OF THE STATE OF MICHIGAN: I have found that probable cause exists and you are commanded to make the search and seize the described property. Leave a copy of this warrant with affidavit attached and a tabulation (a written inventory) of all property taken with the person from whom the property was taken or at the premises. You are further commanded to promptly return this warrant and tabulation to the court.

Issued: ___2/23/12___
       Date

_____ Judge/Magistrate _____ Bar no.

RETURN AND TABULATION

Search was made: ___2-23-12___ and the following property was seized:
                  Date

1. Family photo

_____
Officer

Copy of affidavit, warrant, and tabulation served on: ___left at scene___
                                                       Name

Tabulation filed: _____
                  Date

A copy of the first search warrant. This search warrant was obtained within hours of my sister filing a missing persons report and after she was told the only thing that Detective Shultz could do was email, call and knock on our door. There was an unmarked white van outside our home during this execution of the search warrant, with a plain clothes man standing guard on the corner of our property. Who joined the Petoskey Department of Public Safety? It is unprecedented to receive a warrant that quickly, unless there is visual reason to suspect a crime has occurred. A civil lawsuit could have been filed against this search warrant on a basis of a violation of our civil rights.

STATE OF MICHIGAN JUDICIAL DISTRICT	SEARCH WARRANT	CASE NO.

TO THE SHERIFF OR ANY PEACE OFFICER:

Police Agency
Report Number: Petoskey DPS / 826-2012

_____ Detective David Schultz , has sworn to the attached affidavit regarding the following:

1. The person, place, or thing to be searched is described as and is located at:

▮▮▮Jefferson Street, Petoskey, Michigan and more particularly described as being a white two-story, stick-built residential structure with a white detatched single vehicle garage located to the rear of the residential. The residence has a covered front porch which faces Jefferson Street. The structure is located on the west side of Jefferson Street and is the third house south of the Pearl Street intersection. The number ▮▮▮ mounted or attached to the facia board of the covered porch; any outbuildings at said address and any motor vehicles found on the curtilege.

2. The PROPERTY to be searched for and seized, if found, is specifically described as:

Tim Medsker (DOB: ▮▮▮), Sabrina Medsker (DOB: unknown), and/or Joshua Medsker (DOB: ▮▮▮) or any evidence of the whereabouts/location of any of the identified persons; any computers, CPUs, internal and external hard drives, digital memory storage devices located in any digitial camera(s) at said address, digital memory devices (including but not limited to flash drives, floppy discs and compact discs) and the examination and contents of all digital memory devices and "hard drives" located at the above location; and all firearms and ammunition located in the above area(s) to be searched.

IN THE NAME OF THE PEOPLE OF THE STATE OF MICHIGAN: I have found that probable cause exists and you are commanded to make the search and seize the described property. Leave a copy of this warrant with affidavit attached and a tabulation (a written inventory) of all property taken with the person from whom the property was taken or at the premises. You are further commanded to promply return this warrant and tabulation to the court.

Issued: _3-5-12_
    Date

                                  Judge/Magistrate   _P25-46_
                                                                            Bar no.

RETURN AND TABULATION

Search was made: _3-5-12_ and the followingproperty was seized:
                   Date

        SEE Tab / Return

Schultz
Officer

Copy of affidavit, warrant, and tabulation served on: _left on Table_
                                           Name

Tabulation filed: _____
        Date

A copy of the second search warrant executed at our home on 3/5/12.

Sent: Monday, May 05, 2014 11:39 AM
To: ██████████parksidefcu.com
Subject: Fwd: Re: Medsker Banking

██████ ,

Explain to me what: PAYCB140502-0003 is (see bleow). Also, what exactly
is the delay in having given the 'Payment Order', please get that out
of BOA.

Here is an email that I received:

--- Original Message ---
Date: 5/5/2014
From: "Edouard ██████" <edouard.██████████.com>
Subject: Re: Medsker Banking

Good afternoon Mr. Medsker,

I will now explian what the transfers department just told us about the
report that we made.

001-00-1358811 The report for the transfer of $8500.00 About this
report, they said that we received the instructions for this transfer,
we call this as an "instructions order" but in order that we can
deposit this transfer into your account, the bank sender needs to send
another order called "Payment Order", but this order was never
received and the transfer probably is going to be cancelled because of
the guarantee period.

001-00-1358819 The report for the transfer of $17000.00 In this
transfer, happens almost the same, we received the instructions order
but the payment order was not received until 05/02/2014, so this
$17,000.00 is going to be deposited on 05/06/2014.

They said also that the bank that sends the transfer has an investigation
about the transfer of $8500.00 requesting this information on the report
001-00-1358811 and the reference number for this investigation is
PAYCB140502-0003, with this you can ask your bank for more
information.

**A final note about our wires. According to our bank in Panama there was an investigation
into the money transfer of $8,500.**

A final picture. Brandon ended up fleeing out to Montana from Michigan, around six months after we left. This picture he dubs, 'The Picture from Hell' was perhaps the same car that had been following him around and harassing him late and night. This car was spotted at the Manistique, Michigan State Police post, where Brandon also had an address listed on his driver's license. As he was leaving to Montana he was eating across the street and noticed this car, taking the picture before he left.

On the Run!

What happened next is told how it happened. This is the truth and we stand by it, regardless of what others think. I had prayed to God for help should a situation ever arise, to know when the proper time to head off, to go on some long term camping trip would be. Never had we imagined such a scenario, an America that was battered, failing, but still clinging on; one where our time had run out. Someone or something set these people after us, we were now targets, enemies of the state.

We sat looking at the camera screen with the image of the gold Volvo frozen on there. This was serious, we were tired, but could we even stay in our home? We didn't know what to do, so I left Sabrina and Joshua downstairs and went upstairs to our room. Here I asked the Most High what we should do, not really thinking I was going to get a response, but I was hoping for one. This was too much for us, we needed an answer, we either had to run or not.

I opened up my bible, to around the middle and began to read Psalms chapter 89-91. When I read chapter 91, the Spirit spoke to my heart.

"He who dwells in the secret place of the Most High shall abide under the shadow of the Almighty. I will say of Jehovah, He is my refuge and my fortress; my God, in Him will I trust. Surely He shall deliver you from the snare of the fowler and from the destructive pestilence. He shall cover you with His feathers, and under His wings you shall take refuge; His truth shall be your shield and buckler. You shall not be afraid of the terror by night, nor of the arrow that flies by day, nor of the pestilence that walks in darkness, nor of the destruction that lays waste at noonday. A thousand may fall at your side, and ten thousand at your right hand; but it shall not come near you. Only with your eyes shall you look, and see the retribution of the wicked. Because you have made Jehovah, who is my refuge, even the Most High, your dwelling place, no evil shall befall you, nor shall any plague come near your dwelling; for He shall give His angels charge over you, to keep you in all your ways. In their hands they shall bear you up, lest you dash your foot against a stone. You shall tread upon the lion and the viper, the young lion and the dragon you shall trample underfoot. Because he has set his love upon Me, therefore I will deliver him; I will set him on high, because he has known My name. He shall call upon Me, and I will answer him; I will be with him in trouble; I will deliver him and honor him. With long life I will satisfy him, and show him My salvation."
Psalms 91

I immediately prayed and what happened next took me by surprise. There wasn't a voice that I physically heard, but it was as if I was spoken to, suddenly this very distinct 'Run!, Go!, Run!' was heard. There really is no way to properly explain how this happened, but in faith I immediately obeyed. God knew we were innocent.

Going downstairs I told Sabrina we had to leave, we had to go. I explained to her what had happened and told her that we must leave within 5 minutes, we will decide after what to do and where to go. She went and gathered stuff for baby Joshua, I went and set off part of my emergency plan.

We had two lock boxes well hidden in the house. I grabbed both of those and dragged them into the kitchen, here I opened them up dropping the contents on the floor. Silver and gold coins hit the floor and our home bank cash reserve was put into a smaller, hardened box along with the coins. When my father had passed away he left me just over $5,000, not needing the money, I immediately put it into bullion. We grabbed all of the cash, dumped out the bin that the backpack vacuum was stored in, which was a large Rubbermaid container with wheels, grabbed our handgun and threw everything we were taking with us into that container. The front door went open and we walked several blocks to a little neighborhood that was on some dead end street up the road. Here Sabrina and Joshua waited as I grabbed the truck.

With it being cold outside, I hustled. The truck was several blocks away, but I made it there in a few minutes. Cruising to pick up my family, we loaded the truck with the few possessions we had managed to grab and headed north for several blocks, exiting town the quickest way, into the country of Petoskey. We were now on the run, though we hadn't yet planned on leaving the area.

Brandon was long asleep when I tried calling so we went to Harbor Springs, to the local branch of our bank that was located there. Inside I withdrew several more thousand of dollars worth of cash. There we did spot a gold Volvo parked down the street. This interesting car had a business card taped to the window. The business was not a local one, we can not recall what or where it was, but it was a micro business, a one man show. In the back of the car where tons of file folders in boxes. We didn't really think that it was the same car, we will never know. There I picked up the phone to call my mom.

Thursday, February 16th, 2012

It is now Thursday, February 16th, 2012, and I am speaking to my mom for the last time, for awhile. We usually spoke on the phone every week or so, not too often, not too far apart. I wanted to tell her what was going on, but she was talking about family and things they were up to, I just didn't know how to approach it. How do you explain something like this to family? We had never once told them of any problems we had in the past, they knew nothing of it. We really didn't know what was going on for sure, so we told each other goodbye and ended the conversation. Coincidently, my mom had a plan underneath another party for her cell phone also, it was not in her name.

We drove around for a couple of hours, getting lunch and then finally driving back into the outskirts of the city limits of Petoskey. Going by Taco Bell we noticed a gold Volvo in the lot, apparently eating lunch there, we didn't stop, kept driving. After picking up a copy of the Petoskey News-Review newspaper, we headed back out to West Conway Road, between Harbor Springs and Petoskey, where we sat in a large gravel parking lot of an industrial and storage area of Petoskey. There we contemplated what to do. We began to call on rentals that included all expenses.

One of those rentals was in Oden, Michigan, just north of Petoskey a few minutes. For $450 this studio apartment included everything, it was $900 to move in with the deposit. The landlord seemed anxious to rent the place out, we decided to give it another day before we made such a move. In the meantime, we called Sabrina's mom, Kathy.

Surprisingly, though her mom works midnights, she answered right away. She knew something was wrong while talking to Sabrina and asked what she could do to help. Sabrina told her that we needed a hotel room for two nights, outside of Petoskey. We couldn't use our credit card and needed her to rent that. Some people had come after us and we had to lay low. Her mom, instead of asking a million questions, agreed. A few minutes later she called back with a hotel booked for us in Alanson. Sabrina also asked her if she come over and help us move some things out of our house for awhile, she also agreed. She would be there as soon as she could get there. It was late afternoon and we still had janitorial contracts to fulfill that night. Checking into the hotel room, we made arrangements to have Brandon come and work for us, so we could get our work done quickly. He agreed and we met up later at the school that we cleaned.

That night we would see that we could no longer work, we had gone hot. Our stomachs ached from the stress and our appetites were low. We decided that to get all of the Thursday night work done, we would split up. We would all split up at one account that we did, outside of Bay Harbor, and drop Sabrina off. Our equipment was stored at every business and I still had the other backpack vacuum in the truck from the night before. We could make it, we didn't need any more supplies. While Sabrina was cleaning that building by herself and taking care of Joshua, Brandon and I would work with Dan to get the work done as fast as possible. It should be noted that Dan knew nothing of what was going on, except that we were trying to complete the work in record time.

We began with an alarm installation company that we cleaned. We were in and out of there in less than 20 minutes. Then we went to a downtown Petoskey business and equally broke out the work in less than a half an hour. We were riding around in Brandon's car. The truck, due to Sabrina's insistence, had been parked on the rear backside of the building she was cleaning, out of sight. Sabrina had Brandon's cell phone left with her and I had mine. As we went to leave the downtown business, Brandon and I noticed an almost identical truck to ours, pulled over in the Family Video parking lot, just down the street from where we were. There were two city of Petoskey police supervisor vehicles with their lights on behind it. They quickly turned off their lights and left, less than a minute later. Meanwhile all three of us guys went up to clean the school.

Surprisingly, as the kids would be on mid-winter break and off for the next few days, the school wasn't in that bad of condition. In just over an hour and fifteen minutes, we declared the task complete. Everyone was rushing around, cleaning. Brandon then went to drop Dan off at his apartment in Petoskey. On the way there we had a phone call from

Sabrina, there was nothing we could do, Dan would end up hearing part of the conversation. Here was a panicked Sabrina calling.

A few minutes after we left her there to clean, a Pontiac Aztec showed up in front of this now closed business. They got out of their car and back in, slamming the door. They peeled out of the parking lot. Next a city of Petoskey patrol car entered the parking lot, driving slowly around the front of the building and then leaving. Finally a semi-truck was in the adjacent lot, oddly shining off and on his lights. He did have a view point of the building and I would totally disregard this for a long time, but both times he flashed his lights was when Sabrina came into his view from a window in the business and then police would drive through the lot again. The building was now dark, with the exception of the upstairs bathroom light. Sabrina watched as the police were driving back and forth, speeding by on the highway. Was there really a problem? The police entered the lot again, finally leaving.

She was asking what she should do, should she cover Joshua up with blankets and go through the bit of woods to a back road? Should she wait? Not knowing whether she was in real danger, I relayed to her, with Dan in the car, that we were going to have to run from the police, even though we didn't do anything. Stay put, unless you really felt you were in danger, be prepared to come out of the building through the back door to get into the truck. Get the engine warming and we would be there soon. Dan of course now wondering what that phone call was about, inquired. I responded with the fact that I was just a man who knew too much, not somebody who did something illegal. As we dropped him off, I made sure to pay up all of his earnings through that very day. It wouldn't be until a year later that we actually found out that the FBI is known to use semi-trucks in operations. Whether or not that was a coincidence, there is more to the Aztec.

One day, after we spotted the gold Volvo, there had been an Aztec that seemed out of place in our neighborhood, the same color, same looking model that Sabrina saw. One of our neighbors across the street, close to our house, had a woman show up in this Aztec carrying some sort of paperwork. She remained in their house one afternoon and left before school was let out. Now, knowing the lengths that the FBI and other federal agencies have been known to go through, that remains an unanswered question. Sabrina remained calm at the building in Bay Harbor, as we were on our way, as it was getting to be late at night. Brandon had dropped me off, we got in our F-150 and all agreed to meet up back at the school.

Having seen a truck nearly identical to mine pulled over in downtown Petoskey and with the pressuring of Sabrina, I opted to go the back way to Boyne City and use the country roads to head up to the school in Petoskey that we had already cleaned that night. I knew there was a chance that the city of Petoskey police department had become involved in what appeared to be a federal problem. While we were still hoping to be proven wrong and if there was questions that needed to be answered, an agent, from whatever law enforcement division could have left a business card or made a phone call, so that we might clear our name, we decided to mostly avoid driving through Petoskey in our truck.

At the school Sabrina and Joshua would hang out for hours. Brandon and I had a plan, we were going to scope out my neighborhood, watching carefully for anything odd, grab a bunch of stuff and bring it back to the school where we would load it into our truck. Living on virtually no sleep, we were quickly getting ready to go, when it suddenly occurred to me to grab my RFID key for the Petoskey News-Review.

We serviced the Petoskey News-Review three times per week, usually Monday, Wednesday and Friday. They had done a great remodel throughout most of the building and replaced the locks with RFID key badges. The badge, when placed near or touching the sensor by the door, would unlock it. These were becoming more and more popular, we had four such keys for different businesses we cleaned, one being our pass for Bay Harbor. With that now in my pocket, Brandon and I headed and parked in a friend's apartment building parking lot, near downtown Petoskey. There, without making ourselves known to that friend as it was late, we began to head down to 7-Eleven for some munchies to eat while watching the house.

Sabrina and I wanted answers, the best way seemed to be looking from the outside. After our 7-Eleven trip, now being just after midnight, we began to walk through downtown and were in the Petoskey News-Review parking lot, cutting across the back lot. There were others still walking around downtown, also heading from 7-Eleven with their nightly snack. As we neared the sidewalk from the Petoskey News-Review parking lot, a city of Petoskey police supervisor SUV was driving on the adjacent street. When he neared our location, he slowed down to a crawl, the window was put down on the passenger side, as he now crept slowly with his patrol vehicle, staring out the window into the poorly lit parking lot. He continued to head down to the end of the street slowly, which was only a few car lengths away and make a right turn. Now he was in the front of the Petoskey News-Review, with us coming up along the same building. We could see, in the reflection of the windows of the post office that is across from the Petoskey News-Review, that he was making a U-turn, he would be back. At that moment we were only a few feet away from a rear door entrance to the Petoskey News-Review, quickly, at my lead, we ran into the back of the building entering a dark, windowless room, where the newspapers where stuffed with inserts. From inside the building we could hear that police SUV enter the back parking lot.

We went to work our way to the front of the building, but as we entered the printing press area I could see there were reporters still working in a mostly dark office building. Oftentimes there would be reporters coming in to cover a news story. On this night it appeared that the sports writers were at their desks, answering phone calls from coaches giving details about the games that had been played that night. This happened often. What we were trying to do is get to a place in the building that would allow us to see what was going on outside. With no windows in the back, we didn't know. Was the officer out back with a flashlight trying to find me? Had he recognized me? We retired to the darkness of the back of the building and waited for around twenty minutes. Once again we headed off in the night.

We found a place in a park not too far from the Petoskey News-Review where we were able to sit without being seen and watch any traffic that traveled up Howard Street, towards my home. For nearly a half an hour we watched seeing only one police car head up and a few other cars. Nothing seemed out of the ordinary, so we continued our journey.

Walking the back way towards our home, we stopped at the vacant house across the street from our home, watching carefully from the backyard. We could hear a car, once, travel on the other street behind us, but saw nothing. There were no walkers, no life in the neighborhood at all, it was normal. Not one car traveled down our street, after a few more minutes we ran across the street into our yard, entering the back door. Inside Brandon would sit and watch that one camera that we setup to work at night time looking out our upstairs window, viewing the side street outside. We wouldn't know it at the time, but he was watching a paused screen, not really watching anything. While he was busy doing that, I began to collect some items, including those from a list that Sabrina had given me.

With a couple of bags of needed items, our cat Storm in his cage, placed neatly at the bottom of the stairs, we decided how to get the items out of the house to the car parked several blocks away. Knowing nobody was home in the rental house next to us, we decided to place these items in the driveway next door, that would not be seen, unless someone walked or drove by directly. Here those things sat with Storm as we began to jog back to Brandon's car. We would be on our way back to pick them up in a few minutes.

Arriving a few minutes later, we jumped out of the car in the neighbors driveway and quickly gathered the few things I had managed to pack up. With Storm now meowing, we put him into Brandon's car. Off we went, quickly heading back up to the school to meet a worried Sabrina. At this point my confidence had increased in the Lord, I wasn't sure what was going on, but trusted that if something was going on, He would keep us safe. After all, it was Him who had warned us.

With us retiring to the hotel room in Alanson, Brandon headed back home. He wondered what was going on also and though he had no known problems, he contemplated whether or not he would be next. Before he left we all sat in the parking lot wondering if that mysterious phone interruption that he had, as we discussed his portion of the Obamacare series had anything to do with this. We were left wondering what the reason was, but decided to shut down the website, perhaps they would go away?

That article had pushed the limits of free speech and I knew it when I edited it. Though it was within free speech, a comment ringed, asking a question about whether or not patriots realized that this piece of legislation could destroy their country and whether or not they were willing to take a stand against it. Could this have been seen by the federal government, who was apparently already keeping tabs on us, as a call to arms, a threat? It had been no such thing, but in a world where the government was creating database after database and watching so many Americans, who knew? Were they convinced we were domestic terrorists now set on the destruction of the country? The website would be taken offline. With it now into the early morning, our family would sleep for a little bit.

Sabrina's mom Kathy had arrived. She owned a trailer on a piece of property in Conway that we would stop at. At her trailer we discussed the situation and told her that we needed her to rent us a U-Haul trailer. We were going to go and lay low in the U.P., moving our supply of dry foods, clothing and many other things out of the house. We would rent a place up there that included utilities and take it easy for a year. Our truck would have to be left in her yard, they were looking for the truck and we wouldn't be able to openly drive it. A small town, aside from Marquette, would seem to be a perfect place to stay, a walkable town, somewhere in Michigan's upper peninsula. Stopping at our bank one more time, I once again withdrew a large amount of money. We now had $30k in cash, plus around $10k in bullion on us.

Kathy was to get our house emptied out slowly into a storage unit while we would be living in the U.P. We would keep up on the rent on our house until that was done and our communication would cease, until we would come out of hiding in a year. This was the plan. Kathy looked at us, then began to stare at the road ahead, driving towards the U-Haul rental place. She said she was sorry, but we had to have done something illegal and was now having second thoughts about helping us. She didn't want to be involved, she was ready to go back home. With our assurance that we had not committed any crimes and her finally believing us, she decided to help. Now she had become angry at this system of repression that was unleashed against us. How dare they mess with her kids? What could be done about it though?

Kathy rented the U-Haul trailer not far from where she owned her trailer in Conway. We bought the hitch for her truck to haul the trailer and headed back to Alanson to grab some food and then back to the hotel room. We all sat there, confused by the situation. We discussed it, trying to decide what to do. Sabrina and I had a lot of work that would normally start up later that Friday afternoon. Should we even bother? I began to seek the will of God on the matter. After prayer, I walked around thinking about it, the decision had been made. We would no longer go to work, we couldn't safely complete our work, we would have to leave.

There had been too much evidence that a problem had begun. We couldn't debunk that with us being pulled over by the Michigan State Police, my sister getting a phone call, changing our address and people showing up, one seemingly taking a picture, the other a now known undercover police car with a Michigan municipal plate. The icing on the cake was that it appeared that the city of Petoskey police department had been vetted on this case at Big Boy and were now actively pursuing us. They had that silver F-150 like ours pulled over, had been by the building where Sabrina had Brandon's cell phone and was cleaning. It seemed that I would have gotten stopped the night prior in the Petoskey News-Review parking lot, if I didn't grab that key. How could all of this be coincidence, how? It couldn't and we knew it. What we didn't know was what would happen if we stayed. We didn't know their intent, but felt that if we returned home late one night, they would arrest us or worse. What was going on?

We knew that we could technically not do any work on Friday and still get the work done over the weekend. Normally we had Sunday off anyway, so aside from missing the library's Friday cleaning in Boyne City's, we would just clean it on Saturday. A simple explanation should do, if they called, as on occasion we requested to work on a Saturday instead of a Friday and they never had a problem with that. There was still time to change our mind, though we would end up going forward with our plan. Hoping that if we were wrong about the situation, somehow God would make it known to us within the next day, then we could continue on with our lives. Plus with Kathy there, despite the lack of sleep, we could really bust out the work over the weekend. She knew most job sites, she worked after Joshua was born a few times, helping out greatly. We had very few words to say to each other after our long discussion, it was a very troubling time.

Friday, February 17th, 2012

Around 9pm, on Friday the 17th of February, 2012, God would begin to quickly reveal to me that we didn't have a choice. The right decision had been made, we would flee, not under the circumstances we had planned for, but we would indeed run for our lives. We remembered how there seemed to be some protection from God regarding our Plan B materials in the storage unit. It seemed odd to us that the very day we came up there, prepared to move the items, we happened to be there the same day our storage unit was involved in that auto accident. With this in my mind, I was absolutely sure in getting all of our stored food and supplies out of the house, as well as the clothing that we had, some bedding, many things I thought would be taken. The plan was that Kathy would drive us up to a place in the U.P., go to our storage unit there, where she would help unload, then she would head back to her home. We thought we had it all figured out. Before we would go to our house, we would watch out for a couple of hours, making sure it was safe. We all met at the school.

For us it was a perfect night, the school had started its mid-winter break that day, there was no cleaning needed, it was our day off from that job. There Sabrina and Joshua would wait, while we parked the U-Haul trailer on the back of the school lot. The idea was that we would park away from the house, walk there, pack up stuff, place it outside, pick it up with Kathy's truck and bring it to the school, where we would load it into the U-Haul trailer. We would make two or three trips there, repeating the process. Getting things out of the house had worked for us the night before, so we thought. What was about ready to happen would give us all nightmares for some time, including Kathy. At the moment my confidence was strong that God would allow us to get these things out, after all I had purchased them. Why wouldn't He, we now needed them?

Snow was starting to fall in Petoskey, getting heavier and heavier. With the street lights partly darkened from the snowfall, a beautiful winter landscape, like a famous painter's picture of a nice winter town, had surfaced outside. Kathy would park her truck in the back of the Petoskey News-Review parking lot. She waited inside the building as Brandon and I got some snacks and coffee from 7-Eleven for the night. This time no one was in the Petoskey News-Review, the weekend had hit, work could wait, unless a true news story needed immediate attention. This was Petoskey and that usually didn't happen.

In the front of the Petoskey News-Review office we had a perfect view through the large windows, reclining in the new comfortable office chairs. We were looking at the intersection of the bottom of Howard St., the road which connected to either Pearl St. or Jennings St., both of which accessed our street, Jefferson Ave. For over an hour we all sat there, nothing seemingly going on. There was hardly a car driving by due to the snow and only one city of Petoskey patrol car going up the road and returning fifteen minutes later, much longer than would be necessary if they were just checking on our house, the officer appeared to just be doing a routine patrol. Knowing that getting truckloads of our items out of the house would take a long time to complete we had to get going, it was getting very late.

We walked up Howard St., taking a direct route to get to our house quickly, then we turned off onto Pearl St., heading towards Jefferson Ave., where our house was. When Sabrina and I moved into the house, the backyard, though nice, was an overgrown wreck. I had spent nearly a hundred hours clearing brush and debris from the yard, ending with a massive pile that had to be hauled to the city lawn waste dump. All of the shrubs, someone of them 8" tall, had been carefully cut and manicured using an electric hedge trimmer and the 100' extension cord that we had for business, as well as our ladder. We had placed gardens in the yard, carefully planning and growing a beautiful, fully loaded, organic garden. Everything had grown nice, except our melon garden that failed. The black raspberry patch had been cut back with all of the dead removed, this care provided a large bounty of fresh berries for weeks in late summer, some of which were still in our freezer. Grass was planted on a bare patch that had been covered with roots, it grew well, even though it took two separate seedings for the grass to provide proper ground covering. A clothesline had been erected in the yard, as well as a couple of bird feeders that we had connected to a 4x4 post, cemented in place and viewable from our kitchen table. An American flag hung proudly from our porch, next to the neatly trimmed evergreen bushes by the front of our house. Our yard looked good, despite the fact that winter had now set in. We received comments from our neighbors on the large improvements that had been made. While doing all of the work on our yard, I had noted that there was a little space between the fences of our neighbor's back yards, enough that someone could walk between this space to get behind our garage in our back yard, without going on the main sidewalk. We were only a couple of houses down from the connecting Pearl St., as we approached Jefferson Ave., on a snowy night. For the first time I would lead all of us through this forgotten path and enter our back yard.

Once in the back yard we entered the back door of our house, coming up through the laundry room of our home. There I assigned everyone tasks. With flashlights in hand and careful to not shine them towards the windows, Brandon would be the lookout, Kathy would be in charge of packing up all of our dry food, I would gather most of the clothing for our family and bathroom necessities. This is when I found out that Brandon had been watching a paused screen on the video camera system.

Unpausing the screen we realized that there was still no image from the camera on it. For whatever reason the camera upstairs, perhaps due to the elements or the cold, had ceased to provide a clear enough image. With snow still falling in the night sky, Brandon would have to do it the old fashioned way, the way we had seen on movies growing up. He would take a fold up chair and watch out through the blinds on the front door. He was instructed to barely open a blind and peek out, not to make his presence obvious by having the blinds bunched up while surveilling the neighborhood. Kathy was beginning to get things packed up, working the food pantry found underneath the stairs. Boxes where starting to be piled everywhere and a roll of black trash bags were pulled out of the office business supplies. These strong mil trash bags could hold a bunch of weight, as long as the items wouldn't break, things could also be placed in these bags. All of us began to do our assigned tasks.

Brandon knew that if he saw anything he was to immediately let me know. While it would be possible that a car could drive down the street or the police, though not yet their usual 3:30 am trip, I wanted to know about it. He was instructed that no one should be walking by on the sidewalks. I went upstairs rushing to empty out many things from our walk-in closest and dresser drawers in our bedrooms.

We had tons of clothing, linen, shoes and miscellaneous items filling up our walk-in closet, our dressers were full of newer clothing. We always kept a couple of extra pairs of new shoes, new jeans, extra socks and everything else on hand. As part of our emergency plan that we had in place and with the recent jump in prices of goods we had seen the few years prior, we were always prepared to have a very bad year in business. As I was filling trash bag after trash bag with clothing and brand new organic luxury sheet sets and bedding, I began to drag these full bags downstairs, tossing them into a pile in our living room. Our house was already very full, we had ample things and had bought a large wooden play pen for Joshua that filled the middle of the living room. Plus, as we often thought ahead, we already had a nice wooden table with a couple of children's chairs down there. We had thought to perhaps have one more child in a year or so. Kathy had packed up most of the dry storage food and I was finishing on bringing bag after bag of our stuff downstairs to be piled in our now completely cluttered living room. At nearly 2am in the morning I heard Brandon holler as I was finishing up my task upstairs. He had seen headlights on the other side of Pearl St. The car parked somewhere on the side of the street.

I was determined in thinking that God would allow me to get all of these things out of the house, perhaps there was some sense in having bought it all? It sure seemed like it, wouldn't it be necessary to take and have these things, as we laid low and took a year off in the U.P.? I told him to keep his eye open. About fifteen minutes later he hollered again. A woman had went by walking a dog. Right then I should have known something was amiss, but with my mindset strongly assuming I would get these things out of the house, I wasn't ready to give it up.

Quickly I peaked out the upstairs front window, looking off into the snowy night, careful to not allow any noticeable movement in the blinds and looked. That woman walking the dog looked like the same one with the Michigan state police bag from Big Boy. Even though it was snowing and night time, it sure looked like her. I couldn't be certain, but thought it was. Still, I thought, we must get these things out! I questioned Brandon about whether or not he thought she saw him looking through the blinds and how far he had them open. He hadn't listened, there he had bunched up two or three rows of blind that he was holding with his hand and watching out. This was not keeping low, it was being obvious! He didn't know if she had seen him, but when she walked on the sidewalk on the other side of the street with her dog, she had looked directly over at him. Angry, I went back upstairs, why didn't he listen? Now I began to pack up our stuff even quicker, Kathy had made some serious head way on the food and was doing an excellent job, we were almost ready to get her truck and start hauling load after load out of the house. Finally another holler would come from Brandon.

The neighbors on the corner of Pearl St. and Jefferson Ave., kiddie corner from us, had a large yard with a poly white picketed fence. Brandon could see headlights shining on the fence, the car was somewhere on Pearl St., on the side of the road, pulled over. I glanced out another window, seeing the headlight beams lighting up part of the fence, still I continued packing. I told Brandon not to worry about it, Kathy continued. Now as I was starting to get a bit of common sense returning to me, I began to wonder about all of these events going on outside our house. It was now just after 2:30 am and in just over a half an hour, we had a walker with a dog, probably from that car that was parked on Pearl St., and another car that pulled up on the other end of Pearl St., that connected to Howard St.

I knew my neighborhood, I was often up late at night. I would go outside to smoke sometimes and just enjoy the beautiful night. Nothing ever happened and no one ever walked by. What about all of these new faces jogging by our house and walking dogs, faces that we had never seen before. We knew who our neighbors were, we saw them walking their dogs or just taking a leisure walk. Could these actually be law enforcement agents? Then I began to think again on how I was pretty certain this was the same woman who attended that meeting at Big Boy with the Michigan state police bag. I had seen her walk by at Big Boy, myself not noting that her bag was from the Michigan state police, Sabrina was the one that noticed that. She never looked in my direction, but just headed to the meeting room in the restaurant. Could it really be? In the ten minutes it took me to realize that I could be wrong, though not understanding how I could be wrong about getting all of these things out of our home, I glanced out the window again. Those headlights were still reflecting on the fence!

Now I had to investigate. Walking downstairs I instructed Kathy and Brandon. Both Brandon and I had our cell phones, I told them that I was going to investigate the situation. They must listen and listen well, if the phone rang, drop what you are doing and come out the back door immediately, we must go. They stopped their work for a minute and waited as I went out the back door.

Taking this forgotten path behind our garage, that I had found between the property fences, I pushed my way through. Coming out from behind the neighbors garage towards

Pearl St., I peaked out to see who had their headlights on. It was a city of Petoskey patrol car. Literally within a second of glancing over the headlights on the car turned off, the patrol car just sat there. I went back on the forgotten path into our backyard, behind our garage and picked up the phone.

A few seconds later both of them emerged from the back of the house. They all knew we had been caught, these law enforcement agents knew someone was in our house, we would have to run. Kathy made sure the back door was locked and we went to the very rear of yard. Now we hopped the back fence in our yard and went up towards Howard Street, avoiding Pearl Street. There we crossed the street, running through the snowy roads as the snow was still falling heavily. A few inches had now collected on ground. Right before we crossed the street, we saw there was another city of Petoskey patrol vehicle, the supervisor SUV, heading up Jennings St., towards where we lived. We ran faster.

Crossing the street, we cut through a foreclosed property to a half street alley out behind it, that connected a few of the property owners back yards. From there we worked our way down towards Tom & Dick's party store, a couple of blocks from our home. There was yet another car heading up towards our home, the gold Volvo. Somehow these agents now knew we were at the house, we continued to run. Taking a longer way to avoid the more open downtown area, we finally worked our way to the Petoskey News-Review parking lot and hopped in Kathy's truck. We would take the back way out of town, driving next to the stadium and work our way through a few country roads up to the school that we cleaned. We had failed, though we escaped, we had failed.

With it now late into the early morning hours, we picked up Sabrina and Joshua, dropped the U-Haul trailer back into the lot in Conway and headed back to the hotel in Alanson. We chatted with Brandon for a few minutes and called it a night, with him heading back to his Topinabee home. Now we knew the right decision had been made to cease our business, immediately, with no notice.

What could we do? We couldn't operate a business under these terms. Having to flee for our lives, as they seemed to be getting smarter about finding us, we spoke about what was now one of several incidences that had occurred recently, showing us that we did have a problem. We thought of the phone call all over again, the changing of the address, people showing up, the gold Volvo, the still disbelievable meeting at Big Boy, the woman with the Michigan State Police bag and even though we didn't have absolute proof, there was only one way to find out; try to resume normal life and see what happens, go home, leave the lights on, drive around town. We weren't willing to take that risk, we were not criminals, these agents had no logical reason to have this sort of manpower being used against us.

We also knew that we had a few problems in the years prior. The TWIC card, the recent driver's license problem, the FBI car parked down the street long ago, the phone lighting up and the recent static on the line that had just been fixed. There was evidence prior to this night that had made us wonder if we were not just on some sort of watchlist, but if perhaps there were people actively pursuing us. That night we would get a bit of sleep, the next day we would take off, not knowing what our future held.

Before we had left the school, I had pondered what to do. Not cleaning an office building is one thing, very bad to do, especially with a customer like the Petoskey News-Review and others, weekly customers could survive, but the school couldn't have any lapse in cleaning. The kids needed a clean school each and every day. They would return Tuesday from their mid-winter break to attend school, but who would clean the school on Tuesday night. I couldn't give our customers any heads up, we had to get safely somewhere else. Plus we were not completely certain about what we were doing, there were some doubts, even though it had become apparent that it was not wise to continue on with life in the Petoskey area. When we went to pick up Sabrina and Joshua, I took my keys to the school off of the key ring and jotted down our employee's name and phone number on a piece of paper.

Dan knew how to clean the school, he could do the entire thing if need be. I didn't leave any other message, just the keys, Dan's name and his phone number up by the school secretary's desk. At least they would have a chance. We wouldn't know it at the time, but by Tuesday morning the director had called up Dan and would be in the process of making arrangements for him to start cleaning the school that night. He had left messages on my phone, emailed me, that if I didn't respond, though he did not know what was going on, he would assume I had quit and hire Dan. I'm glad he did, the school never missed a day being cleaned.

Saturday, February 18th, 2012

Finally Saturday morning, February 18th, 2012, had come. That morning we gave Storm, our cat, to Kathy. It was very sad morning, a day of tears. Brandon had arrived at our hotel room in Alanson, he was planning on also going with us. He didn't know if he would be next on these people's list and called off of work, under a different guise. I had grabbed an old laptop from the house that we rarely used on the night that Brandon and I had successfully gotten things out. It had been bought years prior, in 2005, from Dell, sitting in new condition, but now aged. Prior to leaving we made one more stop at a gas station in Alanson to stock up on food supplies, we needed a few snacks. There I would pick up the cell phone, my mom's number was entered, but I just couldn't press send button. My concern was that she would freak out, immediately call the police or CPS and then our flight plan would be done with, we would get caught. With our truck backed up near Kathy's residential trailer, right in the heart of Conway, we would give the title to her mom. I would make one more phone call, this time to Shannon.

Shannon was in the process of having another child, his other half was in labor as I spoke. He was awaiting the birth, but his girlfriend still wasn't fully dilated. In a few words, I told him that our house had been surrounded by agents, they had found us, we didn't know why they were after us, but we were running for our lives. He, understanding of these things, bid me farewell, he knew to also watch out for himself.

Shannon had for much of his life lived at his parents trailer in the absolute middle of nowhere. For some reason, we had noted over the years, there was always static on the line when we spoke to each other. He had used a cell phone and assumed it was poor service as we often spoke on the phone. He didn't usually have a reception problem with other people, so he was aware to keep an eye out for trouble. Shannon, Brandon, plus Sabrina and myself were often the ones in attendance at the bible studies or church services held at our house. Shannon, though not always having the time to do so, would join us at La Senorita, playing basketball or bowling, we were a tight knit group of friends. That would turn out to be the last phone call that we would make. Sabrina and I both now had knots in our stomachs. We began to make our move.

Heading north on the highway towards the Mackinaw Bridge from Alanson was a hard trip. We had clothing for Joshua, as well as the necessities, Joshua was breastfed exclusively, he had just recently turned three months the very day the phone call happened to my sister. Sabrina's mom, around the same size as her, had given her most of the clothes she had packed as we had both been wearing the same clothes for a few days. On the way towards the Mackinaw Bridge, as we neared Pellston, we saw that a deputy had yet another silver truck pulled over. We pondered whether or not that was just a coincidence, though we had left our truck behind at Kathy's place. We had told Kathy to not worry about us, we were going to rent a place and had plenty of money to make it a year. We were going to await to see what would happen, in the meantime she was instructed to empty our house. She was also told that if we didn't get a hold of her in a few days to get the birds.

We had two parakeets that we were going to get out of the house that night that all of the trouble arrived. Being unsuccessful in our attempt to do so, they were left at the top of the stairs and given enough food and water for a week; in the dim light of the nightlight, that was in the hallway, still left on, the birds were placed. I never did make it back upstairs, but had fed them that night a bunch of food and fresh water, for whatever reason, prior to seeing the police car awaiting around the corner. Now we were approaching the mighty Mackinaw Bridge that connected the Upper Peninsula to Michigan's Lower Peninsula. We wanted to know why all of this was happening.

Knowing that the bridge had been hardened by Department of Homeland Security grants and riding up front with Kathy, as Sabrina and Joshua were in the back, I began to read a newspaper crossing the bridge. We didn't want any of the face recognition camera software on portions of the bridge to detect me, should someone be looking. After we passed the toll booth on the other end I put the newspaper down and we ended up at the McDonald's in Saint Ignace, sitting in the parking lot.

We all went into McDonald's and ate lunch. Why was this happening? We wanted answers, but none came. As we sat there eating our meal we discussed this. Everyone agreed that the right decision was being made and Kathy promised secrecy. She would tell no one. In the prior couple of days only her phone and Brandon's phone had been called, with the exception of the call to Shannon. After lunch we went to the corner of the parking lot where both her truck and Brandon's car was parked. There we loaded

Brandon's car, not telling her exactly where we planned on going. She knew we would be in the U.P., but not where. Those goodbyes were very hard.

Brandon and I took both of our cell phones that he had under his plan and broke them, tossing them into the woods behind McDonald's. We would lead these agents that far and then drop off of the map. The phones we had kept all the way up to the last minute, as we wanted to make sure that if somehow someone called with information that showed us we were dead wrong in our conclusions, some sort of reasonable explanation, we would get it, now it was time to part ways and head off.

Saying our final goodbye to Kathy she offered to give us her truck, right then and there. She had just purchased this brand new GMC truck months before, her lifelong dream of owning a brand new truck like that, here she was willing to give it to us. We couldn't accept it. We were already sad that with the birth of Joshua she now had acquired this payment. She had bought the truck to be a good grandmother and make many visits from across the state to see him. So far she had done just that and was well loved by baby Joshua. Here in the parking lot we were in the process of leaving, not knowing the future. Was God forewarning us, would Plan B be necessary soon, was that what this was about? We had always wondered how we would get to the U.P. during a full fledged national emergency. That turned out to not be the case, as we would soon find out.

As Kathy's truck left the lot and headed back toward the mighty Mackinaw Bridge, we got in Brandon's car with me driving. We were going to head to Munising, a small city an hour or so north, to find a rental and keep low. There was only silence in the car for quite some time, no one dared say a word, we were all overcome by what had happened. How our lives, all of them, were seemingly normal just a couple of weeks prior to this. We would end up hiding under His wings.

Under His Wings

Saturday Evening, February 18th, 2012

We arrived in the small town of Munising, Michigan, in the Upper Peninsula, along the shores of Lake Superior. Here we found a mom and pop motel and rented a room using a fictitious name and paying with cash. It was a Saturday evening now, February 18th, 2012. We had all of the warm clothing that we needed for Joshua, Sabrina had to purchase a few clothing items for herself as well. Going and grabbing some dinner we retired that evening to the hotel room absolutely exhausted. We were now in hiding but what was going on?

Brandon wasn't sure how long he would be there or even if he would stay. We no longer had the means to contact people we knew, it was too dangerous. At the moment we still would not use the laptop in case they somehow knew that I owned it. Later we would find out that the police were asking questions about the laptop that someone told them we owned, they wanted to know details about it, but no one knew anything. We also decided to buy some red hair dye for Sabrina, which made a slight difference and Brandon got a buzz cut from a pair of hair clippers we had bought. My hair would remain the same, for the time being. Finally in our room with two double beds we all sat down and decided to have a bible study.

As the study was opened in prayer, I prayed that God would give some guidance about what to do. In what I would never recommend, I opened the bible up and read the first chapter that I saw, that chapter was Psalms 88. Part of that chapter spoke to my heart.

"You have removed my acquaintances far from me; You have made me and abomination to them; I am shut up, and I cannot go out; my eye has become faint because of affliction. Jehovah, I have called daily upon You; I have stretched out my hands unto You. Will You work wonders for the dead? Shall the dead arise and give thanks to You? Selah Shall Your Lovingkindness be declared in the grave? Or Your faithfulness is Abaddon? Shall Your wonders be known in the dark? And Your righteousness in the land of oblivion? But unto You I have cried out, O Jehovah, and in the morning my prayer comes before You." Psalms 88:8-13

"Lover and friend You have removed far from me, and my acquaintances into darkness." Psalms 88:18

Tears began to flow down our faces, but could it just have been a coincidence, I decided to flip to another portion of Scripture and read it. The next was Proverbs chapter 3. Here once again we all felt God speaking to our hearts.

"Trust in Jehovah with all your heart, and lean not unto your own understanding. In all your ways acknowledge Him, and He shall direct your paths. Do not be wise in your own eyes; fear Jehovah and depart from evil." Proverbs 3:5-7

"My son, do not reject the chastening of Jehovah, and do not loathe His correction; for who Jehovah loves He corrects, even as a father corrects the son with whom he is pleased." Proverbs 3:11-12

"My son, do not let them depart from your eyes; keep sound wisdom and discretion, and they shall be life to your soul, and grace to your neck; they you shall walk in your way safely, and your foot shall not stumble. When you lie down, you shall not be in dread; yea, you shall lie down and your sleep shall be sweet. Do not be afraid of sudden terror, nor of the devastation of the wicked when it comes. For Jehovah shall be at your side, and He shall keep your foot from being caught." Proverbs 3:21-26

With that, we had a renewed confidence in the Most High God. We knew that in obedience to Him we would not get caught. We would take refuge under His wings. While we did not know the future, we slept that night, getting well rested, trusting in Him. Was it not Him who had warned us? Did he not show us ahead of time that we had a problem? Now we were safely away. The next morning Brandon and I would work on a project.

We purchased two TracFone cell phones and a couple of minute cards with cash at a dollar store in the local area, splitting the purchases between us. Going to a public computer at a coffee shop, we used the computer and setup the phones with fictitious names and addresses. Once we had them all activated we had an emergency line of contact. Though there were rules regarding the usage of these cell phones.

Brandon would only use the phone at predetermined times. Each phone call would setup another time, ours would remain on, but his phone would remain off. I had seen a bag that blocked cell phone signal against detection and being interested in privacy rights, had purchased one a few months prior. Brandon would keep his cell phone hidden in the car, turned off, battery removed, in the signal blocking bag. When he knew to call our phone, he would take and drive miles away from his house in Topinabee, making a few turns while driving to ensure he wasn't being followed. Then in the middle of nowhere he would call us. He also would make sure to not take any other cell phone with him while doing this, there could be consequences.

We didn't know it at the time, but the FBI had been building Operation Stingray that would cause cell phones to bounce off of fake towers. They would use this very method to find people by narrowing down on who might be a terrorist and watch these phones. They would find from the information they collected easily those that had regular registered cell phones, verses those who were using prepaid cell phones. From there it was a narrowing down process, using whatever methods they had decided to guess which phone numbers belonged to those on their watchlists or the watchlists of the Department of Homeland Security.

Leaving Sabrina at the motel room with Joshua, we began to walk around the town trying to see if we saw any For Rent signs, something that we could move into right away. We also grabbed a local newspaper. Finding one sign we inquired, but they would only rent to one person, not a family of three. Brandon was planning on returning to work soon.

Sunday, February 19th, 2012

We had talked about his decision to return to his home in Topinabee all day and it seemed to make sense. If Brandon had any problems that seemed to cause him to flee he would trust that God would help him get away and find a way back up to our motel room or rental. In the meantime, he would try to get to the bottom of what was going on, keeping an eye on our house and keeping us informed of any new information that he found out about. It was now Sunday, February 19th, 2012, no one except Brandon, Kathy and Shannon, knew we were missing. Our customers were still off of work from the weekend, with the exception of the library, they would not know that their buildings had yet to be cleaned.

The thought of what would happen as the phone rang off the hook the next day, Monday morning, troubled Sabrina and I a lot. Our life was in that business, we went out of our way to keep good customer relationships with all of our clients. We were really hurt about what was going on and worried about whether or not the school would be affected. There was nothing that we could do, we were now certain we had to run, though we didn't have any answers. There didn't seem to be much to rent in Munising, which was surprising and we began to talk about looking elsewhere in the U.P. For the meantime we would pay for an additional two nights in the motel.

Once per day we checked the Petoskey News-Review website and a couple of other local news sites, to see if there was any information about a raid on our house in Petoskey, but nothing showed up. Finally late on Monday night Brandon decided to call his grandparents home, where he lived. Walking a few blocks away with his new cell phone in hand, he tried to get any information that he could. He also called McDonald's where he worked as a manager in Indian River, Michigan, just a few miles away from Topinabee.

Brandon would often stay at friend's houses for quite a few days, not returning home. His grandparents were used to it, so they were not worried at all. Brandon would come back to the motel room with some news, the city of Petoskey police department had contacted his grandmother to see if she knew where we were, knowing that we were good friends with Brandon. She didn't know and the conversation was ended at that. Brandon didn't tell her he knew where we were, he was just calling to tell them he was all right in case they began to worry and to make sure nothing was amiss. McDonald's told him that he would have to return to work on Wednesday, he didn't have a choice. Coming back to the motel with these new revelations, we began to decide what to do.

It was finalized that Brandon would indeed go back, but first he would help us to find a place to stay and be settled the next day. We would have to drive around to other cities until we found a rental. He had to work Wednesday evening or else he wouldn't have a job. In the meantime that Monday morning my sister had found out I didn't clean the family factory over the weekend.

Her husband had called her Monday morning and asked if she knew why I would not have cleaned the factory. She didn't know and left a message on our business line that I would get later on, wondering on the message if I decided to forget about them and take a mini vacation, she was not pleased. However, she would begin to worry about us, eventually my mom included. Now with the realization from Brandon's grandmother that the police were actively trying to find us, we knew we had done the right thing. We couldn't have stayed, we would have to find a place to lay low for awhile.

Tuesday, February 21st, 2012

The next morning we got up early, it was Tuesday, February 21st, 2012. Not knowing if we would come back to the motel we put all of our belongings in Brandon's car. We began to head towards small towns on the way to Marquette, stopping at each one of any size, hoping there was a rental. We didn't want to have to find one in Marquette, Michigan, as we were concerned about it being too big, but with needing to find a place soon, we had seen rentals available online there.

Our trip did eventually lead to Marquette. The couple of rentals on the way that we called did not answer their phone. Arriving in Marquette we began to look for apartments. The apartments we called on were not ready to be rented yet, it was a college town. The rental market was tight. There was a short term weekly rental building in Marquette, but they also had no current openings, the building was full of college students. We began to head towards Houghton, Michigan, still a drive from Marquette. They appeared to have a couple of available rentals in the newspaper. Our decision abruptly changed.

Houghton was also a college town, wouldn't it be more of the same? We decided to head south towards US 2 that ran somewhat alongside the upper portion of Lake Michigan. Now Sabrina and Joshua were asleep, though it was only afternoon and Brandon was sitting in the front passenger seat. We were going to go through Manistique and had some concern about this. We didn't want to be seen if they were looking for us, that would be where they would look. If we weren't in Petoskey they would assume it was Manistique. Nervous about driving through the town I remembered those verses we read and continued on, knowing we would be fine. God could be trusted.

Just as we were entering Manistique, on the side of the road was an unmarked white SUV, shiny, clean and brand new. The SUV had three antennas on top of the vehicle, a sure sign that it was law enforcement. The man in the SUV was staring at all of the traffic going by. His vehicle was positioned facing all of the incoming traffic, on an angle, giving him a view of all of those who were driving into Manistique. Looking at him out of the corner of my eye, I kept my hands on the steering wheel staring ahead, so as to not draw attention. Brandon was looking ahead also and did not notice the vehicle.

When we exited the other end of town and I was certain that there was no more law enforcement officers waiting on the opposite end of Manistique, I told both Sabrina and Brandon what I saw. I couldn't tell them sooner, as I didn't want that instant head turning action that to a law enforcement agent would be a sure sign of a potential suspect. Now we were on our way, in another half an hour we would arrive in Escanaba, Michigan.

Not too far from the northern border of Wisconsin, Escanaba is a small town, but complete with everything that is necessary for today's modern lifestyle. Not a town of booming economic growth, but it has survived the shrinking U.P. economy. With it now becoming late afternoon we were out of options, it would have to be Escanaba. Thoughts had played into our head about going to our former congressional candidate friend's house that was somewhat nearby Manistique.

We knew that she had a cabin on her property and would likely not mind the company. We all recalled late one night on our way home from her house, just as we were leaving where she lived in the middle of nowhere, a Michigan State Trooper immediately appeared right behind us and followed us for several miles. We had told her this happened to us and she mentioned to us that on occasion she had seen them watching her house. If anyone was watched in this country, those who run a liberty based campaign were probably not only blacklisted, but watched carefully. I had heard the story about Governor Jesse Ventura's odd incident that happened to him while he was in office. We didn't think her home was a safe place to go and didn't feel that God was leading us in that direction.

Finally we arrived in Escanaba and began to drive around near the old downtown neighborhoods looking for For Rent signs. In a matter of minutes there were four of them found, it now seemed like we were in the right town. One of these places, an upstairs apartment in a converted house, seemed perfect. Sabrina got a hold of the landlord on our new cell phone. With her using a different name and pretending to be a single mom with a new child, she arranged to meet the woman landlord in a few minutes. The place did require electricity in the tenants name, but Sabrina had negotiated with her about a different option, a steady year round price. The landlord having done something similar for one tenant years ago, agreed to think about it. I would park a few blocks away, Brandon and I would go for a walk while Sabrina would drive the car to meet her, taking Joshua with her. The plan seemed good, Sabrina would rent it, I would hardly come out, she would take care of the grocery shopping and purchasing things that we would need for up to a year. By then surely this would all die down and we could reestablish ourselves somewhere. For now we just needed a place to stay and lay low.

As Sabrina drove off to meet with her, Brandon and I began to walk down the sidewalk discussing things. I thought this would work out, the place seemed perfect from the outside. Brandon knew he would be heading home in a few minutes, after helping us get some groceries for our new place. Sabrina would figure out where the nearest grocery store was and if there was a bus system in the area. We would communicate via our secret phone network and he would help us investigate, the eyes in our home area, to get to the bottom of this. He also spoke of going to an attorney friend that he had, though I suggested we didn't have enough evidence to go to him, where was the proof? As we were walking and talking on the sidewalk we came to a four way stop.

To the left of us was a Michigan state trooper who had just pulled up to the stop sign, heading in the opposite direction we were walking. Without looking intently at him, we crossed the street knowing that he would give the right of passage to us, as was the law. Crossing the street this trooper began to move his car forward, his car literally crawling along. He pulled into the very end of a driveway on the corner and sat there. We glanced over, continued walking and turned down an alley that was just up the road. The second we were out of view we took off running and put ourselves in a position where we could see his car from way down the street. For nearly 5 minutes he sat there, finally backing up, going the opposite direction he had been traveling, making a right, following where we had been walking as he drove down the alley we had just ran down. Did the Michigan State Police have a be on the lookout (BOLO) advisory for me? Had something come across his computer screen telling him to be watchful for us at the beginning of his shift? We found that incident very odd. We came back towards where Sabrina was to pick us up and waited for her, sitting on some stairs of a local church.

Finally after a few minutes she arrived and we got into Brandon's car. The landlord had begun to ask questions, things went awry, she didn't believe her story. Sabrina couldn't answer how she could afford to live there with cash, without a job and where she was currently living. The idea had failed. With the possibility of the Michigan State Police now thinking we might be in Escanaba, just a half an hour drive from Manistique where there had been an undercover SUV looking at all incoming traffic, we began to leave the town not knowing where to go. We thought of our friend once again, almost ready to head in that direction, but finally as we were heading north out of town a motel came up on the side of the highway. I decided that I would try one more thing, I would see if I could rent a room longer term here, for ten days.

Walking into the motel lobby, a kind gentlemen, one who claimed to be a Christian from the bible verses that were found throughout, rented a room to me in cash. He didn't ask any questions as I filled out the form using a fake name. He said he would get the car information himself in a little bit, but Brandon would be gone before that happened. One thing struck me as odd, the way he said it, he would put us in the room that was right behind him. This room was the only room that could not be seen from the traffic on the highway. If I was outside smoking or just sitting on the available chair, I could not be seen. We moved our bags into the room. Brandon and I agreed to contact each other late on Thursday night. We weren't planning on calling each other often, but would setup another time to contact afterwards. In the meantime he was planning on scoping out our neighborhood to see if things were still going on.

Wednesday, February 22nd, 2012

The next morning, Wednesday the 22nd of February, 2012, my sister and my mom were now beginning to get worried. The thought that we had went on some sort of irresponsible trip and just ignored the family business was passing, concern was now setting in. She had tried calling my cell phone and stopping at the house. They began to wonder, but would give it one more day. She didn't want to go to the police, she figured we had a reasonable explanation.

In the meantime we found that our new motel room was located near a mall, a McDonald's and a grocery store. All of this could be accessed with walking on the side of the main highway for a few blocks and then through connecting parking lots. There was even a Shopko for diapers, of which we now needed as we no longer could use the cloth ones we had been using. Once per day we would take a trip to purchase food or anything else that seemed necessary. During much of the day, with absolutely nothing to do, we would both spend time with Joshua, read our bibles for quite some time, discuss the situation and wonder how it was going to end. We weren't miserable, but were very anxious on knowing how to resettle ourselves somewhere. Could this be for the purpose of Plan B or could we just move to another state, renting a car to get there? There were many questions and few answers, we knew we needed more information to make a final decision, we would have to wait. On Tuesday morning, before we left Munising, we had an odd experience.

We had taken time on that Monday night at the motel room in Munising and wrote letters to many family members, complete with envelopes addressed to them. We were ready to tell them what was going on. The idea was to mail a whole package to a friend who would receive it. Inside would be a letter to this friend instructing them to drop the other letters in the mail. This way we wouldn't have a postal stamp from the U.P., in fact it would have been from out of state. As Brandon and I made our way to the post office on that Tuesday, they were closed. We didn't think it was a holiday and there seemed to be no explanation, so we ended up hanging onto the letters. Those letters, had they made it out in the mail, would have caused some serious problems for us, we would have told those agents who were now looking for us, that we knew they were trying to find us. Instead of them just thinking they weren't quite quick enough in collecting us, they would know that we were in hiding, which would diminish their hope in finding us and cause them to immediately use more drastic measures to locate us.

Thursday, February 23rd, 2012

On Thursday, February 23rd, 2012, we would finally be reported missing by my sister. That morning my mom and sister were now deeply concerned. They knew a lot of the accounts that we had in Petoskey and began to call some of our accounts. After the phone calls were made they found out that we also hadn't cleaned those buildings either. My sister didn't want to go to the police, but she now did, knowing something was wrong.

Entering the Petoskey city municipal building, she worked her way to the police department to file a missing persons report on us. She met with a detective there and sat down. He asked her some questions and she told him her concerns. He looked at her and said that he couldn't do anything about it, there was no reason to believe we were missing, we probably just didn't want contact. At this point she got angry and told him that she knew us, knew this was totally unlike us and he ought to do something. He asked for our cell phone number, email address and home address. He promised her that he would email me, which he never did, try calling us and knock on our home door, leaving his business card. My sister was satisfied with that at the moment.

Two hours later my mom drove by our house and saw city of Petoskey police cars and a unmarked white van parked in our driveway. There was a plains clothed man standing at the end of the driveway. She pulled into the end of the driveway, in a panic, thinking something terrible had happened to us. The man at the end of the driveway stopped her. He questioned her, what she was doing there and who she was. She explained herself and he told her she had to go, she could park up the street, he couldn't refuse that, but she could not be on the property. He gave her no explanation as to who he was or what was going on as she moved her car just down the street. In a panic she was on her cell phone trying to figure out what a white van would be there for. Someone told her that they could only think that there was a tragic accident or crime that had taken place. A few minutes later everyone would leave the house, with the police stopping to tell her that they were in the house with a search warrant to get a photograph and that they didn't find anything wrong.

The city of Petoskey police department hadn't called my sister to tell her that they were going to get a search warrant, but literally right after she left, detective Schultz, whom she had spoken to, managed to get a search warrant. With this van outside my house, we have a theory on what probably happened while they were inside our home. Not knowing how long they were in the house prior to my mom's arriving, we know that they left soon thereafter.

The house was a disaster. Just days before it had been all neat and orderly, everything in its place, but since then there was a backpack vacuum lying on the floor, with all of its parts, from grabbing the container when we fled the house. On top of that there were partially packed up boxes stacked high in the living room and trash bags full of clothing, shoes, linen and other items tossed everywhere downstairs, mixed with some other miscellaneous belongings. Upstairs there were a ton more trash bags with clothing shoved in them, stuff from the cupboards in the bathroom tossed on the floor, as I picked through the back stock that seemed most valuable. The birds where still in the cage on the top of the stairs. In the bedrooms the dresser drawers were open, partly picked through, with clothing all over the floor. Pulling the bedding that we had as extra back stock, down from the shelves in the closets in haste had caused an avalanche of things that were neatly stacked up, stored away. At the top of the stairs, near the birds, there was rifles in bags, ready to be hauled out. Next to those were ammo cans, full of brand new boxes of ammunition. The key of it all was the kitchen.

In the kitchen there were two fire proof boxes on the floor, mostly emptied, with some paperwork that we had left on the kitchen floor. Then under the table, which it would eventually be found on top of the table when we returned, there was a TracFone box, the phone and components to it missing. Our assumption had always been that they thought they found gold. What they found was nothing.

The TracFone had been purchased by Brandon and stored away at his grandparents house for their use, should there ever be a problem. He too had a locked closet with some food, batteries, a gun and ammo, a flashlight and some other miscellaneous provisions for his family. He didn't tell his grandparents about it, but figured because they saw no necessity of getting even an extra case of food he would do it for them. When we saw the gold Volvo, I had asked for the phone as I didn't have time to go and get one, he gave it to me.

Our initial thought right after seeing the gold Volvo was to go and rent a storage unit in Petoskey, store things and then rent an apartment with everything included in the area. By now we were really thinking that was what we should have done, but at the time we really couldn't get ourselves to believe that the situation was as bad as it turned out to be. So I never got around to getting minutes for the phone or using Wifi somewhere to set it up. We had never used a prepaid phone before. The TracFone phone remained in the truck, never having been setup or turned on. Our theory is that an investigator would immediately assume, due to the serial numbers on the left behind packaging, that the phone was going to lead them right to us. With the numbers on the package they must be able to figure out where the phone was now located. If that is the case, they were wrong, there was no phone to be found.

A few days later we would finally be in the local news. The Petoskey News-Review would print an initial article immediately, at the request of the Petoskey police department, then they would run their own story later, mentioning that we also cleaned for them. We also landed on 7&4 News, as well as 9&10 News, the local news stations for television viewers in northwest Michigan. We had decided that we would begin to check the news using the laptop.

Once per day I would walk over to the mall in Escanaba and pull up the news, checking only once and leave any articles open on the browser to read back at the motel room. We didn't want to check multiple times per day, as we knew that it was possible for them to track the IP address of people viewing stories. Certainly one of these federal agents would consider that we would view a story written on us? If there were too many of the same IP addresses on the same day, it would give them a reason to be suspicious and an investigation into that lead could ensue them in locating us, at least close enough to where we were staying.

There was something that happened when we left Petoskey and went up to Munising, before finally settling temporarily in Escanaba. That very next day, even though we didn't have an opportunity to speak to Kathy, she began to have extra traffic up and down her street. As well as that, all day and all night long, 24/7, a vehicle, usually an SUV with tinted windows, would sit in a parking lot across from her home on the outside of the Alpena area, facing her house. She would see them occasionally get out, standing and looking in her direction, but never approached them. She knew we were in big trouble and knew they sat there trying to locate us. When Brandon returned to Topinabee he also immediately began to have the same problems.

At the Indian River McDonald's, where Brandon worked as a manager, strange vehicles immediately began sitting in the parking lots once he returned to work . Over the course of the nearly three weeks that we were in hiding, Brandon would have a serious of strange events happen to him. The local Tuscarora police department in Indian River, Tuskies as the officers are known locally, paid him a visit on Thursday, two days after he had returned from dropping us off in Escanaba. The Tuskies had stopped in on Wednesday, but Brandon wasn't at work at the time, then they had gotten his schedule for the next day. They knew who he was as they often ate at McDonald's. This was on Wednesday the 22nd of February, the day before we were reported missing and the day he retuned to his home. On Thursday one of the Tuskies would stop by during the early evening and question him whether or not he knew where we were. He stuck with his story that he did not. The officer then asked him if he knew that we were survivalists. He didn't acknowledge that and the officer thanked him for his time. Detective Schultz, from the city of Petoskey, would also give him a call, asking him if he knew where we were, Brandon also told him he did not. Detective Schultz told him he didn't believe him and would be in contact with him again. Over the course of the time we were in hiding there were many things that would happen to Brandon.

Once when Brandon was at his grandparents home in Topinabee, he got a phone call from detective Schultz. Schultz wanted to know what type of car he drove. Brandon told him and then, while still on his grandparents phone speaking to Schultz, noticed that there was another car, with a man inside of it, sitting right behind his car. As he looked out the window at the car parked behind his, the driver proceeded to burn out of his driveway. Technically it was Brandon's grandparents car. The car was registered in their name and they had the insurance on it. Brandon paid his portion of the insurance, keeping the car maintained and putting gas in it. The understanding was that the car was his, once in a while his grandparents would have to use the car, other that that they let him do with the car as he pleased.

Another time there was a strange man outback in the woods with an iPhone behind McDonald's. Brandon looked over at him while taking out the trash and he went deeper, hiding in the woods. This man would eventually walk into McDonald's, asking Brandon how he was doing and get some food. On another night the same man would come through the drive thru and order food. Brandon couldn't help but notice the Michigan State Police binder left on his backseat. There was more, unlike Kathy who just had people sitting in the parking lot across from her house all of the time, these agents were more active with Brandon. Detective Schultz had wondered where Brandon went when he had taken the time off of work. One night after work, as Brandon was talking to another employee who was about my build and height, in the dark, outside the back of McDonalds, a woman walked up, snapped a picture of him, got into a truck with another man who was waiting and drove off immediately. He stood there not knowing what to do.

We talked, this new information would come across my way late at night as the phone would ring waking me up in our motel room in Escanaba. In my conversations with him, well after McDonald's had closed for the night, I asked him to call Kathy on the guise if she knew where we were and find out if anything was going on. After this conversation we would get some of the details of what she was also dealing with. The rest wouldn't come until after we would speak to her again in a couple of weeks.

A few days after we were reported missing, but as she had already been closely watched, a sheriff's deputy from Alpena county paid a visit. As he introduced himself, he hollered at her, *"what did your son-in-law do!,"* he then explained that the purpose of his visit was for her to give detective Schultz out of the Petoskey police department a call. Schultz couldn't get her number, my family didn't have it. Kathy called and Schultz knew she had our cat, we are not sure how he came to know that, but she told Schultz that a six foot blonde haired man dropped him off one day, not saying anything to her, just dropping off our cat. Schultz called her out on that story, but she stuck to it. Both Brandon and Kathy had done one smart thing. They had both called our now broken cell phone and left messages asking where we were, Kathy a couple of times.

A few days later and the police showed up once again at Kathy's house, this time with CPS. This CPS worker had a lot of questions, some of which Kathy wrote down for us to read later that she had found odd. Aside from telling them that Joshua was not there, which they very satisfied with, they asked several questions:

"What version of the bible do they use?"

"Who comes to their bible studies?"

"What is Northern Michigan Lighthouse?" This was a website that I was working on, sort of a small Christian ministry, it was not yet completed, the website was under construction when this happened.

Is it wrong to have bible studies at home? Is it wrong to have a Christian website? Is it wrong to use a certain version of the bible? There are all sorts of cults out there and bad things everywhere. None of them are illegal to participate in, we have the freedom of speech, the freedom of religion. The CPS worker also asked about drugs, abuse and a host of other questions. We would later find that the Petoskey police department had filed a report with them.

In the meantime I followed up with Brandon that he check up on the truck, the house and tell me what is going on. He refused to stop at the truck's location, he knew he would have no logical reason to be there, whereas, if he went by my house he could simply say he was looking to see if I were home. Late at night, after closing McDonald's, he went on a trip to my house. Now as we were reported missing almost a week from the filing by my sister, he saw some disturbing things. We did not know about the search warrant at the moment. Brandon drove by my house, it looked normal.

What wasn't normal was that during the middle of the night at the bottom of Pearl St. and the Howard St. intersection, the usual way we would return home, was an SUV parked with three men standing outside of it, seemingly keeping a lookout. Brandon then went down a few blocks towards Tom & Dicks and as he passed the rail road tracks just beyond that, suddenly a gold Volvo appeared from the darkness and started to follow him. He drove making several turns and finally the gold Volvo no longer followed him. As he told me this on the phone late on night, he would no longer agree to drive by the house at all. He began to talk about getting us an attorney, he felt he would soon need one himself. We still didn't think an attorney could help us, but he would eventually do so anyway.

We wouldn't know the scope of what was going on until afterwards. The news seemed to die down about us locally, it was no longer on the main portion of the websites, seemingly buried with new news. We figured that was it, a few local news stories and they would give it up. In the meantime we had been following our new routine, waiting on God, reading the bible, going to the mall or McDonald's for a bit and watching some television. We were very anxious to know what was going on, but it would still be another week or so.

Eventually I walked down to the office at the motel and gave an excuse that we decided to extend our stay, telling the owner we were from Chicago, a city which I knew well and were just trying to take life easy for a bit. I paid for more nights at the motel. If need be we had actually discussed staying at that motel for an extended period of time, we could afford it. The police would end up calling a lot of our friends.

They spoke to Nathan and Garrett, who at the time both lived in the Orlando metro area, both of them were shocked to find out we were missing as they hadn't heard anything of it. They spoke to Sabrina's sister who would find out on the phone that we were missing. She knew nothing of it. They also spoke to our employee Dan. Dan had heard a bit of that conversation I had with Sabrina while we dropped him off at his house, so they called him to answer questions about us.

On the phone they would question him on whether or not we mentioned going anywhere. He had recalled that I told him I would like to go to Chicago eventually, though Sabrina and I didn't have any plans yet. He asked Dan what sort of things we talked about, what I talked about. He questioned him about our business activities. Dan didn't know much, we didn't talk a bunch. I could tell he wasn't interested in politics, so I rarely said any comment, except a complaint or two about Obamacare. Our conversations were usually about work or his work plans for our company. Dan had rode around with Brandon and I the last night we went to work, so after this interview the police would now know we knew they were looking for us.

The phone rings and detective Schultz is now questioning Brandon about how he had heard that I would use his car and how often I would ask to borrow it. Really Brandon didn't know what he was talking about, we had once used his car prior with Dan to get a couple of jobs done, but that was because once per month Sabrina cleaned for the women's domestic abuse shelter in Petoskey. We had wanted to finish work early that night to go to Walmart and then out to eat at a 24 hour restaurant, so while she was cleaning there, we were cleaning elsewhere using Brandon's car. Sabrina and I were always worried about driving other people's cars in case we were to get in an auto accident. We didn't want the responsibility. One night while Brandon is telling me this, I asked him to go ahead and tell Shannon the details and see if he was having any problems.

The next morning Brandon is on his way out to the trailer and modular park where Shannon is living in a rent to own home. Brandon arrives and not wanting to stir up anything with Shannon's girlfriend and their new baby, they decide to go for a walk. As they step outside Brandon notices a car sitting across from Shannon's modular, in a future development section of the park. There is a woman sitting motionless in the car with a wire going up to her ear, not too far from Shannon's front door. He motions to Shannon and asks him to follow him.

As they are walking down the road this car is slowly following them. They stop, the car stops, with the woman staring at them from a few car lengths away. Finally they move on and can hear the car slowly crawling behind them. Once again they turn around and finally the woman stops right there. The go around the corner and she doesn't follow them. He gives Shannon a brief explanation of what was going on. Shannon claims that was the first time he saw anything, he hadn't noticed anything out of the ordinary. After we would speak to him again, he would see this car once in a great while for the next couple of months.

Finally detective Schultz calls Brandon up and tells him that he was thinking of calling him down for questioning, that if we didn't show up soon our story would go viral in the news. We all thought he was bluffing, but we would find out later from my sister that Schultz wasn't, they were going to use the media to try and find us. They had already begun right away, with a small press release that they asked the Petoskey News-Review to print about us within a day after my sister Kelly reported us missing. They had been trying to get my sister to talk to news stations down in the Detroit area. For some reason they thought we were down there. In the meantime, they also released an article in major city newspapers, both in Phoenix and Orlando. Schultz finally got into contact with Sabrina's dad, knowing we were familiar with the Chicago area where her father resides. He also did not know we were missing and found out through that phone call.

In the meantime my sister Kelly had some weird questions and comments being asked to her about us. One was that there was a CPS investigation and that Sabrina had received no prenatal care, plus that we had left the hospital without being discharged, Kelly objected strongly that neither of these allegations were true, which they weren't. Schultz then went on to discuss the jaundice, of which Kelly knew that we had received treatment in Charlevoix for Joshua, my mom had brought Sabrina McDonald's for dinner and stayed with her awhile, as I was working for the business. Schultz added that we had opted out of taking the newborn blood screening test. This was true, we opted out, as was allowed, from having Joshua's DNA stored in a national database.

On another occasion my sister was told that we had went to a cult church when we lived in Florida. Aside from visiting the church that Nathan went to one time, which was a large Baptist church, we had never even attended church in Orlando. At the time we were not following God, but living like the world. Schultz finally produces a large list of addresses and asked Kelly which ones that her and my mom knew we lived at. Kelly recognized several of the addresses, but several of them she did not. The list had addresses from all over the country. From the description given, it was much more than where we had actually lived. He then would call her and tell her what he had heard.

A psychic had told them that we were off in the woods, heading to a cabin to follow a visionary named Joseph. When we heard that comment afterwards, we really began to wonder if they weren't trying to find us through the media, our friends, plus detective work. Would the federal and state agencies that were using the city of Petoskey police department have killed us and called it a murder-suicide? Afterwards when we would read the news articles and the comments, we learned of the McStay family that the media had compared our case to.

Some serious research had shown me that at one point the Department of Homeland Security had actually been involved in trying to find the McStay family, how is that even possible? Why would they be involved, doing national security, in locating a missing family? We also read that Summer McStay had often given out fake names while purchasing things, so had we. That the family had taken and looked into Mexico during an online search, we had also. They bought Spanish software, so had we. It looked to us that the McStay family crossed in Mexico on foot. Did they make these same people mad? We wondered and still ponder. Even with an arrest in their case now, I still hold questions and will note that the arrest of Chase came very shortly after we first released the copy of this book, prior to this edit. I have thought before to call someone from the McStay family and ask them if Joseph was a 'conspiracy' theorist or whether he spoke against the government or was politically active. Perhaps they wouldn't even know, we didn't really talk about the articles that I posted on Brandon's website to anyone. My sister would also find out about this website from the police.

Kelly was asked if she knew that I was involved with an extremist group and posted extremist articles online. How did Schultz know about the website? They had not yet done the second search warrant to take our computers. When I posted on the website I always used the alias, Logan, never my real name. Brandon's name and picture was on the website, but not mine! Running two businesses in the small town of Petoskey, I avoided being publicly involved in these types of politics that would be contrary to business. We were well known to many business owners and had friends who owned businesses, where we did some of our shopping. Aside from that, we scooped the yards of many prominent people throughout the area. While we didn't usually have prolonged conversations, we knew them and they appreciated our service.

After the second search warrant was issued, Kelly would then be asked more questions, about the books we read, our collection of bible study books and finally a CD sermon that I had from a fundamental Baptist preacher named Paul Washer who was preaching about whether or not people were really saved. This CD sermon, according to Schultz, was radical religious material, in fact, it was in reality just a conservative Christian sermon, old-fashioned, the type that you would have heard in some churches during the 1950's. Even if it had been radical, it wouldn't have been illegal.

Detective Schultz even contacted the Christian ministry website, A Voice in the Wilderness (www.a-voice.org), where I had signed up years prior to be on the email mailing list. A few times a week a Christian study, a hymn and an article about a Christian topic would make its way into my email inbox. He wanted to know my beliefs on the Rapture, he also asked this person if he knew where I might be or which online boards that I visited. An email of the exchange would be sent to my inbox with a message from the website owner, that apparently I was missing.

Finally Kelly gave into the continuing pressure by Schultz to go to the media. Despite the fact that city of Petoskey police department insisted that it appeared we left on our own accord, as Schultz knew that Kathy had our cat and he also knew that our landlord had received an envelope with two $300 money orders to pay our rent for March, they still decided that media would be used to find us. She found herself talking to those same local stations, 7&4 News plus 9&10 News, then it went to the Detroit area. Even some radio stations did interviews with her about us. We wouldn't know of this, as we thought perhaps googling our name would be a sure way for us to be found. We only ever saw the second set of news pop-up on local news station websites. Our hope was to tell our family soon what was going on, but there were still people watching Brandon and Kathy constantly, we were not out of the woods yet. Kelly wouldn't take all of this lightly, she had some troubles about some of the questions that had been asked also.

Even though she didn't know of our political actions, she did know that we thought 9/11 was a government cover-up, she knew that we thought you should have some storable food. She also was the one to receive that strange phone call just prior to us missing. She began to ask Schultz if we were in trouble, she told him about the phone call and brought this to his attention several times. Schultz insisted each time that we were in no trouble at all. She explained to him that I was not an extremist, she knew better. After all, a comment would come out of this about whether or not we went camping. Where did that come from? Detective Schultz would also tell Sabrina's sister that we owned a lot of guns. We didn't, we owned some guns.

Why was the city of Petoskey, as they pushed Kelly into doing interviews with what would turn into a media frenzy with people such as Nancy Grace, so candid about how it was just as if we up and left? Most articles would quote the city of Petoskey police chief, John Calabrese, speaking of how everything was orderly in our house, only one article would mention that we were in the process of packing things up. In reality our house looked as if a bomb had gone off. The city of Petoskey police department would mark on the items taken from our house during the second search warrant, our surveillance notes that were found near our camera system. Right on that note was camera times and possible suspect cars, including the gold Volvo.

The city of Petoskey police department, which were acting under the guise of a missing person case, collected information for whatever federal agencies had originally asked for their cooperation and assistance. They would ask Brandon whether or not he helped hooked up our camera system or who helped set it up. They apparently didn't think I could do such a thing, running cables around the house. He told them it was me, indeed it was. They were under the assumption, as they would tell Kelly, that the camera system was hooked up to the internet and that I could view the house from a computer outside of our home.

They even questioned Don our landlord for quite some time. We have all respect for Don and at the end of the matter he told us we could remain in the home if we wanted to. He would tell me that we were good renters, good people, he liked us, but was only angry that the media had shown the address on the house once. He thought they shouldn't have done that and knew it wasn't our fault. When we received our refunded deposit, there was a note from him deducting $100 for time spent with the police. Both times the police had a search warrant, they would go to him to get the key and return. This meant that within a matter of minutes of knowing facts about us, after Kelly reported us missing, they were in the process of contacting our landlord, getting the keys, getting a warrant and going inside, completely opposite of being able to do nothing as they had told Kelly. Family had also expressed concern about our birds.

Kathy, when she spoke to Schultz, wanted to go and get the birds out of the house. He told her, after she told him she had a key, that if she went into the house she would be arrested. Kelly and one of her husband's family member, both requested to get the birds out of the house. In fact, this unnamed extended family member got angry and yelled at them to at least bring her birds. According to Kelly, they were assured by Schultz that they were fed plenty of food when they came into our house, he had taken care of them. The birds would be stiff at the bottom of the cage when we came back. To us, it was a sign of how angry these people were, that they didn't manage to achieve their means. We wrapped the cage with a comforter that was laying on the floor, with bird feathers scattered everywhere. They had indeed run out of food and water. As we sat in the motel room in Escanaba, wondering what to do, things were about to change.

One of Brandon's friends, the same person that had his picture taken with Brandon late at night by that woman at McDonald's, was woke up to a phone call one day by Schultz. Did he know where we were at? In anger, he told detective Schultz that he woke him up, to not bother him he had only met us once. Another of Brandon's friends likewise received a phone call. She knew us better than this other friend, but we never once hung out with her independently, without Brandon. She just happened to be on Brandon's family and friends plan. Brandon had been using his phone that had been connected to the website, for his personal calls, as the other had been broken. Over a year later when he would be going through his paperwork he would see the incoming calls to that phone in the middle of the night that would reach his voicemail, as he was not taking a phone with him while he would visit friend's homes outside of work. These calls would all be 1-000-000-0000, occurring while we were in hiding, that will be explained more in depth. Detective Schultz once again threatened to bring Brandon in for questioning, he told him that he knew he wasn't being honest. Brandon had helped to hide us and he was trying to get answers to what was going on. With this threat from Schultz, Brandon picked up the phone at his grandmothers house and made a phone call to his attorney, a meeting was setup two days later. That phone call made a big change.

All of the sudden, though we wouldn't piece it together for a few weeks after doing our own investigation talking to our friends and family, researching the facts, that phone call to his attorney brought instant relief from the spooks that were watching both him and Kathy. They disappeared, things returned to normal immediately. The parking lot across from Kathy's house was once again empty, traffic returned to normal. The amount of people walking dogs or jogging nearly vanished. They were gone! Brandon hadn't talked again to Kathy and wouldn't speak to her until after the ordeal was over, but we had already heard from him that things seemed to quiet down. Now, we agreed that he should speak to his attorney on our behalf.

Attorney Peter O'Rourke might be mostly retired, but he still does some cases for people and on occasion will help out those whom he desires to. He has an impressive resume and pictures in his house, including meeting a former President. He was a municipal city judge, a commander during active military duty, served on various boards and associations in the state of Michigan and is still greatly involved in the local community. Mr. O'Rourke is well connected and holds a book of contacts of attorneys that he recommends to people in need of one, for various reasons.

Brandon had gotten into some trouble while in high school, the counselor there was friends with Mr. O'Rourke and the two met up, becoming friends. Despite their huge age difference and wealth gap, Brandon and him just hit it off right. Brandon was always welcomed to come over, in fact, he could have stayed in his guest house for free, in exchange for some lawn work. For Brandon, staying at his grandmother's house with his family was fine. He was never picky, if he had food to eat and a place to crash, he was content. Brandon went in to meet up with Mr. O'Rourke, he explained to him the situation, as Mr. O'Rourke listened. The only question he had for Brandon was whether or not we actually did something that deserved this, had we committed a felony or not. Brandon told him the facts and assured him that we were what he said we were, honest, hard working people, who had only made the wrong people angry. At that point Mr. O'Rourke agreed that if we decided so he would take our case, but we would have to be the ones to call him, it could not be through Brandon. A friend of Brandon's was a friend of his.

The advice he had given Brandon was that it was just best to go back, let them arrest us, as it seemed to him that was what they were going to do, and then once the charges were filed, he would have access to the paperwork and he would go from there. With this new information, we became hesitant again. We thought for sure the only thing they were going to charge us with was domestic terrorism or some made up heinous crime. We hadn't done anything, it would just be a kangaroo court. We withheld from calling for a bit. In the meantime things would change again. Detective Schultz would call Brandon one final time, this time with a serious question.

"So you want to flee the country?," Schultz said on the other end of the phone line. Brandon immediately denied such a notion, wondering how Schultz knew that this had been discussed? Now Schultz told Brandon he would probably call him back to setup a time to speak to him in person. At the moment Brandon was in the middle of his shift at McDonald's. He stepped outside to smoke a cigarette and pondered what to do. Picking up the phone, he called a friend, he needed a ride. Now he would assume that this was going to affect him, despite the fact he hadn't seen anything in a few days, he thought they were looking at him, how did they know that he spoke of fleeing the country? That day he walked out of work, no notice, no nothing. His ride picked him up and he rode silently to be dropped off at the motel in Escanaba, where we were staying. I knew he was coming, the phone had rang, the secret phone and he told me that he knew we were right, he felt he was also in immediate trouble, he was heading up there.

We would later find out that a file he had sent me to proof edit had spoke about leaving the country, not bothering to be politically active and settling elsewhere. Brandon did not even have a passport and had made no plans to flee the country. It was an idea, it was free speech. Later that night after he arrived we would look through some files on the laptop computer we had with us. We had a copy of nearly all of our files on there, there we would see what Schultz knew about. We still didn't know that he had a search warrant executed at our home again, that same day. There we began to read some of the articles that were placed on the website, double checking that there was nothing illegal said. None of the articles called for violence against the government or taking up arms.

Now we pondered what to do. Were we actually going to activate our emergency plan? We seriously considered figuring out how to get to a major city, perhaps Philadelphia, where we could just live simple lives, renting a cheap place. Could we make it to Mexico? What about Canada? At the moment we weren't aware that the Customs and Border Protection had been keeping an eye out for us to cross the border. A few minutes after Brandon had walked out of McDonald's would go by and detective Schultz would try to call Brandon back there. McDonald's answered and couldn't find Brandon, he was gone. Then Schultz would call Brandon's grandmother and ask where he was at, her only response would be to tell Schultz that whatever he said to him must have made him run, the conversation ended. Now grandmother was wondering what was going on, she knew there must be trouble, that we wouldn't up and leave our business for a good reason. She had warned Brandon many times, *"that stupid website of yours is going to get you into trouble!"* Brandon would be reminded of that by her with an 'I told you so' over and over again. Finally he arrived in the evening up in Escanaba.

His ride dropped him off and we all spent a few moments telling them goodbye. This was the first person that we personally knew and had seen, in what appeared to be a very long time. In the motel room both Sabrina and Brandon thought we should just go camping for a bit, despite baby Joshua. We had all of those special clothes for him, winter was ending, the weather had warmed up, God could provide. Across the street there was a nice, new 4-wheeler for sale. The price tag was just under $10k. They thought it was a good idea to purchase it, I disagreed, telling them to let me wait a bit longer. I had been praying about this situation since it started.

Unlike when we got to Munising and I knew that God spoke to my heart through the bible, there had been nothing else like that happening. We rested safely in knowing we wouldn't get caught, but still didn't know what to do. I had read the entire bible and was rereading portions of it during that time. There seemed to be no answer, should we just assume it was a camping scenario, what about trying to get to Mexico? How long could we wait in the motel room? We just didn't know.

The next morning, on March 7th, 2012, nearly three weeks of being in hiding, things changed, God spoke once more through His Word. We were not aware that our news story had gone viral, we hadn't seen ourselves in the news on the local websites in the past couple of days.

Escaping Michigan

Wednesday, March 7th, 2012

Waking up the next morning in the motel room with everyone still asleep, I opened the bible to read, a good start to the morning I had now become accustomed to. Having recently read the entire bible, I decided to reread Psalms and was working through that book. I began at the chapter I left off at, but never made it past reading that one chapter. The following half a verse stood out to me, God spoke to me heart through that verse, could I be right, could I trust Him, was I wrong?

"...they devised a plot which they were not able to accomplish." *Psalms 21:11b*

As everyone else was getting up for the morning I spoke of this, though thinking I would be embarrassed should I be wrong. I thought that this verse that spoke to my heart meant our situation was over. The night before we had determined that we would call the attorney, Peter O'Rourke, as a last ditch effort. Walking over to the mall that morning I spoke to Mr. O'Rourke. It was now March 7th, 2012, the day the case would be closed, at least the missing persons case from the city of Petoskey police department.

Mr. O'Rourke asked how we were doing and essentially told me the same thing that he had told Brandon. I explained to him that I thought it was due to political activities and I didn't know if he could help. He asked, *"what would it take for me to convince you to come home?"* I couldn't think of anything off the top of my head when finally he suggested that he would get a letter, both from the Michigan State Police and the city of Petoskey police department, that I had no wants and no warrants. We agreed to speak later in the afternoon.

That morning Mr. O'Rourke made some phone calls and arranged a meeting with both John Calabrese, the chief of police in Petoskey and a representative from the Michigan State Police. Sitting in a room at the table, he told them that he wanted a letter that we had no wants or warrants. Both of them refused. Once again he restated that he demanded a letter while speaking directly to the Michigan State Police, they flat out refused, they would give no letter. Finally the representative from Michigan state police told him that he would have to ask the commander of the Gaylord post. Looking at Calabrese, Mr. O'Rourke now demanded a letter from him. He still refused. Finally he told Calabrese that he would go to the media and tell them that this family wants to return home and you are preventing them. Calabrese then agreed to write a letter and grabbed a note pad, starting to write on it. Mr. O'Rourke then told him that it would have to be on an official letterhead, reluctantly Calabrese agreed.

When I spoke to Mr. O'Rourke at our arranged time that afternoon, I assumed he had gotten a letter from both the Michigan State Police and the Petoskey police department. He didn't tell me this story, of the difficulty in getting a letter until after he picked us up. He told the city of Petoskey police department to drop the case, we were no longer missing. They refused to do so unless I contacted my mom via cell phone, he couldn't understand why that was necessary, but I complied. Dialing my mom, I told her that I was fine, as we heard some terrible clicking on the phone line, something was still amiss. For those who wondered, Sabrina never spoke to the police department, nor did anyone speak to her when the city of Petoskey police department issued a press release that we were alive and well, that I had contacted a family member, that the case was now closed. Even the attorney at that time the case was closed, didn't speak to Sabrina.

We didn't realize how big the story had gotten. After the initial phone call in the morning to the attorney, we had decided to actually check the news. Right there on Yahoo!, our story was prominently displayed as the number one news article. To our shock our story had went national. Even Good Morning America had done a story about us that very day! As we sorted through these stories we simply had to close the computer, it was too much to deal with.

As a side note, people often thought the comment in news articles about *"looks like something spooked them"* from the city of Petoskey police department was odd, hopefully now you understand why that comment was made. The ordeal was far from over, but we were coming back home. We didn't want to trouble Mr. O'Rourke to pick us up, he had done enough, we assumed we were going to rent a car in Escanaba to return home. It turned out there was no car rentals available in Escanaba, so the next morning we called Mr. O'Rourke to make arrangements to pick us up. He agreed, but we would have to wait until Friday morning as he was already preoccupied for the day. That afternoon we called every single friend and family member having to buy more phone cards. Out of precaution Brandon rented a room in cash so that we could continue to stay at the motel, in case anyone showed up due to the cell phone calls and a location now being known. Should anyone have asked at the front desk they would have went to the wrong room, we were now staying in the room that Brandon rented.

There were mixed reactions with our family. My mom and sister had been so worried about us, at first there was anger, though they would hear our side of the story. Others listened to the story and asked what we were now going to do. A lot of people would ask *"would these things just go away?"* We told them how God had kept us safe through the ordeal. Still there was this clicking when talking to both my mom and sister, as well as a few others that could be heard. There was one phone call that I would make that would add another strange portion of this entire ordeal.

Picking up the cell phone, I called my buddy in the Chicago area, PM. Speaking with him he would tell a story to me that was hard to believe that happened the same day he had found out we were missing, this would also be the day that we had spoken to our new attorney and our story had hit national news. The grocery store where I had worked at in Whiting, Indiana, had received a fax with our whole family's pictures on it, showing Joshua as missing and endangered. They immediately called PM at another location and faxed it to him. There he and his wife began to discuss what was going on, thinking it might have something to do with politics. He picked up his phone and sent a text. His text, that we never received, was *"what the #$@% is going on? R U alright?,"* a few minutes later someone texted back to his cell phone, *"he's fine."* He then picked up the phone and calls our cell phone number, a man answers. He asks for me, the man simply tells him that we am fine. Not knowing what to think he exclaims to the man *"what the #$@% is going on!"* and hangs up. As I am talking to him on the phone and he relays this story, which happened just a day prior to me calling him, I can't even believe it. *"I'll show you the text, I swear,"* he tells me. PM has always been an honest individual, we knew he was telling the truth. Our cell phone was broken and in the woods behind McDonald's in Saint Ignace. We still needed a plan, it just seemed right to get out of Michigan as soon as possible.

About an hour later I called PM back to ask him if we could stay with them for a bit. He told me that him and his wife had just been talking about the same thing and he was going to call me back to tell us to get down there and get out of Michigan. Most people agreed, we needed to leave Michigan, at least for awhile.

Friday, March 9th, 2012

On the way back to Petoskey, with Mr. O'Rourke having picked us up in the morning on Friday, March 9th, 2012, we learned that a second search warrant had been issued for our house on March 6th, 2012. This time they had seized the rifles that were sitting at the top of the stairs, as well as thousands of rounds of ammo in cans, that were also sitting near the bird cage. They took the video camera system, the monitor and the DVR, our surveillance notes, all three computer towers, leaving the computer monitors and keyboards behind. They took quite a few things out of the house. A life insurance policy that had been sitting on a table in our living room in the open, since we left, with a letter that was opened on the same table about changing beneficiaries, still sat there though. We were changing it so that it could go to Joshua if both of us should somehow die. This we had been working on, even prior to the phone call my sister received asking for me.

The policy was a gift from Sabrina's grandmother when she was a child. We had been talking about life insurance shortly after Joshua was born. What if we should get in a car accident? Who would take care of him? I elected to get a new policy as my ten year term policy I had purchased when we were living in Whiting, Indiana was almost up. If I died the money would go to Sabrina, if she also died it would be setup for Joshua in a trust fund that the caretaker would have access to. We had thought about talking to my sister Kelly about the whole ordeal, but were still working on getting life insurance for me.

This turned out to be a task. I went through the brokerage firm where we had all of our policies, both business and personal. We always went through smaller companies, as a small business owner, why not support them? The larger businesses never called us for work. Plus, these smaller companies were usually cheaper and provided better customer service. They began speaking and working with me on getting a new life insurance policy. I knew I didn't want to give blood to get it, no testing, just simply a policy. Usually with policies of $100k or less this wasn't a problem, my policy at the time was for $100k and I had no exam. So we went to renew it with the current company, they denied the renewal.

The insurance agent thought it was because my current policy was already in force, so trying another company that did not require an exam, I applied. Here I was denied again, could it be because I already had a policy in force? She theorized, but called me back the next day with another option. There was another company that she was sure would have no problem issuing me a policy, with this company it had to be $99k or less in order to avoid the medical examination. I went in, filled out the paperwork and waited. A couple of days goes by and she calls me not understanding why, but I was denied again. We gave up on that option and wondered if there was some sort of link between a government watchlist and the life insurance industry. I researched it, it seemed possible, but was unable to prove it. All of that had taken place in late 2011. Surprisingly the police had never taken that life insurance policy that was left in the open on a table in our living room. Wouldn't that policy change request have suggested foul play?

They had found one of the two Tribulation packets that we left hidden in the house and had taken it during the second search. I had made these, as well as those who attended the bible studies also did so. Is it wrong to believe in the Rapture of the church and a coming Tribulation? We know the bible teaches such things, even though many disagree, it is still free speech, not illegal to think or speak about such things. Inside these packets were some letters to whoever may find it, a bible and some tracts about how to get saved. The police also took pictures of our book collection.

We had over 400 books on shelving in our house, many of these books were expensive and rare titles. We should be able to read what we wanted without it being documented. Just because some of those books on the shelves contained titles that were about the Federal Reserve, 9/11, corporations or the medical industry, doesn't make them illegal. In fact many of our books were on United States history, particularly a large collection on World War 2, of which I had a keen interest in. We planned on home schooling so we had books covering every major topic from the inception of the United States to current events. Once again not illegal to own any book, in fact the Bill of Rights protects against being violated in such a way.

Now on March 9th, 2012, we were on our way back home, having been gone around three weeks. Riding in Mr. O'Rourke's SUV, we started to talk about what had happened. I never could get myself to tell him that we thought probably the government had us labeled as domestic terrorists, but we discussed political repercussions that had happened. He too had heard some stories and did not think we were being dishonest, it was just hard to prove these things. He began to prep us for what he thought was about to happen.

He assumed that when we went to the city of Petoskey police department to pick up all of our things that they would want to talk to both Sabrina and I, plus see that Joshua was alright. He thought we might have a temporary problem with CPS, but didn't think they could do very much, aside from talking with us. He would help us with CPS, if need be, but wasn't concerned. We didn't tell him of our plans to leave the area. All we knew was to expect to answer some questions once we arrived at the police station.

On the way back to Petoskey was a state trooper on the side of the road between Escanaba and Manistique, as we went past him he pulled out and followed for a few miles, finally turning around. There were no other problems noted as we continued to head back. Finally after crossing the Mackinaw Bridge, the attorney picked up his cell phone and dialed Calabrese, the chief of police in Petoskey. He told him we were on our way and we wanted our things back once when we arrived.

Mr. O'Rourke asked us if we wanted to go to the media with our story on the way back. One of the family members had tipped off Fox News that this was a violation of civil rights, they would not give any details though. Fox News had emailed one of Brandon's email addresses that they had found linked to his website, asking him to have me give this reporter a call. We certainly did not like the attention we were already receiving and wanted substantial proof to back up our claims. Now that we could talk to people we had more evidence, but at the time we still didn't know a lot of what had happened, we didn't know that the police and the man standing by the white van had been in our house minutes after we were reported missing. Seeking Mr. O'Rourke's advice we were told that if we wanted everything to drop down back to normal, not to talk to the media. He still left that decision up to us, ultimately we decided not to talk. We were thinking about what my family had been through and didn't want to cause any more attention to them. My sister would receive calls from the media for months and months after the ordeal, wanting her to tell them the real story.

Finally I wanted to know what the cost for all of the services Mr. O'Rourke was providing for all of us was. He looked at me and told me he was a very expensive attorney, I had already racked up $5,000. This was true, some people who used him would pay very large sums of money for his representation. He then looked back and said he was going to work a deal. He added up his gas, the lunch he had just paid for at Burger King, before we left Escanaba, the cost of getting some paperwork and smiled. The total would be only $100, no more. We couldn't thank him enough. Even though we could have afforded to give him $5,000 right then, (and would have) we had a whole life to rebuild and we knew that.

A few minutes later detective Schultz called back Mr. O'Rourke and told him that because both of us had concealed carry permits that we would be patted down upon arriving. He told Schultz that we both knew the law and knew that we couldn't take weapons into that building. Schultz had asked my sister Kelly about how often we carried a gun in the truck. She told him all the time, that we kept a gun in our truck; this was no longer true as we started cleaning a school. We were nervous approaching the city of Petoskey, we now knew about the refusal for a letter stating we had no wants or warrants from the Michigan State Police, but I had a copy of the letter from Calabrese and he had used the term *"to the best of my knowledge,"* this wasn't definitive to me.

When the Patriot Act came into being, it created secret courts and secret warrants. With research on the Terrorist Screening Center and the now declassified messages that an officer may see, one point to be made is that the suspect pulled over may have a warrant that does not show up on the officer's screen in their cruiser, a secret warrant. A lot of cases against so called domestic terrorists start off with a secret court hearing, where an arrest warrant is issued. These things are not public and this is not the way our legal system should work. As we pulled up to the city of Petoskey police station I knew at that moment all I could do was trust in God, all of us!

On the way back down, Mr. O'Rourke asked me where our truck was, how come they had not been able to find it? That truck had sat there, surrounded by neighbors in Conway, at property in Kathy's name, unnoticed. That very fact was amazing to us, they never did find the truck and not one person even thought to check that property that was owned by her mom, right there in the same county! Before we got to the police station in Petoskey, Mr. O'Rourke stopped in Conway so we could pick up our truck. We continued our trip, following behind his vehicle.

Joshua was sound asleep in the backseat with Sabrina so just Mr. O'Rouke and myself walked into the police station. We figured I could answer any questions, hopefully, and they could come out and see them in our truck. As we walked in I saw John Calabrese, our eyes connected, he had a very displeased look on his face. After he glanced at me, he walked away into the back of the station. Waiting for us was detective Schultz. We were not patted down, but were told to walk to a side room.

In this side room were all of our things that had been taken with the recent second search warrant, with the exception of the computers. Those we were told were locked in another room and the officer that had the keys was off duty, they wouldn't be available until at least Monday. Now with the expectation that I was about to be questioned, Schultz looked at me and told me to sign these pages and then I could collect my things. Nothing else. I signed the documents. One of the officers, who seemed very friendly, asked if we wanted help loading the ammo cans. We accepted the help and he carried out a couple, placing them in the bed of our truck. With the guns and thousands of rounds of ammo loaded back up, we headed back home, paying Mr. O'Rourke the sum we owed him. He agreed to help collect the computers early next week, if we wanted, but not too late in the week as he would be on his way to Hawaii.

Late Friday afternoon we arrived back at our house. The whole situation had been like a bad dream. Sabrina was a bit worried about staying there, but I knew if they gave us our guns back I didn't expect them to be coming over the weekend. We would only be there by ourselves for one night, family was on the way, Sabrina's mom and sister. That evening while back in the house I got a phone call from my mom. She thought it was best if we didn't talk for awhile, this included talking to my sister Kelly, it was too much for them to handle. We had wanted to go over and visit them before we left, but I simply told them to call me back when they wanted to.

Now was our house bugged, who knew? We began to survey the damage. The dead birds, a black rubber glove left behind, Sabrina's jewelry box downstairs, apparently one of the things they had forgotten to take during the last search. I noticed the paper bag with the unused prepaid cell phone box, out of the bag, on the table. Our back door lock had scratches all on it, as if it were picked. We drove and picked up some food taking it back to our home and began to pack up things.

We always saved enough boxes to move. They were hard to come buy and we had space to keep them. Plus should we ever have had to activate our emergency plan there would be one phone call made to a friend who would pack all of our items up, donate or sell them, however they saw fit. They even had a notarized power of attorney left behind for them to take care of business and were responsible for the pets. Money was also tucked aside for them, of which we had grabbed prior to leaving. They also had a key, so one phone call or letter and we were good on that end. Things didn't happen as we suspected, so we never contacted this person. Packing late into the night, but also taking breaks, we watched as our neighbors stared, though not one of them inquired with us. We had made the whole neighborhood mad apparently, they didn't like the media attention, we don't blame them, but we also couldn't help it.

The next morning Sabrina's mom Kathy and her sister would show up. Then we would realize what had went on outside Kathy's house after we left. The stories were just too much. I would call Dan and find out he was cleaning for the school. I offered for him to take all of the business equipment and supplies that he wanted. He brought over his fiancé and a friend, we spoke for awhile and he took what he thought would be useful. It was all garbage now to us, we didn't need it. Our answering machines were full.

We had phone messages that started from the businesses that were not cleaned that Monday after we had stopped doing the business, with many comments of genuine concern from our customers, only one of them simply calling and telling us not to bother showing up again. Those were mixed with calls from my family and finally more family. Towards the end of the messages we were getting calls from national media networks throughout the country, someone had managed to get our business information, not too hard to do with a simple web search and our newer websites. Only one struck us as odd.

The local hospital had called us, as well as the pediatrician on February 29th, 2012. The pediatrician's office called to let us know we had missed an appointment for Joshua, we never had one setup prior to fleeing for our lives. That same day on the caller ID the local hospital in Petoskey had also called, though they didn't leave a message.

With our added help from Sabrina's family and some help from Brandon, by Sunday morning the entire house, which was a ton of belongings, was all packed up and neatly stacked in the living room. The furniture was all that was left in the upstairs bedrooms. We gave away a bunch of stuff for Kathy to load into her truck and take with her, things we no longer needed. We were heading down to the Chicago area, Hammond, Indiana, to be exact, to stay with our friends for as long as we needed to. We wanted to be gone before Monday morning, so we would say our goodbyes on Sunday afternoon.

Out of the entire time that we were at the house that weekend, there were a couple of cars that drove by slowly. We could only expect people who were curious about whether or not we were back to drive by, it was a small town after all. However, there was one who stopped at the end of our driveway and stared, if looks could kill, I would have been dead. We took note of that one car, though at this point it would be impossible to prove if any spooks were still driving by. Late that afternoon we locked the door and got into the truck to head down to Hammond.

On the way down to the Chicago area, we noted that about every 45 minutes of driving, on the northbound lane of US 131, going to Grand Rapids, Michigan, there was a state trooper just sitting on the side of the road, a couple of them had their lights just flashing, most just sat there. Finally that evening we arrived in Whiting, Indiana, at Arnie's hot dog stand, our first stop.

As we pulled into the parking lot of Arnie's, we noticed that a Hammond police car had gotten behind us a short bit ago. He swung into the parking lot, looking at us and then drove off. We still continued to order our food at Arnie's wondering what, if anything, was going on. Calling PM we made arrangements to meet at his house. He was still at work, but we could go to his house and wait. Instead of doing so we decided to meet him at his job and there followed him back to his house.

We parked in the front of his house, he was on a corner lot, one side nothing but a rail yard and a field across the street. There he told us not to worry as the police never really came through this neighborhood. A moment later another Hammond police officer drove by, we took note. In the meantime, we unloaded the car to a room that was prepared for our family in their basement. PM and his wife told us that we were welcome to stay as long as we liked, they had hoped that we would move back down to that area, in fact, so did family who lived in the same vicinity.

After the whole ordeal in Escanaba we believed that God had in store for us to move to Kalispell, Montana. While we were in Escanaba, awaiting for Mr. O'Rourke to pick us up the next morning, we had looked at a bunch of towns to move to and Kalispell had been at the top of the list. We had never been there, but it seemed like a nice small town with a good economy. At the moment we were not set in our hearts where to go. Living in the Chicago region was good with the friends and family we had, but we simply didn't want to raise Joshua there. We both grew up in small towns and felt it was better than a major urban environment, despite the fact we would eventually look at an apartment right behind Arnie's in Whiting, Indiana. I would ponder a potential job offer in the area, but we just opted not to stay. We had already lived there, done that and had been happy to leave back in 2003. Sometimes places are great to visit, but once real life sets in, the honeymoon with the new city is over, you are no longer a tourist. The next day I would leave to head back to Michigan.

Our house was all packed up, on the office floor there was a gigantic pile of things we were going to throw away. We wouldn't need all of these business materials, we had too much stuff. There was still a storage unit full of our expensive camping gear, four guns and more ammo, as well as our hunting and fishing gear, game cart and a bunch of expensive clothing for everyone. All of this would have to be emptied out of that unit, boxed up at the house and left there to be moved by a professional moving company. Monday morning, one day after arriving in Hammond, I would go to a neighboring suburb in Illinois renting a black SUV that I would use for my trip back to Michigan. Our truck would no longer be seen in Michigan, it would be left in the front of our friend's home in Hammond.

Saying goodbye to Sabrina and Joshua, I took the trip up north. Around 10pm I would be back in Petoskey, several blocks from our old home. Parking my black SUV with Illinois plates and walking a few blocks, I entered the back door of the house. Now the lights would go on and I once again saw I had a ton of messages on our phone. They were all from the media, national networks, many from Los Angeles, Washington DC and New York City, wanting me to call them, they wanted our story. I had yet to realize that there was a problem with the phone that night. We had left only one phone hooked up, The Weekly Scoop line, though all of the phone service was still active at our house, the Aardvark Janitorial phone had been packed. With my laptop in hand, I opened up the computer and began to check my email, it hadn't been checked since we returned.

Reading through my email was a message from the clubhouse manager at Boyne USA, they wanted to know if we still wanted to do both of the golf clubhouses this year, they also knew of a larger insurance agency that wanted a cleaning estimate immediately, one of her friends. I thought about the boat, we hadn't breached their contract and all of our pooper scooper customers, the time to start would have been right then. I added up in my head the total amount of income that we still potentially had with the business, it was over $40k, plus some of our other customers might take us back, we had been well liked. Had we made the wrong decision in moving out of state? Our landlord had offered for us to stay, to go back to normal. Did we really have to leave Michigan now? With all of the media attention and an attorney, could these spooks really do anything?

My thought had been that they could and would use CPS against us. We were now enemies of the state, agencies had come after us, though we still had no concrete evidence, they could use their tools of repression and come up with some bogus charges from a CPS investigation to get their objective, us, one way or another. These bogus charges could end up with prison sentences for both of us. My pondering ceased in a moment, I had noticed the phone.

The caller ID on the phone was active. A phone call had been received that night around the time I got back to Petoskey, it was from 1-000-000-0000. I tried to go through the caller ID, but it wouldn't let me. Picking up the receiver on the phone, I had not a dial tone, but a strange tone. Around this time Brandon would arrive to meet up with me at my house. He had made arrangements for me to stay at someone's house for the next two nights, away from Petoskey. We both sat there looking at the phone.

Unplugging the phone and replugging it in, still the same, couldn't clear this number from the caller ID, same weird tone on the phone. To us that phone was hot, right there, it was a live tap, someone was using the monitoring feature that was built into the phone. This time I unplugged the phone and tossed it in the garbage pile that was there in our soon to be abandoned office. We were ready to go, we did not want to overstay our welcome. Brandon had no problems since we had come back and our street appeared to be quiet again. Walking a few blocks to where I was parked, we would head off to stay the night at this other persons house.

The next day both Brandon and I would meet up with Mr. O'Rourke again at the city of Petoskey police station. We both walked in and I signed to have the computers returned to me. The towers had been partially disassembled and left that way. We were told that we could wait a day or two and they would get someone to reassemble them. I didn't have time, we were ready to go, Mr. O'Rourke would be leaving to Hawaii soon. Taking the computers, I placed them in the back of Brandon's car, not wanting the police to know what I was driving. We left with no questions asked by any of the officers. After loading up the computers I thanked Mr. O'Rourke as he went to continue on with his daily tasks. Parking away from our old home we walked a short distance and waited inside.

That morning I had made an appointment with a professional moving company to give me an estimate. We needed to get all of our stuff loaded up and sent down to Chicago, we didn't want to give the police and federal agencies any heads up that we would not be returning. As I waited I had in my hand I had a receipt from a piece of registered mail that I needed to pick up. Staring out the front door and waiting we saw the city of Petoskey police drive by very slowly in front of our now old home, they looked over and in the front seat was a woman riding as passenger. It was CPS, they wouldn't stop though, our truck wasn't there. They didn't want to give us a heads up, we had been right, there would be trouble if we stayed, it wasn't an option. A few minutes later the scheduled estimator came by.

I accepted the estimate, it had been the only one I would receive and knew that I was going to pay whatever it would cost. I setup for our belongings to be delivered in Hammond, with no specific address, but one I would call them about. We would still have to get a storage unit to put all of these things in. They wouldn't be able to deliver our things for a couple of weeks, but a date was set for them to go in and load all of belongings out of the house. Handing the moving man a key, we shook hands. The deal was set, now I headed to check our post office box down the street and pick up that piece of registered mail.

As I waited in line holding this slip to pick up the mail, I wondered what it was. With my turn next in line I realized that unlike before where I would receive many packages from online orders, there were no orders waiting for me. Likely in my hand I held a court order regarding Joshua. At that moment I walked out the door, whatever it was I didn't need it. For the next six months as Brandon or my sister would check our mail box and send the mail to an undisclosed address, there would always be this slip in the box at least once per month, whoever this was, was persistent. Now we were ready to meet up with another person to go and empty out the storage unit.

Plans had been made, I would drive my rented black SUV, another would drive his truck and Brandon swapped cars with a friend, though they were nearly identical cars, it was a different plate not linking the car to him. We made sure this other person understood the risks, we didn't want someone else to get involved in our troubles. He didn't care, he was up for it. Late that afternoon we arrived at our storage unit up in the U.P. and worked quickly.

Brandon insisted that I bring the American flag from our home. He thought that it would be proper to leave it upside down in the storage facility, that way when they found it the 'patriot in distress' signal would be prominently displayed. I did so as we all quickly loaded everything up in separate vehicles; we did not want one person to have all of these things, though they weren't illegal, we didn't want additional trouble. In less than a half an hour, smoking a cigarette, we closed the door of the storage unit, leaving it swept and unlocked. From there we headed out and made our way back to highway US 2. A few miles on the highway, stuck in a line of traffic of seven vehicles, we, though partially separated with the traffic, were making our way back. There was a state trooper that was coming from the opposite direction, as soon as he passed by I glanced in the mirror, I saw brake lights being hit, he was turning around.

It took the officer a minute to turn around, there was too much traffic and now he was far in the distance in my mirror. A sharp curve was coming up on us. As we were now out of his view a side road was quickly coming up on the left. I gave a hand signal to the truck that was with us that I was going to turn off onto that road, he too had seen the trooper. Brandon a few cars back wouldn't even notice us turning off. Without hitting the brakes I went down the road, flooring the engine and hitting speeds of 100 mph. I would maintain this for a mile and then slow down to a stop a few miles up the road. There I would wait for my new found friend to arrive.

A minute or so later he pulled up behind me. He knew why we had taken this road and we wondered about Brandon. We were near a 'T' in the road and decided to head back towards the highway to see what was going on. As we neared the highway we saw a state trooper had a car like Brandon was driving and like the car he also normally drove pulled over. We thought it was him, but we would find out that behind Brandon was a car also like his. This is the car that would be pulled over, though Brandon would have another, separate, state trooper come up on him and follow him on the way back for quite some time. At that point we went back to the 'T' in the road and took the back way to get home.

Now all of our stuff from the storage unit was loaded into my black SUV and Brandon's borrowed car. We gave the helper the game cart and a few other items that were no longer needed. They had been of no use, the problem that finally did arise wasn't even one we planned for. Heading back to Petoskey around midnight, we watched from a distance to see if any activity was going on around our old home, nothing. From there we pulled directly into the driveway where we unloaded our backpacks, hunting and camping gear, clothing, guns and ammo, into our house, packing everything in boxes and leaving them in the kitchen. Nothing happened outside during that hour that we were there getting everything set, at least not that we noticed. From there we would head back to stay one last night at this friend's house, I would return the next day to the Chicago area.

As Brandon and I realized that it could be years before we would see each other again, we made a plan. The next morning we would pick up a couple of more cell phones and using different computers, we would once again register them with fake names and addresses. Now with both of us having a signal blocker bag, we would take and have a means of connection should there be a problem. Plus the one prepaid phone that Sabrina and I were using would be placed in that signal blocking bag, once we left the Chicago region. That morning we all sat there discussing what had happened when this undisclosed person, who had helped empty out the storage unit, mentioned that it looked like there was a manhunt on his way home on that previous Sunday.

He had traveled from Detroit back up north and on I-75 there had been state troopers every 45 minutes or so on the side of the northbound lane. There I remembered the same thing as we traveled towards Grand Rapids, on US 131, that same day. That couldn't really have anything to do with us? Could they have thought we were heading back from Chicago when we were really going down? Could God have confused their plans? There was no proof of anything, just something we pondered. Later that morning saying some final goodbyes, I got in the black SUV and began my descent back down to the Chicago area.

As I crossed the state line leaving Michigan and entering Indiana, anger hit me, I put my hand out the window with my middle finger up, hoping a camera near the border would take note, forget Michigan I hollered, I will never go back. Our long time home was gone, abandoned. For everything Michigan was, for the reasons we loved it, it was now gone. We would leave thankful to be safe, but angry that anything had even happened. Now as I was hitting the Gary, Indiana, area going towards Hammond, the cell phone rang.

On the other end a panicked Sabrina was on the phone. The neighbors had told our friends that the Hammond police department had a cruiser parked behind our truck for long enough to leave a puddle from their air conditioning on the street. They thought it had meant trouble. Our friend's neighbors knew nothing of us, except that we were some friends of theirs. Room was quickly made in our friend's garage to hide the truck. Now I began to wonder what was going on.

It would have been understandable to have some issues with the Hammond police department. If they had been looking for us in the area as missing persons, they perhaps didn't know that we had been 'found'. It would be reasonable to assume that Hammond police cruiser that drove by us in the parking lot of Arnie's called us in, as well as the one who drove by PM's house, but by now they should know we were not listed as missing persons anymore. The next day Sabrina and I would return the black rental SUV, renting another car right there, we were off to Kalispell, Montana.

A New Beginning

We arrived in Kalispell, Montana, a couple of day after leaving Hammond. We knew that Chuck Baldwin, a former presidential candidate and pastor, had moved out to the area starting a church. He was a leader of the patriotic movement and we thought that perhaps we would tell our story to him and see if he suggested that we go public with our story.

Attending his newly established church on a Sunday, we briefly met him and then were told of a meet-up at a restaurant later in the evening for anyone who wanted to attend. There, with a decent sized group of people, we told our story. The doors were closed to the meeting room. One of those who worked for Baldwin, as Baldwin personally did not attend these dinner meetings, wanted to setup a meeting with him and us. He gave us his phone number and told us to call to make arrangements. At this dinner meeting a woman forced a $20 bill into our hand. Those in attendance suggested we not even bother to risk getting our stuff, we disagreed. If God had allowed us to move our stuff out of the house we would have it delivered to Hammond and drive it out to Kalispell. One man in attendance asked us some weird questions, how to spell our last name, where we rented our rental car from and where we were staying. Not even yet aware of the FBI's vast network of informants, we became suspicious that this group of people were infiltrated.

Leaving the meeting we set off and made some arrangements to view apartments the next day. There were indeed jobs in Kalispell, quite a few compared to most places in the country. That night we would also be looking through the phone book at the things that were in the area. We thought about starting a pooper scooper service, wanted to see how many janitorial services were listed in the phone book, when we finally came across the government section.

Flipping through that section we noted that Kalispell also had an FBI office, as well as one for the Department of Homeland Security and the Customs and Border Protection, the later whose office was just a few miles north in Whitefish, Montana. Recalling those strange questions from this mysterious single man, who traveled back and forth to Seattle, Washington, we decided that Kalispell wasn't for us. We didn't want to escape our problem in Michigan, only to be in an area that we would eventually find out had so many federal agents working in it. Out of fear we left Kalispell and headed back to our friends in Hammond.

My family was now talking to us again. Now we would get details of what happened and Kelly would start to piece together how there were some troubling things during the investigation. She couldn't remember all of the questions that were asked or everything that was said, but the details she provided would only strengthen the fact that we were correct in our flight. She, as well as another family member, would call the city of Petoskey police department, demanding answers. The police department's explanation for the patrol car, late that night, was that someone had some prescription drugs taken from their mailbox earlier that day and they were following up on an investigation into that. That didn't explain their quick entry into our home or many other questions.

Now back at our friend's house in Hammond the police would still drive by, going slowly past our friends home. We noted an undercover cruiser also going by, even though we only had a short stay, there now appeared to be joggers every once in awhile that did not fit the neighborhood of upper lower class to lower middle class hardworking Americans. We didn't really know what happened in this neighborhood, with the exception of our friends who insisted it was a rarity to see the police, which were now common. We eventually took a second road trip after our belongings were delivered to our storage unit in Hammond.

Our road trip led us to explore the Branson, Missouri, area. With all of the online research I had did in the past few days at my friends house, we had decided to check that area out. Branson seemed like a nice area, though when we arrived it was still a bit of a ghost town, the shows were mostly still closed for the season. A tornado had also just ripped through and there was damage everywhere, yet it was being cleaned up. The economy in Branson was alright, how to find a year round job that was full time was a bit concerning, but it looked like a good town to raise a family. I spoke with a few people on how they felt a pooper scooper service would be received, they had positive comments to make about it. There was one thing that this portion of Missouri had and that was cheap rent.

We found a two bedroom apartment nearby in Kirbyville off of a dead end highway near the lake where we would rent an apartment, that even with electricity would only cost around $400 per month. The thunderstorms that would roll through, booming loudly, was just another great thing about this portion of the country. There we would take some time off, selling things on Ebay, using free Wifi hotspots to do so. We kept hidden out there, not being easily found. The only people who knew we moved there were our friends in Hammond and Brandon.

With Arkansas so close to Branson, Missouri, we ended up getting a box with a street address at a UPS store to receive and send mail. First we had tried to rent a post office box, but instead of being so easy to set one up, as we had in the past, there was now additional paperwork requirements. The postal clerk told us that due to a couple of bad apples they had many more restrictions and rules. This was part of the governments fight against terrorism. Were we one of those bad apples?

Selling stuff on Ebay seemed to work and we went to a swap meet a few times north of Branson in Springfield, Missouri. We had too much stuff, our rental U-Haul from Hammond had been overweight and caused trouble driving it down there. We didn't need all of these things, so we reduced a lot of stuff that we never used anyway. We did take note that MANY things we sold on Ebay were purchased in Michigan. Checking some of those addresses that these items would be shipped to, we would find that they were largely higher end homes that were all on the real estate market in downstate Michigan. It made no difference to us, if anyone was looking for us we led them to believe we were in Arkansas.

From Arkansas, we would call family on one of our cell phones. Kept in the signal blocking bag, when we entered Arkansas, we would remove it and call family once per week, seeing if any news had come in. On our other phone we would speak to Brandon, there was no problems that he noted, things seemed to be back to normal. We had opened up a bank account using our still Michigan driver's license, in Arkansas. Some checks had come in from refunds on insurance policies, our return deposit for our landlord, plus we needed an account to put our earnings from Ebay into. Before I left Michigan, I stopped one last time at our bank branch, the one that always asked for more information. There I cashed the paychecks from our business, everyone had paid the prior bill I sent out before we left. While at the bank they once again told me that Sabrina and I needed to give them our driver's licenses. I told them next time we came in we would, though I would never go back. After a few weeks of using this bank in Arkansas I would return to the teller line, the teller being the woman who opened our account.

She instantly recognized me and demanded a working phone number, they had tried to call. They demanded an Arkansas driver's license with an address on it, she was very rude compared to when I had opened the account. In fact, we told her right then that we did not live in Arkansas, but we were looking to stay in the area permanently, our decision had not yet been made. Reminding her of this, I gave her our old cell phone number. She still wanted us to get a driver's license in Arkansas. People can have bank accounts in multiple states, each bank is different, but there are a lot of people who will spend a good deal of time in one state and are part time residents or just long term travelers. We wouldn't go to this branch again.

As we would withdrawal our earnings from Ebay, going to other branches of this bank and there were several that we went to, no one would ever say anything to us about needing an Arkansas driver's license. We did begin to wonder if the Branson area was right for us. It was a beautiful area, people were nice, but with us already having a couple of signs of our trouble not being gone, shouldn't we be where we thought God wanted us?

Both of us took note when we moved into our apartment in Kirbyville of a older woman who rented the apartment next to us. She was outside reading the Bible when we first met her. After a brief introduction she stated how God had provided her both a job and that place in one day, that didn't just happened. She finalized with the fact that *"she lives where God tells her to live."* Given our circumstances and how we knew that God told us to go to Kalispell, but we instead went to Missouri, this was a comment that made us heavily consider our motives.

We moved into our apartment in Kirbyville in late April, by the beginning of June, after having sold many things, we would be giving a notice to the landlord, we would be heading to Kalispell. I had sent resumes to a few restaurants and two had already called me. We had already packed most of our remaining belongings in our apartment in Kirbyville. Even though our anticipated move date was just over a week away, I would get a phone call from a prospective employer in Kalispell, could I make it there in a few days for an interview?

We left the next morning as we had no obligations in Missouri, taking the back country highways with a mix of the interstate, we got to Kalispell a couple of days later in the evening. Eventually I would get a job with a restaurant group in the area, where I would become one of their general managers. We would get a janitorial service running that would eventually have me resigning my new career. We also learned we would have problems, problems that wouldn't go away.

Spooks

We rented a split house in Whitefish, Montana, just north of Kalispell. Downtown Whitefish was absolutely beautiful and we fell in love with the city once we saw it. From there my career took off and over time we would build up a janitorial service that would provide enough income, though not as large as what we had in Michigan. We would quickly realize that after relocating there and changing our registration and driver's license to Montana, using our real address, we had some new friends, or rather fiends, to contend with.

When we first relocated to Whitefish, we setup the camera system and would soon thereafter catch a local police officer at 6am, parking by the corner of our house and walking along the sidewalk in front of our house, turning back as he hit the end of our property line and returning to his patrol car. There would be a man with longer hair and cowboy boots, that we would eventually call Rico. He would walk by our house, get to about the neighbors fence line and turn around walking back past our house a few times per day. One day Sabrina was actually outside when he came by, instead of just reviewing this on camera, she saw him in person. He stopped at the end of our sidewalk, that went up towards the city sidewalk, glaring into the house through the open front door. Sure enough, he had a wire going up to his ear. After he realized he was caught, he soon thereafter would disappear, only to be seen by Brandon and his wife later that year after they would move to Whitefish.

As summer went on our problems became less and less, the events, cars pulling near our house late at night, an undercover patrol car that would travel by on the highway that was only a block from our home that rested on a corner lot, would become less frequent. Here we will recap some stories of problems that we had with the spooks.

That undercover patrol car would suddenly appear late one night at 3am, after I got home from work. We also had seen this same car late at night driving by our home or an adjacent street. On the highway that was visible from the front of our house, late at night we would see this undercover patrol car as frequently as every 20 minutes, but sometimes a week or so would go by without seeing him once. One night he was going by on the highway every 5 minutes, where we could view him from our home, so I decided to walk the block up to the highway to see who was in the car. As he approached where I was standing, suddenly a red light came on inside his car and he sped off. I had never heard of police vehicles using red lights and had never seen such a thing, but an internet search revealed that they had such things, its purpose would make it hard for someone to see into the car, but still allow the officer to see out. After that we only saw him one more time a few days later.

Brandon had been doing fine with no noted problems the entire summer of 2012, working at McDonald's in Indian River. He hadn't been staying at his home in Topinabee very often as his car had been broken down for quite some time. During that time he was seeing a woman, who would in the near future become his wife. Staying at a friend's house out by her parent's house, he would often get a ride to that house after work from her. Finally his car got fixed, all of the work that was slowly getting done by a friend was complete. Now he began to drive his own car again and would once again spend the nights, oftentimes walking around Topinabee.

Topinabee is a nice small town, here Brandon enjoyed owning the town at night, walking for a bit, the peace and quiet in this sleepy little community. He had done this for years and on a rare occasion had been stopped by the police to make sure he was not doing anything criminal. This time things were different.

In the beginning of September, in 2012, Brandon began to have issues, quite a lot like we had prior to fleeing for our lives. Late one night as I was on the phone with him and he was outside his house standing in the light rain, he noticed a van parked not too far away by the empty lot on the side of the road that he lived on. As we spoke, he walked towards the van, out of the shadows a man would appear as he approached, the man entered the van and drove off before he could get a plate number. This gray van would now be seen more frequently in his neighborhood, once even parked on the side of his grandparents property, in front of their home. Finally one day as he just parked in front of his grandparents house he saw the van go by.

His car was once again getting a bit more work done to it, he was borrowing his future wife's brand new car to get back and forth to work. With the car still running from having just arrived, he threw it into drive and began to follow the van. The van took off at a high rate of speed and he pursued. Eventually the speed of the van taking corners was beyond his driving skills and he lost them. Then he gave me a phone call, as it was late at night and I was usually still awake. As I calmed him down on the phone, he pulled into the driveway and got out of the car.

A couple of minutes later a red car would drive by his home slowly. As the car drove by he noted the usual police mounted laptop in the car, a male driver was in this unmarked car. Still standing by his soon to be wife's car, he watched as it turned around heading back towards his house, he hopped in the car. He was furious, what did these people want? I told him not to break any laws, follow the speed limit, this could be a trap, you can not be driving 90 mph on the highway, it is a misdemeanor in Michigan to do so, one that could include jail time!

He agreed and followed at a normal rate of speed, this undercover agent did not speed off as the van did. Finally the red car pulled over on the side of the road, turning onto the beginning of a dirt road and parking. Brandon was afraid to go up behind him, so he drove by slowly. As he went by he saw the man snap a picture of the license plate or back of the car, the flash being seen, as it was night. Now they had him driving his soon to be wife's car. Within a week, this same red car and grey van would be seen in the McDonald's parking lot late at night. They would always drive off if he tried to approach them.

His soon to be wife lived in Onaway, just a few miles east of Indian River. There he would often spend many times talking to her outside late at night. Now the red car would be spotted a couple of times, once pulling into her driveway in the middle of the night and once hiding up the road from her house. Also the gray van was spotted once in the same area. Brandon was concerned, but he was also ready to propose.

His proposal included the warning, *"if you marry me, you marry a terrorist,"* she would say yes and understand that, though he was innocent, she would likely become entangled, if she hadn't already. Not knowing where these problems were going to lead they both decided that after their early October wedding, just a few weeks after he proposed, that they would move with haste. Due to the uncertain situation, they were going to relocate to Whitefish.

We had an extra bedroom in Whitefish, the street level of the house that we rented had three bedrooms, one we didn't even use. In mid-October, they would relocate, taking what they could in their car out to Montana. Soon thereafter they would both have jobs and begin work. Their arrival included a temporary flare up of trouble.

In the meantime Kathy had some trouble flaring up from time to time. While we were living in Missouri, our location only know to PM and his wife, plus Brandon, she was having cars with tinted out windows or SUV's drive by and also park across the street in the parking lot, with the windshields of their vehicles facing her house. They would sit there sometimes the entire day. For her this would happen quite a bit soon after we left Michigan and then happen less and less frequently. Even after we moved out to Montana, around holidays and if she had to bring a loaner car because her work vehicle was getting maintenance done at the shop, then they would suddenly appear again. Finally one day she took action.

She walked across the street away from the SUV, as if she was going to a store. Suddenly she came up on the SUV and knocked on the tinted window. As the window was lowered, there appeared a man sitting in the driver's seat. She hollered at the man asking what the #$%! he was doing watching her house. He looked at her and simply replied, *"you need a doctor."* She then told him if he didn't leave she was going to call 911. She walked back home and looked at the SUV, the engine started up and he left. For nearly six months afterwards, not one vehicle parked in this unused portion of the gravel parking lot. Even the employees at the local market had spoke to her one day, wondering why people were parking back there. Finally they began to appear again, once in awhile. When we were briefly out of the country, they were there again. As of August, 2015 once again these spooks have appeared two times. Now in late 2016 they have not been noted in over a year.

We had a video camera keeping a careful eye out, though by now we never watched the footage, unless we actually noted something. Most days if anyone did drive by, we wouldn't know amongst the traffic, we didn't see something too often by the fall of 2012, only every few weeks. The night after Brandon and his wife arrived we would suddenly have late night joggers going by on the street, the same people around 1am and then 2am. They would jog by once more the following night, but after that we never saw them again. A car the next day, a white normal looking car, would drive by every 15 minutes for hours and hours in front of our house, that we didn't catch happening with the normal traffic, but caught it reviewing the video camera footage later that evening. We were all sick and tired of this, what was now seemingly harassment.

At that time we decided to fully educate ourselves about Freedom of Information Act (FOIA) requests. We began to file some requests off to various federal agencies, the city of Petoskey police department, the Michigan State Police, as well as other various law enforcement agencies where we had lived or where they may have used the local police to locate us as we were reported missing.

FOIA's take a long time to go back and forth. The city of Petoskey would give us some things and upon a second request would give us more. We noted that several exemptions were cited against giving us all of our file. One of those exemptions was that they were not the holders of those records. We would learn, that even if a local police agency was involved in a federal operation, they would only be responsible by law to give out so much information, the rest, would have to be done through the requesting federal or state agency that had asked the city of Petoskey to assist them. This proved to be a problem.

We did, however, learn a few things from the bits and pieces now coming in. The city of Petoskey police department had worked with the Department of Homeland Security while supposedly involved in a missing persons case, where they publicly stated that they believed we left on our own accord! The Customs and Border Protection had been involved, a thing call RISSNET had also been utilized in trying to find us, with the MAGOCLEN division of the Great Lakes region. We hadn't even heard of them, but after looking them up realized that it might have been RISSNET that worked on searching our hard drives, thus the real reason our computers weren't available right away when we returned to Petoskey. This RISSNET would also take and provide loans to law enforcement agencies, including high tech equipment used to surveil and try to gather evidence against suspects. We would also learn from my Michigan State Police request, that there was several exemptions given to me, one reason listed was my FBI #.

The FBI proved to respond fairly quickly. As I read the letter, it stated that they had searched their records and no record was found. They were lying! How could they get away with that, then I reread the letter, printed on it was the following:

"For your information, Congress excluded three discrete categories of law enforcement and national security records from the requirements of the FOIA. See 5 U.S.C. 552(c) (2006 & Supp. IV (2010)). This response is limited to those records that are subject to the requirements of the FOIA. This is a standard notification that is given to all our requesters and should not be taken as an indication that excluded records do, or do not, exist."

Researching this paragraph found at the bottom of the FOIA response from the FBI, we learned that it was a Glomar response. Soon thereafter we would find that other Americans who were politically active would receive the same sort of responses. The idea was simple, if someone was under federal investigation or indictment and they wanted to know, they could simply file an FOIA on themselves and find out what that federal agency knew about them. They could then use this information to change their plans for their criminal activities and know what things to do to try to avoid getting caught. There is logic in having such laws, but in our case, it was simply being used as a tool to further their political repression against us, we were no longer politically active at all, we hadn't been for a couple of years prior to them coming after us, aside from me writing for Brandon's website.

Months were going on as we began to expand the amount of FOIA's that we were filing, sometimes getting a bit of information, other times not. Out of the many federal agencies that we filed with, we would end up getting many Glomar responses, apparently the United States Secret Service was one that I truly didn't have a record with. For Sabrina we only filed a few. In the end I had received the following Glomar responses:

Federal Bureau of Investigation (FBI)
United States Marshal Service
Transportation Security Administration (TSA)
Department of Homeland Security (DHS)
Drug Enforcement Agency (DEA)
Financial Crimes Enforcement Network (FinCen)
Immigration and Customs Enforcement (ICE)
Central Intelligence Agency (CIA)

The Glomar response from the US Marshal Service was creepy and Brandon would likewise receive the same response. Their duties, aside from the Witness Protection Program and prisoner management, is to pursue wanted criminals. Their job is to locate a fugitive and arrest them, so why would we even have a Glomar response with them? We would follow up with some of these federal agencies and further pursue them, usually getting the same response.

For instance, with DHS, we finally got through using the Office of Intelligence & Analysis, then they would also give us a Glomar response, both Brandon and myself. Many times we received back letters from DHS telling us that we needed to provide more information to properly perform a search, including what agents we thought were involved, the dates, the sub department and even why we thought such a file might exist. Finally, frustrated, we both sent out a letter demanding some information, giving some time frames and refusing, citing our Fifth Amendment rights, to not suggest why we might have a file, then came the Glomar response. Other federal agencies would send information that we had files, but they would not release them and cited exemptions, some of these were the same ones listed above, replying on appeals we had filed.

TSA would eventually send me a copy of my TWIC card application, but the comment section on the bottom, the purpose for which I had filed as I wanted to know the reason for my instant denial, would be exempted. An appeal would be filed, they would acknowledge receiving it and notify me when they made their decision, we are still waiting.

Brandon would file with the Bureau of Alcohol, Tobacco and Firearms (BATF) as he only had a small situation that would have suggested that he had trouble before our whole situation ever happened. While purchasing a handgun in Indian River in 2009, his name was flagged, three days later he would go back and pick up the gun, this happened twice that year. He was also the campaign manager in Cheboygan county for Linda's next attempt to take the U.S. Representative job around the same time of these temporary denials. When the BATF replied they gave him a negative response, citing insufficient information, but told him he could appeal their decision within so many days. The date on the letter, though the envelope was just postmarked, made it already too late to file an appeal. We would both file with BATF now, as usual certifying the letters through the USPS. They never responded to either of us, were still waiting on that nearly two years later.

When Brandon had moved out to Montana and we began to file FOIA's, him and his wife kept their Michigan license plate and driver's license for a bit. They needed to find jobs and get secure here, if not, they would return to Michigan. To Brandon it seemed right to throw a bone to DHS by mailing his FOIA request to his grandmother and have her send it out, certified. He did so with all of his FOIA's at first and his DHS response, unlike the several pieces of mail I received from them, his came back registered mail through the postal system. Being a small town like Topinabee, where everyone knows everyone, his grandmother was able to sign for him, going against their intended purpose. Brandon's Michigan State Police FOIA response came in an official state envelope, the letter completely crumpled. His grandparents couldn't even believe seeing that as his grandfather scanned it and sent it to his secure email address. Something similar would happen to both of us.

In the fall of 2013, we decided to just see if the DEA had a file on either of us. We hadn't filed with them, but now we were running out of agencies. Both of ours would come to Whitefish, Montana, where we had a residential street address we used for all mail through a local UPS store. Here we would get them, both registered mail and a Glomar response. Apparently this agency had used these FOIA requests to actually learn where we were at or at least prove we were in the area. Montana has a very strict laws regarding privacy on individuals and their driver's license information. In fact, they allow under that law to use even a regular post office box as the listed address on your driver's license. A warrant for someone to get an individual's information is needed in nearly every case.

In the meantime, we at the time are still calling attorney Mr. O'Rourke occasionally and he begins to try and find out if any search warrants for information have ever been put on Brandon's former Verizon account. We remembered that someone had answered the phone and replied to a text message when PM found out we were missing. After several attempts, Verizon never responded to Mr. O'Rourke. In the end we had some information but couldn't get anyone to hand us our files. We finally in the late winter of early 2013 visited with an attorney in Kalispell.

This attorney is a well known political activist. We arranged a meeting with him via phone and he agreed to speak with us, to see if he could help or what could be done. As we walked into his office in Kalispell we noted a man was sitting in the parking lot across the street, with his passenger window down, in an SUV. We kept with the assumption that he might have been on break from a local business and eating lunch, walking inside the attorney's office. There we spoke briefly of why we were out in Montana, showed him some of the paperwork that we had and then awaited his advice, we only had a total of an hour paid for, though he wouldn't charge us as the meeting ended going over. He explained the trouble with trying to go after the government for harassment. He had a case that he had been working on for some time and one that he took over from another attorney. This case was a simple freedom of speech violation against the Kalispell Police Department and even that had yet to be resolved. He also told us that we would need to hire a full time attorney to work on our case. Finally he warned us about the results if we hired an attorney, which we couldn't afford anyway.

That attorney might get some more paperwork, perhaps enough that a lawsuit could be filed. However, proving harassment wasn't enough. We would have to prove malice on the part of the government. We would have to prove it was due to political actions we had taken. The reason was simple, if someone at some point called DHS, the FBI or anyone else that started an investigation about us, these agencies were allowed to do so. Here we would add a few notes from research. Generally the FBI does have some practices for civil rights protection. Most investigation are ended within six months, some will continue, with approval, for up to a year. At that point a supervisor will decide whether or not to extend it. There are some checks and balance left, though not always, it is a case by case basis. What would happen after our meeting with the attorney the next night is the most noteworthy problem we ever had while living in Montana.

Around midnight we were back from work and inside our home, I realized that I had forgotten to put the business keys in the center console of the truck. Walking outside, I hit the button on the key ring, unlocking the doors and began to put the keys in the truck. I could hear an engine racing towards me from downtown, off the same street we lived on. At this point I stood next to a tree in our front yard. This car turned the corner, heading down the hill, at a crawl. I walked up near the street corner, just enough to peak over and see where he went, there I saw him whipping a u-turn and heading back up the hill. I ran inside and got Sabrina. We watched as he pulled up to the side of the crossroad, just past the intersection outside our home. There he sat with no headlights on. At this point I knocked on Brandon and his wife's door and grabbed a video camera.

The car then went driving through an alley coming back out onto the street a minute later. He would continue driving. As we went back inside we looked out the window and saw he had come back. He was sitting in the back lot of a neighboring business that had a direct view of our place. We stepped outside with a video camera now hidden in my hand. He then opened his door and got out, walked about 30 feet towards us and stood next to a very large tree. For nearly a half an hour all of us stared at each other, now being late at night. A pickup truck with a topper began to drive around our home a few times, a newer truck in good condition. Finally, as Sabrina was holding Joshua, I hollered aloud in the nighttime neighborhood towards him. *"Leave us alone! You are wasting your money on us, we haven't done anything!!!"* He stood, gave no response, and then a few minutes later walked back and got in his car. He sat in his car for a few minutes, finally he pulled out of the parking lot towards us. As he turned and went past the front of our house, Brandon and I quickly sprang up to the sidewalk to try and get the plate number, too late, he was gone.

At that moment, with it now even later at night, two joggers appeared at the very second we took off to grab a plate number, looking our way they now headed towards downtown. We are not in good running shape, but they took off running and we tried to keep up. As they ran towards downtown, now quite a distance ahead of us, a different vehicle stopped and picked them up, they were gone. Now that same truck that had already drove by a couple of times would come by again. In another half an hour this same car that had started the situation would pull behind this business again and sit, this time for just a few minutes, never getting out. At this point I had called the phone number of a friend, someone I rarely spoke with, about what was going on. He was prepared to come by or make arrangements to get us out of there, if need be. It was then that Sabrina noticed a weird red light coming from the office building upper entry windows adjacent to us.

We pondered what the source of this red light was, as we were well aware of our surrounding in our neighborhood. Walking up towards it we were shocked to see the red infrared of a camera that was pointing at our home. We sat up for another hour and nothing else happened. Having to work in the morning, we all finally went to sleep. In the morning the camera facing our home was once again gone, never to appear the remainder of the time we lived there.

This same car would then drive by at night, sometimes creeping around with their headlights off, three more times that we noticed. Once was when we had gotten back from a small trip to Seattle, Washington, the whole group of us. With each separate event he would either sit in his car on the side of the street or park in that back parking lot again, for just a minute and then he wouldn't be seen again that night. We took the original problem with this man as a direct response for inquiring to try and file a lawsuit against the federal government. Either they were trying to push us into a crime, thinking that we would turn violent, as there were others driving around and those two joggers hiding in the alley or it was simply a warning caused from the attorney's visit the day before. For awhile after that, we did back off of the FOIA's, but we began to try once more.

Late January 2013, as our janitorial business picked up a large client, we are working frequently after I get home from my regular job. This new customer was a Monday thru Friday customer. After a month into providing our service for them, we start to notice late at night, slow vehicles driving by or a car with their headlights off, on the side of the road with a direct view of our truck. One truck that stood out going slow was a Dodge Ram, red, extended cab, newer truck. As our work was around on hospital property, we would drive to a parking lot up the road that could be seen from the highway after working at night to have a cigarette, due to the no tobacco policy enforced on the campus. Standing outside our truck one night in this parking lot, Sabrina notices a red truck parked on the side of a street, just across the highway facing us.

This truck which is facing our direction has no headlights on. Instead of lighting our cigarettes we hop back into the truck, which is still running with Joshua in the back, on our way to go to check it out. As we begin to pull up to the intersection the truck is already racing off, having turned onto the highway. I floor the F-150, following closely. As we come up to Reserve Loop, he suddenly takes a left going down it. We continue on the highway, just a bit, to a shopping center parking lot, turn in and slowly work our way out to the same road he went down. We don't see him at the moment, but as we are finishing the loop we see brake lights up ahead. Sure enough it is that same Dodge Ram, stuck at the traffic light on the other end of the loop.

We get up behind him, just as the light turns green, then he once again roars his engine, I follow the lead. Trying to not speed at all, he ends up getting a ways ahead of me, I'm pushing the limit, nearing 70 mph. When we arrive in Whitefish a few minutes later, with him now a half a mile ahead of me, he pulls off into a grocery store parking lot up ahead. Before we can follow, he is already heading back racing towards Kalispell. Quickly I turn around in another lot and begin to continue to pursue him. He then turns on a highway heading towards Colombia Falls, a small town in the area to the east of Kalispell, we follow him on his way there. Finally he pulls into a bar on the corner in town, a busy place, we keep going straight. About a mile ahead we pull into another grocery store parking lot, completely out of sight, waiting for him to go by. After around five minutes and finally smoking that cigarette we had intended nearly a half an hour prior, we head back. Noticing his truck is still there and not wanting to go into the bar, we continue. Just as we are driving past on the highway, back towards Whitefish, we see his truck slam into reverse and he rips out of the parking lot, heading towards Kalispell on another highway. We head home, giving up.

The next night, as caught on our truck dash cam, several police officers would be driving around the streets adjacent to the building we were working at with their headlights off. One of those police cruisers would crawl in, parking at the far end of the employee parking lot and walk towards our truck. We only had one view on camera and he was out of that view for a minute or so, then he walked back to his car and proceeded to meet up with the other officers driving back and forth with no headlights. All of them proceeded to leave. Had they been looking for a camera? Did a federal agency send them? We don't know.

There are more examples, though less extreme that we could give, the scope given here was the fact that all of us would experience problems, aside when first moving to Whitefish, at least every six weeks. Even with our dash cam hidden away in our pickup truck, carefully watching as our work schedule would eventually be exclusively our business work only, we would only notice things once in awhile. People do strange things while driving, we know that; and people do things on occasion that could be seemed as strange to someone else, especially driving around late at night. There were those times that the likelihood of it being a federal agent was very high. We kept mental notes and would rate the incidences as either slight, moderate or high. A slight problem with a vehicle, as federal agents never seem to use the same one after they were noticed, would become a moderate problem when that same vehicle once again did something odd, even if it were weeks after. Then if that same vehicle would become a problem once more, we might, if the opportunity arose, follow it at a distance. Certainly we didn't want to follow to closely, in case it was just some innocent person driving by, the Dodge Ram had already been seen, so we pursued that vehicle to try and get the plate number, but when a vehicle final hit the level that warranted more investigation and the rare opportunity that we were already all loaded up in our truck with Joshua, ready to go, then we would follow. In every instance of doing so, that vehicle would disappear on side streets or go around in circles in town until we couldn't find them. Once we read that the FBI were called 'wheel artists' and if we were to give them credit for anything, it would be that, there driving skills are superb! I have a few hundred thousand miles driving in all different areas of the country, with only a few very minor fender benders, but their driving skills far exceeded mine. They would just disappear!

Another noteworthy event will be mentioned about Brandon. Not too long after Brandon and his wife moved out to Whitefish, after returned home from work late one night, when Sabrina and I were gone, they had noticed something odd. A man went walking down the street and walked to the front of their car that was parked in front of our next door neighbor's house where a parking spot was still available, he then proceeded back. They followed him from around a block away, he went into a local downtown bar. They also went in and couldn't find him, though there was a back door that led to a parking lot. They did see a man who sat near the bar, who may have had some hair pulled up under his hat, but they just didn't know. As they described this man with longer hair, cowboy boots, his height, dress and even the way he walked, which was distinctive, it was who we called Rico, somebody we hadn't seen for a couple of months. The last time I had seen him was in August of that year, 2012. I also had followed him from a distance, where he also went into a casino bar. Out he came with a man who was holding a camera with a very expensive zoom lens, far more expensive then even a nice Canon digital camera. Later than night he walked one final time towards our house, I glanced over and saw him, he made a quick turn going down the side street and back up the alley towards downtown once again. I went and tried to follow him a minute later, after letting Sabrina know, but he was gone.

One other story that absolutely must be discussed is the phone call that my sister originally received. Numerous hours were spent on trying to discover who was behind this. We paid for some online premium phone number information, but could never figure it out. We did find that the company who owned that phone number had contracts with federal agencies, providing emergency guaranteed phone service that would allow them to have several different backups to keep their phone system up and running during a national emergency. Finally my sister, Kelly, hired a private investigator.

The investigator started his search. That last name given on the caller ID didn't have anyone in the area with that name. There were no listed private investigators there either, which is a state requirement to get a license for such services in Michigan. After the investigator research ended with no answers, he could only guess that perhaps it was a collection agency. He didn't know. After the investigation that phone number did not work for a few days. Finally it worked again.

Doing some very deep searching on the internet I found a total of 8 phone numbers that had similar complaints. All of them had people complaining about someone asking for them, calling their parents or even their job or someone on the line asking them about a relative or someone else they knew. The ironic thing here was every single person who answered the phone refused to give them any information. They all found it odd and had all called back, getting the same mysterious message. Until around six months ago {Editors Note: Mid 2015}, the phone number that called us never once had anything that could be found about it, finally I found the number simply listed by an anonymous person online, stating the caller ID information, now the phone number no longer works at all. Brandon and I decided one night to give all of these 8 phone numbers a call. Would someone answer, was there a key that could be pressed on the pad to get to a directory?

Most of these phone numbers had a woman's voice, but two of them had a man's. These numbers were all from different areas around the country and all said the same thing, that this investigative agency does not accept voicemail. After we called them all to no avail, we gave it up. The next night we decided to try one more time, perhaps the pound key would get us to a menu? All of the phone numbers that had the woman's voice no longer worked, they had a busy type noise. The two with the man's voice still worked. Had we actually caused an agency of the government to shut down part of their phone system? Now I would hire a private investigator.

This private investigator went and looked at the phone number that originally called my sister. What he knew for sure was that it was a VOIP number. This private investigator would also tell me that he thought it was a trap line. I had never heard of such a thing and looked it up online. A trap line is a phone number that an investigator uses to try and contact someone they are trying to find. Trap lines used in federal investigations will likely have a pen register on whoever they call. The assumption is that once the person they call, in order to try and find who they are looking for, hangs up, regardless of information given to the agent or not, they will likely call the person that the agency is looking for, thus getting their phone number and therefore location. In the case with my sister they had called her home phone, but she texted me from her cell phone, this would defeat the purpose of a trap line. The owner of the phone number would never be found out, despite our efforts.

We eventually got fed up with all of the harassment. Though it would only happen once in awhile, in late 2013, we decided to prepare and leave the country. Having given up on getting more information, having tried every avenue we could think of with FOIA's, having worked with two separate attorneys about the whole ordeal, we were over it. There seemed no recourse and we couldn't understand why the FBI and whoever else was involved, which now was at least DHS, ICE and the CBP, wouldn't close the case. They apparently had nothing on us, why wouldn't it be let go? With that we began to sell everything we owned, everything; months later in March of 2014, we would take our bags, rent a car and go, way south, to Panama.

Tropical Paradise

For the exact reason that we know we are not the only people with these sorts of problems, though ours is unique in many ways, we will not detail our trip to Panama. We did, however, cross over into Mexico through Tijuana.

Once in Tijuana we stayed at the hotel Ticuan, overlooking the downtown area. Here amongst the graffiti and poverty, in comparison to the United States, we were actually happy. A great weight had been lifted off our shoulders as we took and sat there. We would be there for a couple of days, eventually arriving in Panama.

Panama was a great place, a tropical paradise. They had a program where we were in the process of forming a corporation, starting a web advertising business based on bringing expats and local Panamanian business owners together, living in the city of David.

This hot city was remarkable. Full of life and modern amenities, we quickly fell in love with it. We had been very careful not to reveal our plans to federal law enforcement agencies about leaving the United States, many times a political activist has purchased a plane or bus ticket ahead of time and found themselves charged with domestic terrorism, before they even were near boarding. We won't go into all details here, but all of those tickets are run through government databases that screen the passengers prior. Here in Panama, we no longer had to look out, we could live.

We found a nice rental house in a great community, just on the edge of David, looking towards the mountains heading up towards Dolega, eventually Boquette. Here we furnished this house, a three bedroom, two bath for only $375 per month and bought a 2012 Hyundai Accent off another expat living there. People were friendly and we quickly made ourselves a few friends.

Opening up a bank account did prove much more difficult than opening up one in the United States, but we eventually found a bank that accepted the letters of references that we had and quickly got us an account opened. This had taken a lot longer than we thought. In December of 2013, we both got our FBI fingerprinted background check. We needed a certified copy to apply for citizenship, under an economic incentive of starting a business. That background check had to be clean, our records came back fine. We assumed, the FBI if anything, would consider that we were just trying to get more information, as I filed more than once trying to get a copy of my file. The problem was that Panama would only recognize that document from the FBI for five months, then a new one would have to be received, which took at least two months in Panama. On April 15th of 2014, a bank account was finally opened. The other bank that I had secretly worked with in Panama, before arriving, and thought to have had everything all setup, had denied my account for no reason.

With laws that have been passed by Congress, the secrecy in banking that Panama was so well known for, like the Swiss accounts, had been broken. All accounts from US citizens would have to be reported to Uncle Sam. This required a great amount of extra paperwork on behalf of the banks to file all of the necessary forms. Some banks stopped excepting Americans, other closed their accounts, but all made in much harder to get an account. Prior to 2011, getting a bank account in Panama would have been as simple as opening up an account in the United States.

We had until May 10th to get our proof of funds to the attorney from the bank and THEN have the attorney get it to the government migration agency for approval. As long as the funds were there, we had everything else set to go. Our attorney was waiting on us. Right after opening the account we began the process of wiring money. It turned out to be three separate wires, we both had to have our own proof of funds in our own accounts. With the leftover money that we had saved from our business in Michigan, the sale of every asset we had, turning in and selling all of our bullion collection, as well as that emergency camping gear we still had while living in Whitefish and finally our truck, we comfortably had a good solid year to get our new business to earn enough money to make it down there. By then we would be issued partial citizenship and allowed to stay permanently. We had received a one year visa issued by Panama. In order to be successful we would have to earn a minimum of $1,200 per month, with $1,400 being the goal. With that, we could work, play and just enjoy all of these new things, while continuing to learn Spanish. We knew it was risky, but we took the risk.

We were told that we might have to wait up to a week for the funds to arrive in our bank accounts. A week went by and nothing, finally we hit the very end of April and our concern is growing. What was going on? We took and contacted both the sending and receiving bank, an intermediary bank was also being used, something we had no control over, now we found the wires were being held up at Bank of America. Bank of America was the intermediary bank that we had to use. They refused to respond to our bank in Whitefish. That bank representative would tell us that this was the hardest wire she had ever seen in her life. This representative had worked for the banking industry for quite some time. On the Panama end, all we ever found out was there was some sort of investigation. In the meantime I did some deep searching on the internet.

I found two separate stories of Americans, both politically active, who had similar problems. Their money eventually just showed up, but in both of those cases it was the bank who had told them to check with the United States Treasury, Office of Foreign Asset Control (OFAC). Bank representatives are not supposed to tell the customer if there money is being held up by a request from a federal agency or if they are under investigation. Finally three business days prior to the deadline of needing an application for citizenship accepted, some of the money landed in my account. It would be towards the end of May before the other wires would end back up at the original bank they were sent from. Bank of America refused to send those other wires to Panama, they appeared back in our bank account with no explanation given, never once having responded to the endless requests from the bank in Whitefish about our wires. It seemed we couldn't get away after all, our tropical paradise gone.

We managed to get back into the United States, once again through Tijuana. As we walked through, wondering if they would question us, we had hired a local man who was carrying a lot of our bags on his dolly, but the Customs and Border Protection didn't say anything, aside from asking where we were coming from. They didn't even ask if we had anything to declare. We walked out of their border patrol building to where we had arranged for a ride to meet us and headed back to Montana. We relocated to a place in the same area, quickly I had work lined up and we purchased enough to furnish our house and go on with our lives. We would just have to deal with the harassment. In the process of it all, the decision to write this book was made. It was a very hard choice, one that we went back and forth on, but the feeling was that the world should know the truth.

"Set apart Your wonderful lovingkindness, O You who by Your right hand saves those who trust in You, from those who rise up against me." Psalms 17:7

God's Just Judgment

"For whom the Lord loves He disciplines, and whips every son whom He receives." *Hebrews 12:6*

"My son, do not reject the chastening of Jehovah, and do not loathe His correction; for whom Jehovah loves He corrects, even as a father corrects the son with whom he is pleased." Proverbs 3:11-12

Without the chastening of the Lord, I don't believe that our story would ever have had the necessity of being told. The belief is that I was on the watchlists, noted by some in Washington DC, plus some investigative interest by the Michigan State Police, but without the Lord allowing chastising, my family would never have been one of the few that have been targeted, as of the moment. A Believer, a true Christian, can not go on living a life that is contrary to following Jesus Christ and expect to not have consequences for their backslidden and carnal state.

Likewise the world can not continue on living as if there is no Creator and no consequences for their rebellion and sin. While Believers are not without sin, continuing with a refusal to repent will lead to consequences from the Most High, if the offender is truly Saved. God has provided the Way of Salvation through repentance and believing into His Son, Jesus Christ. He has been patient with mankind, not wanting any to perish, but He was never going to tarry forever. Understand that this is primarily written for those who have been Left Behind and now find themselves in the midst of the Tribulation.

"Do not be led astray, God is not mocked; for whatever a man sows, that he will also reap. For he who sows to his flesh will of the flesh reap corruption, but he who sows to the Spirit will of the Spirit reap eternal life." Galatians 6:7-8

"If we confess our sins, He is faithful and just to forgive us our sins and to cleanse us from all unrighteousness." 1st John 1:9

"Jesus said to him, I am the Way, the Truth, and the Life. No one comes to the Father except through Me." John 14:6

..."testifying both to Jews, and also to Greeks, repentance toward God and faith toward our Lord Jesus Christ." Acts 20:21*

"Truly, these times of ignorance God overlooked, but now commands all men everywhere to repent, because He has established a day on which He will judge the world in righteousness by the Man whom He has appointed. He has given assurance of this to everyone by raising Him from the dead." Acts 17:30-31

"For everyone, whoever calls on the name of the Lord shall be saved." Romans 10:13

"But, beloved, do not be unaware of this one thing, that with the Lord one day is as a thousand years, and a thousand years as one day. The Lord is not slow concerning His promise, as some count slowness, but is longsuffering toward us, not purposing that any should perish but that all should come to repentance." 2nd Peter 3:8-9

Jesus described these days as the days of Noah. Indeed by all appearance we appear to be right about there as it is nearly 2017, but this is being written for those who were Left Behind and are now living in the "time of Jacob's trouble" (Jer. 30:7).

"But as the days of Noah were, so also will the coming of the Son of Man be. For as in the days before the flood, they were eating and drinking, marrying and giving in marriage, until the day that Noah entered into the ark, and did not realize until the flood came and took them all away, so also will the coming of the Son of Man be. " Matthew 24:37-39

"And as it was in the days of Noah, so it will be also in the days of the Son of Man: They ate, they drank, they married wives, they were given in marriage, until the day that Noah entered into the ark, and the flood came and destroyed them all. Likewise as it was also in the days of Lot: They ate, they drank, they bought, they sold, they planted, they built; but on the day that Lot went out of Sodom it rained fire and brimstone from heaven and destroyed them all. Even in the same way will it be in the day when the Son of Man is revealed." Luke 17:26-30

"There were giants on the earth in those days. And also afterward, when the sons of God came in to the daughters of men and they bore children to them, these were the mighty men from antiquity, men of renown. And Jehovah saw that the evil of man was great on the earth, and that every imagination of the thoughts of his heart was only evil all day long. And Jehovah regretted that He had made man on the earth, and He was grieved to His heart. And Jehovah said, I will obliterate man whom I have created from off the face of the earth, both man and beast, creeping thing and flying creatures of the heavens, for I regret having made them." Genesis 6:4-7

"I tell you that He will avenge them speedily. Nevertheless, when the Son of Man comes, will He find faith on the earth?" Luke 18:8

What will man's opinion be of God Almighty? Will those of the world consider and think that His judgment is righteous and just? For one we know that multitudes are Saved during this current time period, but the Holy Scriptures also tell us of another group of people, who despite God's just judgment, refuse to repent of their wickedness.

"After these things I looked, and behold, a great multitude which no one was able to number, of all nations, tribes, peoples, and tongues, standing before the throne and before the Lamb, clothed with white robes, with palm branches in their hands, and crying out with a loud voice, saying, Salvation belongs to our God who sits on the throne, and to the Lamb!" Revelation 7:9-10

"And they blasphemed the God of Heaven because of their pains and their sores, and did not repent of their deeds." Revelation 16:11

The fact is God's judgment is just and His hand of mercy still extends to mankind, even at this very moment to those who are willing and able to accept Salvation.

"Is mortal man more righteous than God? Is a strong man more pure than his Maker?" Job 4:17

"But now the righteousness of God apart from the Law is revealed, being witnessed by the Law and the Prophets, even the righteousness of God, through the faith of Jesus Christ, to all and upon all who believe. For there is no difference; for all have sinned and fall short of the glory of God, being justified freely by His grace through the redemption that is in Christ Jesus, whom God set forth as a propitiation through faith in His blood, to give evidence of His righteousness, because in His forbearance God had passed over the sins that were previously committed, to prove at the present time His righteousness, that He might be just and the justifier of the one who is of the faith of Jesus." Romans 3:21-26

"O let the wickedness of the wicked come to an end, but establish the just. For the righteous God tries the hearts and minds." Psalms 7:9

"But Jehovah shall endure forever; He has prepared His throne for justice. 8 And He shall judge the world in righteousness; He shall execute judgment to the people with equity." Psalms 9:7-8

"Your throne, O God, is forever and ever; the scepter of Your kingdom is a scepter of uprightness." Psalms 45:6

"Adulterers and adulteresses, do you not know that friendship with the world is enmity with God? Whoever therefore purposes to be a friend of the world is shown to be opposing God." Jacob 4:4

"Declare and approach; yea, let them take counsel together. Who has declared this from antiquity? Who has told it since then? Is it not I, Jehovah. And there is no other God besides Me; a just Mighty God and a Savior; there is no one besides Me. Turn to Me, and be saved, all the ends of the earth; for I am the Mighty God, and there is no other. I have sworn by Myself, the word has gone out of My mouth in righteousness, and shall not return, that to Me every knee shall bow, every tongue shall swear." Isaiah 45:21-23

"For evildoers shall be cut off; but those who wait upon Jehovah, they shall inherit the earth. For yet a little while, and the wicked shall be no more; indeed, you shall diligently consider his place, and it shall be no more. But the lowly shall inherit the earth, and shall delight themselves in the abundance of peace. The wicked plots against the just, and gnashes at him with his teeth. Jehovah laughs at him, for He sees that his day is coming." Psalms 37:9-13

"For God so loved the world that He gave His only begotten Son, that everyone believing into Him should not perish but have eternal life. For God did not send His Son into the world to judge the world, but that the world through Him might be saved. The one believing into Him is not judged; but the one not believing is judged already, because he has not believed in the name of the only begotten Son of God. And this is the judgment, that the Light has come into the world, and men loved darkness rather than the Light, for their deeds were evil. For everyone practicing evil hates the Light and does not come to the Light, lest his deeds should be reproved. But the one doing the truth comes to the Light, that his deeds may be clearly seen, that they have been worked in God." John 3:16-21

Understand that these things must take place, this is all part of God's plan for humanity. Satan has deceived the world and due to man's sinful nature, the world has gotten to this point. What you must understand is that not only is the world worthy of God's just judgment, it is deserving.

"And I saw another sign in Heaven, great and marvelous: seven angels having the seven last plagues, for in them the wrath of God is finished. And I saw something like a sea of glass mingled with fire, and those who have the victory over the beast, over his image and over his mark and over the number of his name, standing on the glassy sea, having harps of God. And they sing the song of Moses, the servant of God, and the song of the Lamb, saying: Great and marvelous are Your works, Lord God Almighty. Just and true are Your ways, O King of the saints. Who shall not fear You, O Lord, and glorify Your name? For You alone are holy. For all nations shall come and do homage before You, for Your righteous deeds have been manifested." Revelation 15:1-4

"As it is written: There is none righteous, no, not one; there is none who understands; there is none who seeks after God. They have all turned aside; they have together become unprofitable; there is none who does good, no, not one. Their throat is an open tomb; with their tongues they have practiced deceit; the poison of asps is under their lips; whose mouth is full of cursing and bitterness. Their feet are swift to shed blood; destruction and misery are in their ways; and the way of peace they have not known. There is no fear of God before their eyes." Romans 3:10-18

"The righteous Jehovah is in her midst; He will do no wrong. Every morning He gives His justice to the light; He does not fail, but the unjust knows no shame. I have cut off nations; their towers are desolate. I made their streets waste, so that no one passes by. Their cities are laid waste, without a man, with no inhabitant. I said, Surely you will fear Me; you will receive instruction; so that her dwelling should not be cut off, all that I appointed for her. But they rose up early; they corrupted all their doings. Therefore, wait for Me, declares Jehovah, until the day that I rise up to the prey. For My judgment is to gather the nations, for Me to gather the kingdoms, to pour My fury out on them, all My burning anger. For all the earth shall be devoured with the fire of My jealousy." Zephaniah 3:5-8

Right now, though Israel is the main focus, the entire world is undergoing God's just judgment. What is inevitably going to happen is that each person is going to be judged by God INDIVIDUALLY. There each person will be held accountable for their sin and whether or not their name is written in the Book of Life.

If your name is not written in the Book of Life then you will be cast into the Lake of Fire, where you will remain for eternity, part of God's just judgment. This is a -serious- matter if you can just consider eternity. Yet for those who have repented and believed into Jesus Christ as their Lord and Savior, accepting the free gift of Salvation that God the Father provided for all of humanity, for them a job well done, enter into the rest of your Lord *(Matthew 25:21)*.

Either you can realize the depravity of mankind, including the sin in your own life and seek God while He may still be found or you can be like the other crowd who refuses to repent of their wickedness, joining them in everlasting weeping and gnashing of teeth, in the Lake of Fire.

"Seek Jehovah while He may be found; call upon Him while He is near." Isaiah 55:6

"There will be weeping and gnashing of teeth, when you see Abraham and Isaac and Jacob and all the prophets in the kingdom of God, and yourselves being thrust outside." Luke 13:28

"And I saw the dead, small and great, standing before God. And books were opened. And another book was opened, which is the Book of Life. And the dead were judged according to their works, out of the things which were written in the books. And the sea gave up the dead who were in it, and Death and Hades delivered up the dead who were in them. And they were judged, each one, according to their works. And Death and Hades were cast into the Lake of Fire. This is the second death. And anyone not found written in the Book of Life was cast into the Lake of Fire." Revelation 20:12-15

"But the cowardly, unbelieving, abominable, murderers, prostitutes, sorcerers, idolaters, and all liars shall have their part in the lake which burns with fire and brimstone, which is the second death." Revelation 21:8

"And they shall go out and observe the dead corpses of the men who have rebelled against Me. For their worm does not die, nor is their fire quenched; and they shall be an abhorrence to all flesh." Isaiah 66:24

"For this let everyone who is godly pray unto You, in a time when You may be found; surely in the floods of great waters they shall not come near him." Psalm 32:6

Amen!

Even Unto Death

"For this God is our God forever and ever; He will be our guide even unto death."
Psalms 48:14

This is being written as a warning to those who have been Left Behind. The *"time of Jacob's trouble" (Jer. 30:7)*, commonly known as the Great Tribulation or Tribulation is upon the earth, the Rapture has now happened and those who truly were Christians are with the Lord. There are people around the globe seeking answers, many presumably refusing to believe the lies purported by governments and fellow mankind.

A terrible time for all of mankind has begun as God is carrying out His Righteous judgment against Israel and the world. Now choices have to be made, those who did not fully realize and deny the full true Gospel are likely awakened to a harsh reality, one that will have the hearts of many men failing them: they were Left Behind.

Americans probably have more hints and supposed knowledge about the last days because of the strong Judeo-Christian background of the United States. Around the world many are Roman Catholics, Muslim, worship demons (Hindu) or other false religions, but in America there have always been some talk about the Rapture, the Great Tribulation, the four horsemen, Armageddon, etc. While much of that talk is speculation, false proclamations or even some interesting fictional scenarios, there is the belief amongst many generations that 'the end is near'. This is written for those who are living in that time, the end has come! You are living in the last final days!

You are now faced with a choice, if you are reading this early on during the Tribulation, things might not be so bad and you might assume to have some 'time' to make a decision. Others might come across this while running for their lives, unwilling to accept the mark of the beast or worship the beast or his image. For either, the answer is the same, you need to believe into Jesus Christ, you need a Savior, you need Salvation, you need it now!

"And it shall be, that whoever shall call on the name of Jehovah shall escape." Joel
2:32a

"But what does it say? The Word is near you, in your mouth and in your heart (that is, the Word of Faith which we preach): that if you confess with your mouth the Lord Jesus and believe in your heart that God has raised Him from the dead, you will be saved. For with the heart one believes unto righteousness, and with the mouth confession is made unto salvation. For the Scripture says, Everyone believing on Him will not be put to shame. For there is no distinction between Jew and Greek, for the same Lord over all is rich toward all who call upon Him. For everyone, whoever calls on the name of the Lord shall be saved." Romans 10:8-13

How many people put off learning more of God before such things happened? How many people pondered whether or not the things that they heard bits and pieces about regarding God's truth was realistic or not? How many people heard someone preach the Gospel but put off further consideration due to the cares of this world? Really how many people reading this knew better, knew that they had to do 'better', to change, but either didn't fully understand the Gospel, wasn't prepared to yield their life or didn't seek after God to find Him in the absence of not having any Believer around willing to or actually explain the Gospel to the curious. Now will you dare put it off any longer? Do you make an assumption that you will decide when you absolutely are forced to decide? Do you assume that you will still be alive when you are absolutely forced to decide? Take a good look around, you are not just gambling with your life, your eternal soul is at stake, you will either ultimately end up in Heaven with the Lord or you will be in the Lake of Fire for eternity! There is NO middle ground, do not play around with your soul!

"For He says: In an acceptable time I have heard you, and in a day of salvation I have helped you. Behold, now is the accepted time; behold, now is the day of salvation." 2nd Corinthians 6:2

"And the devil, who led them astray, was cast into the Lake of Fire and brimstone where the beast and the false prophet are. And they will be tormented day and night forever and ever. And I saw a great white throne and Him who sat on it, from whose face the earth and the heavens fled away. And there was found no place for them. And I saw the dead, small and great, standing before God. And books were opened. And another book was opened, which is the Book of Life. And the dead were judged according to their works, out of the things which were written in the books. And the sea gave up the dead who were in it, and Death and Hades delivered up the dead who were in them. And they were judged, each one, according to their works. And Death and Hades were cast into the Lake of Fire. This is the second death. And anyone not found written in the Book of Life was cast into the Lake of Fire." Revelation 20:10-15

What shock and horror for numerous people around the globe when they were with someone who was taken at Christ's appearing! When the Rapture happened, how many nearly fainted, how many died, just due to the shock, horror and awe of the situation, realizing that they had been Left Behind? In all of this there is still good news, God knew beforehand what would happen and He still is providing Salvation to anyone willing and able to receive it. You will have to make a choice.

The obvious logical choice will be for everyone to accept God's free gift of Salvation, the problem with man is sin. Instead of being willing to yield their lives to God, they would rather lives their lives contrary to Him. Now on one hand the choice could be perceivably tougher to unregenerate eyes, as believing into Christ will most definitely equate dying for Him, likely as the guillotine will be used to chop off your head, for failure to go along with the world's ways. Another way to consider it is that things are going to get so bad in the world that men will look for places to hide, they will seek death and ultimately without Jesus Christ, you are eternally doomed to the Lake of Fire.

"And they overcame him through the blood of the Lamb and through the word of their testimony, and they did not love their lives unto death." Revelation 12:11

"This is My commandment, that you love one another as I love you. Greater love has no one than this, than to lay down one's life for his friends. You are My friends if you do whatever I command you." John 15:12-14

"For to this you were called, because Christ also suffered for us, leaving us an example, that you should follow His steps: Who committed no sin, nor was deceit found in His mouth; who, when He was reviled, did not revile in return; when He suffered, He did not threaten, but gave Himself over to Him who judges righteously; who Himself bore our sins in His own body on the tree, that we, having died to sins, might live unto righteousness; by whose stripes you were healed." 1st Peter 2:21-24

"Jesus said to him, I am the Way, the Truth, and the Life. No one comes to the Father except through Me." John 14:6

"For God so loved the world that He gave His only begotten Son, that everyone believing into Him should not perish but have eternal life. For God did not send His Son into the world to judge the world, but that the world through Him might be saved. The one believing into Him is not judged; but the one not believing is judged already, because he has not believed in the name of the only begotten Son of God. And this is the judgment, that the Light has come into the world, and men loved darkness rather than the Light, for their deeds were evil. For everyone practicing evil hates the Light and does not come to the Light, lest his deeds should be reproved. But the one doing the truth comes to the Light, that his deeds may be clearly seen, that they have been worked in God." John 3:16-21

"And when He opened the fifth seal, I saw under the altar the souls of those who had been slain because of the Word of God and because of the testimony which they held." Revelation 6:9

"And in those days men will seek death and will not find it; they will crave to die, and death will flee from them." Revelation 9:6

Your decision will affect your life as you remain on the earth during the Tribulation time period. What do you do regarding your friends and family who worry more about the cares of this world and accept the mark of the beast to be able to continue financially, no matter how rough?

"If then you are raised with Christ, seek those things which are above, where Christ is, sitting at the right hand of God. Set your mind on things above, not on the things of the earth; for you died, and your life is hidden with Christ in God. When Christ who is our life is revealed, then you also will be revealed with Him in glory." Colossians 3:1-4

"Therefore whoever shall confess Me before men, I will also confess him before My Father in Heaven. But whoever denies Me before men, I will also deny him before My Father in Heaven. Do not think that I came to bring peace on earth. I did not come to

bring peace but a sword. For I have come to set a man against his father, a daughter against her mother, and a daughter-in-law against her mother-in-law; and a man's enemies will be those of his own household. He who loves father or mother more than Me is not worthy of Me. And he who loves son or daughter more than Me is not worthy of Me. And he who does not take his cross and follow after Me is not worthy of Me. He who finds his life will lose it, and he who loses his life on account of Me will find it." Matthew 10:32-39

"And brother will deliver up brother to death, and a father his child; and children will rise up against parents and put them to death. And you will be hated by everyone on account of My name. But he who endures to the end will be kept safe." Matthew 10:21-22

"Then I stood on the sand of the sea. And I saw a beast rising up out of the sea, having seven heads and ten horns, and on his horns ten crowns, and on his heads names of blasphemy. And the beast which I saw was like a leopard, his feet were like the feet of a bear, and his mouth like the mouth of a lion. And the dragon gave him his power, his throne, and great authority. And I saw one of his heads as if it had been mortally wounded, and his deadly wound was healed. And all the world marveled at the beast. So they did homage to the dragon who gave authority to the beast; and they did homage to the beast, saying, Who is like the beast? Who is able to make war with him? And he was given a mouth speaking great things and blasphemies, and he was given authority to continue for forty-two months. And he opened his mouth in blasphemy against God, to blaspheme His name, His tabernacle, and those who dwell in Heaven. And it was granted to him to make war with the saints and to overcome them. And authority was given him over every tribe, tongue, and nation. And all who dwell on the earth will do homage to him, whose names have not been written in the Book of Life of the Lamb slain from the foundation of the world. If anyone has an ear, let him hear. He who leads into captivity shall go into captivity; he who kills with the sword must be killed with the sword. Here is the endurance and the faith of the saints. Then I saw another beast coming up out of the earth, and he had two horns like a lamb and spoke like a dragon. And he exercises all the authority of the first beast in his presence, and causes the earth and those who dwell in it to do homage to the first beast, whose deadly wound was healed. And he performs great signs, so that he even makes fire come down from heaven onto the earth in the sight of men. And he leads astray those who dwell on the earth by means of those signs which he was granted to do in the presence of the beast, telling those who dwell on the earth to make an image to the beast who was wounded by the sword and lived. And it was given to him to give spirit to the image of the beast, that the image of the beast should both speak and cause as many as would not do homage to the image of the beast to be killed. And he causes all, both small and great, rich and poor, free and slave, to receive a mark on their right hand or on their foreheads, so that no one may buy or sell except one who has the mark or the name of the beast, or the number of his name. Here is wisdom. Let him who has understanding calculate the number of the beast, for it is the number of a man, and his number is 666." Revelation Chapter 13

"And I heard a voice in the midst of the four living creatures saying, A quart of wheat for a denarius, and three quarts of barley for a denarius; and do not harm the oil and the wine." Revelation 6:6

Choosing Life is not choosing death. For these bodies that we have will certainly pass away, but our souls never die.

"And as it is appointed for men to die once, and after this the judgment"... Hebrews 9:27

The point is that the choice should be simply accepting Salvation by believing into Jesus Christ, casting off all cares and anxieties of this world, even unto death. You can not chose to accept the mark of the beast or worship the beast or his image and still be Saved, there is a line drawn in the sand regarding this, so be warned!

"And when He had called the people to Himself, with His disciples also, He said to them, Whoever desires to come after Me, let him deny himself, and take up his cross, and follow Me. For whoever desires to save his life will lose it, but whoever loses his life for My sake and the gospel's will save it. For what will it profit a man if he gains the whole world, and loses his own soul? Or what will a man give in exchange for his soul? For whoever is ashamed of Me and My words in this adulterous and sinful generation, of him the Son of Man also will be ashamed when He comes in the glory of His Father with the holy angels." Mark 8:34-38

"And He who sat on the throne said, Behold, I make all things new. And He says to me, Write, for these Words are true and faithful. And He said to me, It is finished! I am the Alpha and the Omega, the Beginning and the Ending. I will give of the fountain of the Water of Life freely to him who thirsts. He who overcomes shall inherit all things, and I will be his God and he shall be My son. But the cowardly, unbelieving, abominable, murderers, prostitutes, sorcerers, idolaters, and all liars shall have their part in the lake which burns with fire and brimstone, which is the second death." Revelation 21:5-8

"He who is unjust, let him be unjust still; he who is filthy, let him be filthy still; he who is righteous, let him be righteous still; he who is holy, let him be holy still. And behold, I am coming quickly, and My reward is with Me, to give to every one according to what his work shall be. I am the Alpha and the Omega, the Beginning and the Ending, the First and the Last. Blessed are those who do His commandments, that they may have the right to the Tree of Life, and may enter through the gates into the city. But outside are dogs and sorcerers and prostitutes and murderers and idolaters, and whoever loves and produces a lie. I, Jesus, have sent My angel to testify these things to you, to the churches. I am the Root and the Offspring of David, the Bright and Morning Star. And the Spirit and the bride say, Come. And let him who hears say, Come. And let him who thirsts come. Whoever desires, let him take of the Water of Life freely. For I testify to everyone who hears the Words of the Prophecy of this Book: If anyone adds to these things, God will add upon him the plagues that are written in this Book; and if anyone takes away from the Words of the Book of this Prophecy, God shall take away his part from the Book of Life, from the holy city, and from the things which are written in this Book. He who

testifies to these things says, Surely I am coming quickly. Amen. Even so, come, Lord Jesus. The grace of our Lord Jesus Christ be with you all. Amen." Revelation 22:11-21

"Let not your heart be troubled; you believe in God, believe also in Me. In My Father's house are many mansions; if it were not so, I would have told you. I go to prepare a place for you. And if I go and prepare a place for you, I will come again and receive you to Myself; that where I am, there you may be also. And where I go you know, and the way you know." John 14:1-4

"And I saw another angel flying in the midst of heaven, having the eternal gospel to preach to those who dwell on the earth; to every nation, tribe, tongue, and people; saying with a loud voice, Fear God and give glory to Him, for the hour of His judgment has come; also, do homage to Him who made the heavens and the earth, the sea and springs of water. And another angel followed, saying, Babylon is fallen, is fallen, that great city, because she has made all nations drink of the wine of the wrath of her sexual perversion. And a third angel followed them, saying with a loud voice, If anyone does homage to the beast and his image, and receives his mark on his forehead or on his hand, he himself shall also drink of the wine of the wrath of God, which is poured out full strength into the cup of His anger. He shall be tormented with fire and brimstone before the holy angels and before the Lamb. And the smoke of their torment ascends forever and ever; and they have no rest day or night, who do homage to the beast and his image, and whoever receives the mark of his name. Here is the perseverance of the saints; here are those who keep the commandments of God and the faith of Jesus. And I heard a voice from Heaven saying to me, Write: Blessed are the dead who die in the Lord from now on. Yes, says the Spirit, that they may rest from their labors, and their works follow with them." Revelation 14:6-13

Even during the dark times, know that God cares about those who are His.

"For Jehovah knows the way of the righteous; but the way of the wicked shall perish." Psalms 1:6

"Precious in the sight of Jehovah is the death of His saints." Psalms 116:15

Amen!

We Were Created

"Then God said, Let Us make man in Our image, according to Our likeness; let them have dominion over the fish of the sea, over the flying creatures of the heavens, and over the beasts, over all the earth and over every creeping thing that moves on the earth. So God created man in His own image; in the image of God He created him; male and female He created them. And God blessed them, and God said to them, Be fruitful and multiply; fill the earth and subdue it; have dominion over the fish of the sea, over the flying creatures of the heavens, and over every living thing that moves on the earth. And God said, Behold, I have given you every plant that yields seed which is on the face of all the earth, and every tree whose fruit yields seed; to you it shall be for food. Also, to every living thing of the earth, to every flying creature of the heavens, and to everything that moves on the earth, living creatures, I have given the green plants for food: thus. And God saw everything that He had made, and indeed it was extremely good. Thus, the evening and the morning: Day Six."
Genesis 1:26-31

"For the wrath of God is revealed from Heaven against all ungodliness and unrighteousness of men, who suppress the truth in unrighteousness, because what may be known of God is clearly recognized by them, for God has revealed it to them. For ever since the creation of the world the unseen things of Him are clearly perceived, being understood by the things that are made, even His eternal power and Godhead, so that they are without excuse, because, although they know God, they do not glorify Him as God, nor are thankful, but become vain in their reasonings, and their stupid hearts are darkened. Professing to be wise, they become foolish, and change the glory of the incorruptible God into an image made like corruptible man, and birds and four-footed animals and creeping things. Therefore God also gives them up to uncleanness, in the lusts of their hearts, to dishonor their bodies among themselves, who change the truth of God into the lie, and fear and serve the created things more than the Creator, who is blessed forever. Amen. For this reason God gives them up to vile passions. For even their women change the natural use for what is contrary to nature. Likewise also the men, abandoning the natural use of the woman, burned in their lust toward one another, men with men performing what is shameful, and receiving the retribution within themselves, the penalty which is fitting for their error. And even as they do not like to have God in their full true knowledge, God gives them over to a reprobate mind, to do those things which are not fitting; being filled with every unrighteousness, sexual perversion, wickedness, covetousness, maliciousness; full of envy, murder, strife, deceit, depravity; whisperers, defamers, haters of God, insolent, proud,

boasters, inventors of evil things, disobedient to parents, without understanding, untrustworthy, without natural affection, unforgiving, unmerciful; who, knowing the righteous judgment of God, that those who practice such things are deserving of death, not only do them, but also approve of those who practice them." Romans 1:18-32

Irregardless of whether or not people say that they believe in God, the question that is more relevant is whether or not they believe His written Word. Do they believe that His Son Jesus Christ died on the Cross for their sins? Do they believe that they are sinful and have need for the blood that was shed on the Cross for their sins? Do people realize that ONLY through repentance and believing into Jesus Christ that they can rectify themselves with their Creator? Do they realize that they are deserving of God's just judgment and are doomed to Hell without accepting the free gift of Salvation that God has provided to man through Christ? What most of man believes are hypothesis, educated theories about the origins of Earth and the afterlife from these bodies. They don't believe God.

The other day I happened upon a magazine that had an article about a famous person who had died and seen the light. Knowing that Satan deceives many with such nonsense, I took and read the pertinent part of the article to see if the account was similar to what I had read on previous occasions.

"For such are false apostles, deceitful workers, transforming themselves into apostles of Christ. And no wonder; for Satan himself transforms himself into an angel of light. Therefore it is no great thing if his ministers also transform themselves into ministers of righteousness, whose end will be according to their works." 2nd Corinthians 11:13-15

This person saw the white light and their dead loved family and friends around them. All of these dead ones looked as if they were in the prime of their life, their ailments, old age and other factors that contributed to a degradation of their bodies while still alive, was gone. One of 17,000 documented cases of seeing similar things, this famous person was no longer worried about death and what comes after. They were comforted with this revelation and the fear of death had left them.

Why had they had a fear of death? When God created mankind He instilled in man knowledge of Creation and Himself. Man is not without excuse, deep down they realize that they are in for some big trouble, they are concerned and they should be!

If you are reading this and the Rapture has already happened and you find yourself in the midst of *"the time of Jacob's trouble" (Jer. 30:7)*, better known as the Great Tribulation or Tribulation, than understand that God's mercy still extends to you. This fear of death, this fear of the unknown can be put to rest. All around mankind is the glorious handiwork of God's Creation. Satan will do his best to convince the people of the world that God's Word is not as He says. He will twist the Holy Scriptures, push theological theories that are unbiblical (such as theistic evolution) and try and convince the world to rebel against their Creator, but you, dear individual, should consider these things and realize that you are a sinner...lost without Jesus Christ.

When everything was Created, God called it *"extremely good" (Genesis 1:31)*, yet afterwards Adam and Eve were deceived by "the serpent" and sinned. Every man born needs a Savior due to this. There is not a single person born who has not been born in sin, indeed who is not a sinner.

"And I saw an angel coming down from Heaven, having the key to the bottomless pit and a great chain in his hand. And he laid hold of the dragon, that serpent of old, who is the Devil and Satan, and bound him for a thousand years; and he cast him into the bottomless pit, and shut him up, and set a seal on him, so that he should not lead astray the nations any more till the thousand years were finished. But after these things he must be released for a little while. And I saw thrones, and they sat on them, and judgment was committed to them; and I saw the souls of those who had been beheaded for their witness to Jesus and for the Word of God, who had not done homage to the beast or his image, and had not received his mark on their foreheads or on their hands. And they lived and reigned with Christ for a thousand years." Revelation 20:1-4

"And you being dead in trespasses and sins, in which you formerly walked according to the course of this world, according to the ruler of the authority of the air, the spirit who now works in the sons of disobedience, among whom also we all formerly conducted ourselves in the lusts of our flesh, fulfilling the desires of the flesh and of the mind, and were by nature children of wrath, just as the others; but God, who is rich in mercy, because of His great love with which He loved us, even when we were dead in trespasses, made us alive together with Christ (by grace you are saved), and raised us up together, and made us sit together in the heavenlies in Christ Jesus, that in the ages to come He might display the exceeding riches of His grace in His kindness toward us in Christ Jesus. For by grace you are saved through faith; and that not of yourselves, it is the gift of God; not of works, that no one should boast. For we

are His workmanship, created in Christ Jesus unto good works, which God prepared beforehand that we should walk in them. Therefore remember that you, being Gentiles in the flesh; who are called uncircumcision by what is called the circumcision made in the flesh by hands; that at that time you were without Christ, being aliens from the commonwealth of Israel and strangers from the covenants of promise, having no hope and without God in the world. But now in Christ Jesus you who once were far off have been made near by the blood of Christ. For He Himself is our peace, who has made both one, and has broken down the middle wall of separation, having abolished in His flesh the enmity, that is, the Law of commandments contained in ordinances, that He might create in Himself one new man from the two, thus making peace, and that He might reconcile them both to God in one body through the cross, thereby putting to death the enmity." Ephesians 2:1-16

"Behold, I was brought forth in iniquity, and in sin did my mother conceive me." Psalms 51:5

"Therefore, just as through one man sin entered the world, and death through sin, and thus death spread to every person, because everyone sinned. For until the Law sin was in the world, but sin is not accounted when there is no law. Nevertheless death reigned from Adam to Moses, even over those who had not sinned according to the likeness of the transgression of Adam, who is a type of Him who was to come. But the free gift is not like the offense. For if by the one man's offense many died, much more the grace of God and the gift by the grace of the one Man, Jesus Christ, abounded to many. And the gift is not like it was through the one who sinned. For the judgment from one offense was unto condemnation, but the free gift from many offenses is unto justification. For if by the one man's offense death reigned through the one, much more those who are receiving abundance of grace and of the gift of righteousness will reign in life through the One, Jesus Christ. Therefore, as through one man's offense judgment was to every person unto condemnation, even so through one Man's righteous act the free gift is to every person unto justification of life. For as through one man's disobedience many were declared sinners, so also through one Man's obedience many will be declared righteous. Moreover the Law entered that the offense might abound. But where sin abounded, grace abounded much more, so that as sin reigned in death, even so grace might reign through righteousness unto eternal life through Jesus Christ our Lord." Romans 5:12-21

"But now the righteousness of God apart from the Law is revealed, being witnessed by the Law and the Prophets, even the righteousness of God, through

the faith of Jesus Christ, to all and upon all who believe. For there is no difference; for all have sinned and fall short of the glory of God, being justified freely by His grace through the redemption that is in Christ Jesus, whom God set forth as a propitiation through faith in His blood, to give evidence of His righteousness, because in His forbearance God had passed over the sins that were previously committed, to prove at the present time His righteousness, that He might be just and the justifier of the one who is of the faith of Jesus. Where is boasting then? It is excluded. By what law? Of works? No, but through the law of faith. Therefore we conclude that a man is justified by faith apart from the works of the Law. Or is He the God of the Jews only? Is He not also the God of the Gentiles? Yes, of the Gentiles also, since there is one God who will justify the circumcised by faith and the uncircumcised through faith." Romans 3:21-30

You must look away from all of these theories that man has created. You must BELIEVE God who is our Creator, for we will ALL STAND before Him. We will all be held accountable. If you name is not written in the Book of Life *(Rev. 20:12)* than you will be cast into the Lake of Fire for eternity. There is nothing more important than for you to grasp that indeed God is true, He has the words of eternal life.

"Let it not be! Indeed, let God be true but every man a liar. As it is written: That You may be found just in Your words, and may win the case when You are judged. But if our unrighteousness demonstrates the righteousness of God, what shall we say? Is God unjust who lays on wrath? (I speak as a man.) Let it not be! Otherwise, how will God judge the world? For if in my lie, the truth of God has abounded to His glory, why am I also still judged as a sinner? And why not say (as we are slanderously reported and as some affirm that we say), Let us do evil that good may come? Their condemnation is just. What then? Do we surpass them? Not at all. For we have previously charged both Jews and Greeks, that they are all under sin. As it is written: There is none righteous, no, not one; there is none who understands; there is none who seeks after God. They have all turned aside; they have together become unprofitable; there is none who does good, no, not one. Their throat is an open tomb; with their tongues they have practiced deceit; the poison of asps is under their lips; whose mouth is full of cursing and bitterness. Their feet are swift to shed blood; destruction and misery are in their ways; and the way of peace they have not known. There is no fear of God before their eyes." Romans 3:4-18

"Then Simon Peter answered Him, Lord, to whom shall we go? You have the Words of eternal life. And we have believed and understood that You are the Christ, the Son of the living God." John 6:68-69

How much thought does man give to setting up a life for his family? A man will get married, have children, want to provide food and shelter for his family and finally will want to have enough left over to be able to provide for them until he dies. Yet without Christ there should be much wailing and crying regarding the loss of a loved one, without Christ there is no hope.

You may have made many mistakes throughout your life, you may have many regrets and you might firmly grasp your sinful state, knowing that you have a great weight upon your soul, but what is the recourse?! You must look at the present, you must look towards the future, you must act and set things in order from this point forward.

There is nothing you can do about the past, there is nothing you can do but mourn for those whom have died that you have loved. There is little you can do about the sinful errors of the past, but what you can do is realize your state as a sinner who is deserving of God's eternal punishment, realize that your sins have entrapped you, that you are lost and without hope and repent! Repent and believe into Jesus Christ who died on the Cross for your sins! Why or why will you die?!

"The soul who sins shall die. The son shall not bear the guilt of the father, nor the father bear the guilt of the son. The righteousness of the righteous shall be upon himself, and the wickedness of the wicked shall be upon himself. But if a wicked man turns from all his sins which he has done, keeps all My statutes, and does what is lawful and right, he shall live life; he shall not die. None of the transgressions which he has done shall be remembered against him; because of the righteousness which he has done, he shall live. Do I delight with pleasure in the death of the wicked? says the Lord Jehovah, and not that he should turn back from his ways and live?" Ezekiel 18:20-23

Will you not change, will you not have a heart that yields unto your Creator, will you not desperately seek the Most High God while you still can and with such eagerness explain Salvation to those loved ones who are still around you. God's Salvation extends to all mankind who are willing to come to Him, He is merciful, He is kind, He will forgive you of your iniquities, you will have life through His Son. If only you would put off the hardness of your wicked heart and be rectified to your Creator through Jesus Christ our Lord and Savior, if only!

Eventually during the Great Tribulation, the plans that man has in his heart regarding what he will do while he spends his time here on Earth, will fade away. God's just judgment will be seen visually, the cares of this world will turn into how to survive. The choice will have to be made whether or not to deny your Creator and accept the mark of the beast and/or worship the image of the beast. You will see loved ones who are faced with the same choice, but you o' man will be held accountable individually.

Making decisions based upon what it acceptable to family or friends is not going to help you in the day of Judgment.

"And I saw a great white throne and Him who sat on it, from whose face the earth and the heavens fled away. And there was found no place for them. And I saw the dead, small and great, standing before God. And books were opened. And another book was opened, which is the Book of Life. And the dead were judged according to their works, out of the things which were written in the books. And the sea gave up the dead who were in it, and Death and Hades delivered up the dead who were in them. And they were judged, each one, according to their works. And Death and Hades were cast into the Lake of Fire. This is the second death. And anyone not found written in the Book of Life was cast into the Lake of Fire." Revelation 20:11-15

Going along with the masses is going to do no good when you are cast into the Lake of Fire for eternity. Words cannot convey the seriousness of the situation, you must realize that you are lost in order to be Saved. You must understand that irregardless of what opinion anyone might hold to how one gets to Heaven, God has made these thing known and provide a firm, solid and true path. That path is only through Jesus Christ, there is NO other way.

I wish that you and every one who reads this would realize what odds you are up against. I would love to sit down and point out the deceptions of this world and allow you to see clearly that Satan has deceived the far vast majority of mankind. Yet I know that there are some who wouldn't listen, no matter the amount of evidence that is presented to them. There are some who would even believe, but due to the hardness of their heart, would refuse to repent towards the Most High God, their Creator. This is not written for them, it is written that you, dear reader, might consider YOUR ways, you might consider YOUR eternal destination, that you would realize that YOU are a sinner and that YOU would repent and believe into Jesus Christ. For those who will listen, understand that the merciful Almighty God is willing to pardon you of your iniquities and provide Salvation to you. His hand is mighty, He is the mighty God, the Creator and He will restore all things. Will you be there when that happens or will you suffer the eternal consequences of refusing to believe His Word?

"And he brought them out and said, Sirs, what must I do to be saved? So they said, Believe on the Lord Jesus Christ, and you will be saved, you and your household." Acts 16:30-31

"For the wages of sin is death, but the gift of God is eternal life in Christ Jesus our Lord." Romans 6:23

"Jesus said to him, I am the Way, the Truth, and the Life. No one comes to the Father except through Me." John 14:6

"The Lord is not slow concerning His promise, as some count slowness, but is longsuffering toward us, not purposing that any should perish but that all should come to repentance. But the day of the Lord will come as a thief in the night, in which the heavens will pass away with a loud noise, and the elements will be dissolved with intense burning; both the earth and the works that are in it will be burned up. Therefore, since all these things will be dissolved, of what sort ought you to be in holy behavior and godliness, looking for and earnestly hastening unto the coming of the Day of God, through which the heavens will be dissolved, being set on fire, and the elements will melt with intense burning? Nevertheless we, according to His promise, look for new heavens and a new earth in which righteousness dwells. Therefore, beloved, looking forward to these things, be diligent to be found by Him in peace, spotless and without blemish; and consider that the longsuffering of our Lord is salvation; as also our beloved brother Paul, according to the wisdom given to him, has written to you, as also in all his epistles, speaking in them of these things, in which are some things hard to understand, which the unlearned and unstable twist, as they do also the rest of the Scriptures, to their own destruction. You therefore, beloved, since you know this beforehand, beware also that you not be led away with the error of the wicked, and fall from your own steadfastness. But grow in the grace and knowledge of our Lord and Savior Jesus Christ. To Him be the glory both now and forever. Amen." 2nd Peter 3:9-18

"Behold, I stand at the door and knock. If anyone hears My voice and opens the door, I will come in to him and dine with him, and he with Me." Revelation *3:20*

Amen!

Afterword

We still live in Kalispell, Montana. In 2015 we finally went back into Michigan to visit with family, taking heavy precautions. Since then some family has made in out here a couple of times to visit. In early 2016 we started another janitorial service, which is what we are currently doing again full time.

God helped us get that janitorial service up and running in record time. With an official start date of March 1st, by the end of April I had my notice in at my job and by June 1st we were both fully employed and engaged in the business. Is God done working in our lives, for certain the answer is no. What the future holds is in His hands.

As mentioned in the introduction we began to file a bunch of FOIA's in mid 2015, some of which is still ongoing with both Senator Daines and U.S. Representative Zinke trying to get the FBI to actually follow the law in regards to my request. When or if these are resolved, we will post them on the website (www.ofmissingpersons.com).

Brandon and I are working heavily on trying to warn people to repent and believe into Jesus Christ. The hour seems so late and it just seems like the right thing to do. We do this through All Will Stand LLC, our website (www.allwillstand.org).

As far as problems, oddly, with the exception of a hexacopter drone with a mounted camera that flew in our backyard area (we have this on camera), while talking to media back in late 2014, we have nothing major to note. Sure there are oddities, Brandon had the hardest Rural Development loan ever known to Wells Fargo, they actually had to call Washington D.C. to see why it wasn't getting the usual rubber stamp. He also was banned from entering Canada for no logical reason. We still occasionally have clicks or static on our phones, his credit and debit cards sometimes cease to work and other things of that sort, but what we haven't had is problems with walkers, joggers, cars or other suspected federal agents. There is not one solid piece of evidence of any local ongoing investigation. If any investigation is ongoing, it appears to be done from the nation's Capital.

We thought for sure we would have problems when we came back from Panama, but that turned out not to be the case. Could it be by living there our case was transferred to the CIA, as we were no longer under FBI investigation but CIA jurisdiction? We don't know, we don't have the answers. The decision was simply made to have this book put back up for sale.

Realizing that there was God's just judgment on my family's behalf against us and looking at how the world seems to be ripe to soon experience His judgment, it seemed good to have a warning to those who will be Left Behind. Yet perhaps it could also plant a seed or water someone's heart to repent and believe into Jesus before then. As we come into 2017, we don't know what the future holds, but our story will remain out there for the world to read.

Seek God!

CONTACT

Support Files

For some files that provide evidence of our story and any updates to our FOIA requests, please visit: www.ofmissingpersons.com

Media Contacts

For all media contacts, please email us via the contact page on our website: www.ofmissingpersons.com

Contact Information

Tim & Sabrina Medsker
704C E. 13th St.
Suite 221
Whitefish, MT 59937

Please visit the website for updated contact information. If the Rapture has occurred there is no point in trying to contact us, we are home with the Lord.

Christian Writings
www.allwillstand.org

www.ingramcontent.com/pod-product-compliance
Lightning Source LLC
Chambersburg PA
CBHW050116280326
41933CB00010B/1130